Fishes

Rare and Endangered Biota of Florida
Ray E. Ashton, Jr., Series Editor

Florida Committee on Rare and Endangered Plants and Animals

Ray E. Ashton, Jr.
FCREPA Chair (1989–91)
and Series Editor
Water and Air Research, Inc.
6821 SW Archer Road
Gainesville, Florida 32608

Paul E. Moler
FCREPA Chair (1992–93)
Chair, Special Committee
on Amphibians and Reptiles
Wildlife Research Laboratory
Florida Game and
Fresh Water Fish Commission
4005 S. Main Street
Gainesville, Florida 32601

Daniel F. Austin, Co-Chair
Special Committee on Plants
Department of Biological Sciences
Florida Atlantic University
Boca Raton, FL 33431

Mark Deyrup, Co-Chair
Special Committee on Invertebrates
Archbold Biological Station
Route 2, Box 180
Lake Placid, Florida 33852

L. Richard Franz, Co-Chair
Special Committee on Invertebrates
Florida Museum of Natural History
University of Florida
Gainesville, Florida 32611

Carter R. Gilbert
Chair, Special Committee on Fishes
Florida Museum of Natural History
University of Florida
Gainesville, Florida 32611

Stephen R. Humphrey
Chair, Special Committee on Mammals
Florida Museum of Natural History
University of Florida
Gainesville, Florida 32611

Herbert W. Kale II
FCREPA Chair (1985–86)
Chair, Special Committee on Birds
Florida Audubon Society
1101 Audubon Way
Maitland, Florida 32751

Allan Stout
FCREPA Chair (1987–88)
Department of Biological Sciences
University of Central Florida
Orlando, Florida 32816

Daniel B. Ward
FCREPA Chair (1983–84)
Co-Chair, Special Committee on Plants
Department of Botany
University of Florida
Gainesville, Florida 32611

Special Committee on Fishes

Carter R. Gilbert
Florida Museum of Natural History
University of Florida
Gainesville, Florida 32611

Stephen A. Bortone
Department of Biology
University of West Florida
Pensacola, Florida 32504

R. Grant Gilmore
Harbor Branch Foundation
Route 1, Box 196
Ft. Pierce, Florida 33450

William F. Loftus
South Florida Research Center
Everglades National Park
P.O. Box 279
Homestead, Florida 33030

Franklin F. Snelson, Jr.
Department of Biological Sciences
University of Central Florida
P.O. Box 25000
Orlando, Florida 32816

James D. Williams
U.S. Fish and Wildlife Service
National Fisheries Research Laboratory
7920 N.W. 71 Street
Gainesville, Florida 32606

Rare and Endangered Biota of Florida

VOLUME II. FISHES

EDITED BY

CARTER R. GILBERT

Chair, Special Committee on Fishes
Florida Committee on Rare and Endangered
  Plants and Animals

UNIVERSITY PRESS OF FLORIDA
Gainesville, Tallahassee, Tampa, Boca Raton,
Pensacola, Orlando, Miami, Jacksonville

This volume was made possible in part by a grant from Florida Power and Light Company

Library of Congress Cataloging-in-Publication Data

Rare and Endangered Biota of Florida, Fishes / edited by Carter R.
  Gilbert.
  p.   cm.
  Includes index.
  ISBN 0-8130-1121-3 (alk. paper). — ISBN 0-8130-1122-1 (pbk. : alk. paper)
  1. Rare fishes—Florida.   I. Gilbert, Carter Howell, 1930–   .
QL617.73.U6R37   1992
333.95'6137'09759—dc20   91-31922
                                                                    CIP

The University Press of Florida is the scholarly publishing agency of the State
University System of Florida, comprised of Florida A & M University, Florida
Atlantic University, Florida International University, Florida State University,
University of Central Florida, University of Florida, University of North Florida,
University of South Florida, and University of West Florida.

Orders for books should be addressed to:
University Press of Florida
15 NW 15th Street
Gainesville, FL 32611

Illustrations for *Acipenser brevirostrum* and *Acipenser oxyrinchus*, and a composite
drawing of *Atractosteus spatula*, are from Sears Foundation for Marine Research,
Yale University, *Fishes of the Western North Atlantic* (New Haven, 1963) volume 3,
and are reproduced by permission of the publisher.

Contents

Rare

Species of Special Concern

Foreword

In 1978, not long after I became executive director of the Florida Game and Fresh Water Fish Commission, I was privileged to be associated with the production of the initial six-volume Rare and Endangered Biota of Florida series. That series has enjoyed enormous popularity (each volume was reprinted at least once, most two or three times). It has served as the definitive reference compendium on endangered and threatened species in Florida and is widely recognized as among the most authoritative and comprehensive such works in the nation. I am proud the commission was integrally involved in that initial work, and likewise proud that we were involved in producing this revised series.

In the forewords to the initial volumes, I and my predecessor, Dr. O. E. Frye, Jr., acknowledged the momentum of endangered species conservation to that point, and how the series was a significant contribution in that regard, but admonished that we must not rest on our laurels—much remained to be done. Although much has indeed been done in the interim, I am disappointed that we have not approached the level of progress I had hoped we would attain by now. As the species accounts herein clearly demonstrate, many Florida species are perilously near extinction, and many of the factors leading to that dire circumstance are still with us. The composition of the current official state lists—42 endangered, 28 threatened, and 47 special concern animals, along with 199 endangered and 283 threatened plants—is compelling evidence in and of itself that our progress has been relatively minor (by comparison, there were 31 endangered and 54 threatened species in 1978). There are several reasons for this much-less-than-hoped-for progression, but primarily it has been related to insufficient funding at both the state and federal levels. And without proper funding, the necessary manpower and other resources cannot be emplaced to address many critical needs. So we face the dilemma of either addressing the needs of only a few species so as to maximize effect, or spreading our resources thinly among many species, minimizing the effects on an individual basis.

This is not to say, however, that we have not made some substantial strides forward in the last decade or so. Through an innovative translocation strategy, we have reestablished in Florida the previously extirpated

Perdido Key beach mouse and significantly expanded the range of the Choctawhatchee beach mouse; because of stringent protection and rigorous application of "Habitat Management Guidelines for the Bald Eagle in the Southeast Region," Florida's bald eagle nesting population has grown to more than 550 pairs (as of the 1990–91 nesting season); the brown pelican and Pine Barrens treefrog have been delisted because of increasing populations and/or because our research efforts have provided new insight into those species' true status; nearly 50 manatee sanctuaries have been established in which boat speeds are restricted during the winter congregation period; our research since 1978 has resulted in more knowledge about endangered species biology, habitat needs, and the like, than during all previous time cumulatively; considerable endangered species habitat has been secured through CARL (Conservation and Recreation Lands), Save Our Coasts, Save Our Rivers, Save Our Everglades, and other land acquisition programs; and various information/education programs have resulted in a significant increase in public awareness and support for endangered species conservation. These few examples demonstrate what can be done with adequate resources and commitment, but in fact represent only the proverbial drop in the bucket in light of the total needs.

I hope this revised series reinvigorates our resolve and commitment to endangered and threatened species conservation and we will be able to cite a multitude of such examples by the time a third revision is necessary. These volumes provide an authoritative and comprehensive database from which to embark on such a course, and I congratulate and personally thank each researcher, writer, editor, and individual whose committed efforts have culminated in this exemplary work.

Colonel Robert M. Brantly, Executive Director
State of Florida Game and Fresh Water Fish Commission

Preface

"Thirty years ago Florida was one of the most extraordinary states in the Union, but being flat and quite park-like in character (a large part of the country consisted of open pinelands) it was an easy state for man to ruin, and he has ruined it with ruthless efficiency." This quote from Thomas Barbour's *That Vanishing Eden, A Naturalist's Florida*, written in 1944, is ever more appropriate today. He continues his lament—"A large part of Florida is now so devastated that many of her friends are disinclined to believe that she ever could have been the Paradise which I know once existed." Barbour was talking about the loss of natural habitat in Florida from 1915 to the early 1940s. Imagine what he would think today!

Within the FCREPA volumes, the emphasis is on specific plants and animals that the committee considers to be endangered, threatened to become endangered, or species of special concern (those species apparently in danger but about which we need more information). However, as one reads through the species accounts, there is a continuing theme of habitat loss or alteration by man. Since Barbour's days of study in Florida, the loss and degradation of natural habitats have accelerated beyond human comprehension. We are faced with the possible reality that the only thing which will cause a decline in the loss is that there will soon be no land left to develop.

We are also faced with the fact that we actually know very little about the fauna and flora of this state. When challenged to protect a species or develop regulations to prevent extinction, we are inevitably confronted with the fact that we know little about their life histories, let alone what is needed to preserve a population through biological time. We are also faced with the dilemma that there probably is not enough time or money to allow us to study these organisms, let alone experiment with management techniques. Our ecological knowledge of interspecific interactions and biological communities is even less. Yet we do know that once certain biological needs are not met, we lose another species and another community. The biological communities of this state are being compromised time and again by all levels of government, simply to serve the hunger for growth and development.

We are the first generation to realize that not only do we have local or regional environmental concerns but we now have to be aware of serious global degradations of our air and water. Global warming, acid rain, increased ultraviolet radiation, and degradation of our oceans are making us realize for the first time that our species may well be jeopardizing itself as well as the lowly gopher tortoise and tree snail. We are realizing that the world's biodiversity and the biological engine that drives many of the necessities of all life are being used up or changed by our overpopulated species. If we know so little about individual species and communities, how can we be prepared to understand the complexities of the biosphere, let alone the cause and effect of our actions?

Alarms have sounded in the minds of many people around the world, including Florida. The first step toward a solution to all of this is acknowledging that we are causing problems. Loss of uplands not only means loss of wildlife but also that we affect our water supplies, river systems, and ultimately the health of our coastal systems. Our state agencies are in the fledgling stages of creating regulations on development and the organized effort of protecting biological diversity and natural communities. Hopefully these agencies and the people of Florida will begin to recognize that we must increase our efforts to protect our environment and the creatures who inhabit it, not just to use for recreation but for the sake of preserving the machinery that makes our lives as living things possible.

It is these concerns that have been the driving force behind the volunteer-biologists who have unselfishly spent so many long hours putting together the information in these volumes. We hope that through the information provided here more biologists will turn their thoughts from the test tube to the laboratory in the field, funding agencies will realize the need for this basic knowledge, and government agencies will begin to think more on the biological community level and not the species or individual organism level. Most important, we hope that these volumes serve to educate the citizens of Florida so that we may all recognize the need to learn more and work together to make prudent decisions about our "Vanishing Eden."

Ray E. Ashton, Jr.
FCREPA Chair and Series Editor

A Brief History of FCREPA

The Florida Committee on Rare and Endangered Plants and Animals, FCREPA, was founded in 1973. The original group of 100 scientists, conservationists, and concerned citizens was organized by James Layne, Peter Pritchard, and Roy McDiarmid. The chairs of the Special Committees on Terrestrial Invertebrates, Marine Invertebrates, Plants, Reptiles and Amphibians, Fish, Birds, Mammals, and Liaison made up the first Endangered Species Advisory Board to the Florida Game and Fresh Water Fish Commission. These special committees were made up of concerned biologists who were living and/or working in the state of Florida. The first FCREPA meeting was called for biologists to discuss and evaluate the status of Florida's wildlife and to determine which species should be considered for special classification and concern. From this conference, five volumes—The Rare and Endangered Biota of Florida series—were produced. These were edited by Peter Pritchard of the Florida Audubon Society and Don Wood of the Florida Game and Fresh Water Fish Commission. Section editors for the first series included Roy McDiarmid, reptiles and amphibians; Herb Kale, birds; James Layne, mammals; Carter Gilbert, fish; Howard Weems, terrestrial invertebrates; Joe Simon, marine invertebrates; and Dan Ward, plants. Before its completion, the invertebrate volumes were combined under the editorship of Richard Franz.

Following the production of the FCREPA volumes by the University Presses of Florida in 1976, FCREPA continued to meet and support a special section of papers at the annual meeting of the Florida Academy of Sciences. The affiliation of FCREPA was organized under the guidance of Dan Ward, director of the herbarium at the University of Florida.

In the fall of 1986, it became obvious that the original publications were becoming dated and the demand for the publication was great (the volumes had been reprinted repeatedly). Then chair, Herbert Kale, vice president of the Florida Audubon Society, convened the second FCREPA conference at the youth camp in the Ocala National Forest. The committees on each group met and deliberated on the status of the species in their charge. It was decided at that meeting to rewrite the FCREPA series since considerable changes in our knowledge and in the state of the natural environment in Florida made much of the information produced more than 13 years before out of date. Editors for each of the volumes called together those knowledgeable individuals and potential contributors to the future volumes to discuss the status of the taxa covered in their volume. Their recommendations on the status (and the criteria used) of various species were discussed by everyone present at the 1986 meeting.

Under the direction of Jack Stout, University of Central Florida, and each of the section chairs and editors, the arduous task of preparing the new manuscripts was undertaken. Each section chair served as compiler and editor for each volume. Individual species accounts were prepared by biologists who were among the most qualified to write about the status of that species.

Ray Ashton, vertebrate zoologist, Water and Air Research, Inc. was appointed by the section chairs as managing editor of the series in 1988. Paul Moler, research biologist, Florida Game and Fresh Water Fish Commission, was voted as chair-elect (1992–1993). Four years of preparation and coordination, fund raising, and gentle prodding of the seven volunteer editors and the many contributors have produced the second FCREPA series.

Without the thousands of volunteer hours given by many outstanding Florida biologists, and the support from the Florida Game and Fresh Water Fish Commission, Save the Manatee Club, and Florida Power and Light Company, this effort would not have been possible. Royalties from the sales of these volumes and donations to the FCREPA effort are used to keep all the volumes in print and to fund future work.

Ray E. Ashton, Jr.
FCREPA Chair and Series Editor

Definitions of Status Categories

Categories used to designate the status of the organisms included in the Florida list of rare and endangered species are defined below. In the case of species or subspecies whose ranges extend outside the state, the category to which the form is assigned is based on the status of its population in Florida. Thus, a plant or animal whose range barely reaches the state ("peripheral species") may be classified as endangered, threatened, or rare as a member of the Florida biota, although it may be generally common elsewhere in its range.

In the following definitions, "species" is used in a general sense to include (1) full taxonomic species, (2) subspecies (animals) or varieties (plants), and (3) particular populations of a species or subspecies that do not have formal taxonomic status. This use of the term agrees with that of the Endangered Species Act of 1973.

Endangered.—Species in danger of extinction or extirpation if the deleterious factors affecting their populations continue to operate. These are forms whose numbers have already declined to such a critically low level or whose habitats have been so seriously reduced or degraded that without active assistance their survival in Florida is questionable.

Threatened.—Species that are likely to become endangered in the state within the foreseeable future if current trends continue. This category includes: (1) species in which most or all populations are decreasing because of overexploitation, habitat loss, or other factors; (2) species whose populations have already been heavily depleted by deleterious conditions and, while not actually endangered, are nevertheless in a critical state; and (3) species that may still be relatively abundant but are being subjected to serious adverse pressures throughout their range.

Rare.—Species that, although not presently endangered or threatened as defined above, are potentially at risk because they are found only within a restricted geographic area or habitat in the state or are sparsely distributed over a more extensive range.

Species of special concern.—Species that do not clearly fit into one of the preceding categories yet warrant special attention. Included in this category are: (1) species that, although they are perhaps presently relatively abundant and widespread in the state, are especially vulnerable to certain types of exploitation or environmental changes and have experienced long-term population declines; and (2) species whose status in Florida has a potential impact on endangered or threatened populations of the same or other species outside the state.

Status undetermined.—Species suspected of falling into one of the above categories for which available data are insufficient to provide an adequate basis for their assignment to a specific category.

Recently extirpated.—Species that have disappeared from Florida since 1600 but still exist elsewhere.

Recently extinct.—Species that have disappeared from the state since 1600 through extinction.

Analysis of Florida Aquatic Ecosystems

Many publications have described aquatic habitats in Florida (Rogers 1933; Carr 1940; Hobbs 1942; Berner 1950; Herring 1951; Beck 1965; Rosenau et al. 1977; Schomer and Drew 1982; Seaman 1985; Duever et al. 1986; Berner and Pescador 1988; Livingston 1991). Most of the earlier works discussed habitat types in relation to the distribution of various aquatic animal groups. Beck (1965) summarized and discussed the earlier works but confined his own discussion to lotic habitats. The more recent papers present the most complete analyses of aquatic habitats in the state.

In this volume, the classifications presented by Berner and Pescador (1988), which in turn were adapted from Berner (1950), are used to provide perspective on the availability of habitats for fish in Florida. Because of their thoroughness of analysis and their discussion of the importance of aquatic vegetation to the aquatic ecosystem, much of the following is taken verbatim from that publication. Where those descriptions seemed inadequate, supplementary information was excerpted from other papers and from the authors' experiences.

As the first edition of this volume did not include an assessment of Florida's coastal and marine habitats, a general description of those habitats has been included here. Additional detailed marine-habitat descriptions may be found in Gilmore (1977), Schomer and Drew (1982), and Seaman (1985).

Classification of Florida Aquatic Ecosystems

Inland Freshwater Habitats
 I. Creeks
   A. Intermittent
   B. Sand-bottomed creeks with little vegetation
   C. Sand-bottomed creeks choked with vegetation
   D. Silt-bottomed creeks with little vegetation
   E. Silt-bottomed creeks choked with vegetation

Descriptions of Aquatic Habitats

Inland Freshwater Habitats

Creeks

Intermittent.—In Florida, there are relatively few intermittent streams. These few are, for the most part, merely connecting canals between swamps, ponds, or other bodies of water, the levels of which fluctuate continually according to the amount of precipitation. Vegetation is usually abundant but differs from the type found in constantly flowing waters.

Sand-bottomed creeks with little vegetation.—Sand-bottomed creeks —small, shallow, gently flowing streams with sandy beds—vary from as little as 0.3 m (1 ft) to 12.2 m (40 ft) in width and from a few centimeters to as much as 1.5 m (5 ft) in depth. The bottom is composed of loose rolling sand that builds up in midstream into small ridges, behind which small masses of debris accumulate. Large rocks almost never occur in Florida streams, but pebbles may be found imbedded in gravelly riffles where the water becomes quite shallow. There are occasional pools, but they are not a conspicuous element of the streams. The pools are usually small, quiet areas near the banks or at curves. Debris accumulates to a rather marked degree in some of the streams, with almost any obstacle forming a nucleus for the accumulation of much leaf drift, sticks, and other objects. Tree trunks frequently form dams and give rise to riffles, while the tangle of branches and twigs provides a network in which much detritus becomes entangled. Silt accumulates near the shore and in places may produce rather thick deposits, in some streams even forming a layer more than 0.6 m (2 ft) in thickness; however, the silt deposits in the sand-bottomed streams are usually sparse and of little consequence. Near shore, leaf drift becomes a fairly important habitat, for many insects are harbored in this material, and in the almost-stagnant shore pools the leaf debris, interspersed with silt, may be several layers thick. The flow of water in the sand-bottomed streams is never rapid in the sense in which a northern stream is said to be rapid; rather, the flow is gentle, with the surface of the water seldom being broken. Most of these streams are circumneutral to slightly acid, but some may be markedly acidic. Nearly all streams have tinted waters that may vary in shade from almost colorless to a strong tea color, according to the area drained and to the amount of rainfall. Most of the streams drain flatwoods, hammock lands, or swampy areas and are fed by springs or diffuse seepage areas. Vegetation is almost completely absent from the streams, except for a few scattered *Orontium* plants and an occasional clump of *Polygonum* near the quiet shore zone.

Sand-bottomed creeks choked with vegetation.—This type of stream occurs mostly in the northwestern part of Florida beyond the Apalachicola River. The beds of the creeks are composed of fairly loose sand, but instead of being almost bare, as in the type of stream mentioned above, they are covered with dense growths of *Vallisneria, Sagittaria*, and *Potamogeton*, which in turn are thickly covered with algae. Some debris may collect in slower areas near the shore, but in midstream the vegetation is swept clean, although an occasional partially submerged log may lie among the plants. These streams are usually not much more than 6 m (20 ft) across and may be as much as 1.5 m (5 ft) in depth at the center. In deeper parts of the creeks, the vegetation tends to disappear and may be entirely absent from exceptionally deep stretches. The rate of flow is moderate but is seldom strong enough to cause any marked disturbance of the water surface. The creeks mostly drain scrublands and high pine and hammock country, and the water is much lighter in color than that of the sand-bottomed creeks with little vegetation; however, the water is usually slightly acidic, with a pH of approximately 6.0. Silt deposits are less pronounced in these streams than in those of the preceding class, and debris along the shore is likewise less in quantity.

Silt-bottomed creeks with little vegetation.—Silt-bottomed streams are rather common in the northern part of the Central Highlands of Florida. The stream bottom is covered with a layer of silt overlying the sand and varying from a few centimeters to more than a meter in depth. The rate of flow is comparatively slower than that of the sand-bottomed streams, but it is steady and quite perceptible. The water is definitely acidic and usually has a rather strong tea color. The silt bottom is frequently overlain by layers of leaves and strewn with much other debris, but there are few or no plants in the stream proper. Near shore, *Polygonum* and various sedges and grasses may be present, but they are not especially abundant. This type of creek averages about 6 m (20 ft) in width and from a few centimeters to 1 m (3 ft) in depth.

Silt-bottomed creeks choked with vegetation.—These streams are not particularly common in Florida and are confined mostly to the northwestern part of the state. The streams are shallow, 0.3–1.0 m (1–3 ft) in depth, frequently wide, very meandering in their courses, and are some-times braided. In the shallower zones the rate of flow of the water is neg-ligible. The vegetation is dense and may include plants that are character-istic of more slowly flowing or even stagnant water, such as *Ludwigia, Polygonum*, and *Pontedaria*. Other plants also found in the course of the stream include *Vallisneria, Potamogeton*, and *Sagittaria*, as well as many kinds of algae. The silt in the streams is very loose and may be as much as 1–1.3 m (3–4 ft) in thickness. This material is soft, flocculent, and somewhat sticky and at the slightest disturbance stirs up and clouds the water. There is usually a broad floodplain, and during periods of high water the streams spread out widely until all vegetation is completely submerged (except larger bushes and trees). There is a constant flux of channels due to this flooding.

Rivers

Southeast Florida drainages.—Historically, many natural drainage chan-nels cut through the limestone rock ridge that separated the Everglades from Biscayne Bay and the Atlantic Ocean. These drainages varied from shallow, transverse glades that dried seasonally to deeper natural channels like the Miami River and other creeks that maintained flows year-round. The freshwater head of the Everglades, which produced freshwater springs on the ridge and even in Biscayne Bay, was lowered when the natural stream channels were dredged to drain the marshes and to provide flood control. Few natural stream courses remain in southeast Florida, as most are now replaced by box-cut canals. Originally many of the canals were open to salt water, allowing intrusion inland during the dry season. This intrusion is now prevented by salinity-control structures near their mouths. Descriptions of the canals are found in Beck (1965) and Loftus and Kushlan (1987). The small littoral zone in most canals prevents luxuriant growths of aquatic or emergent vegetation. Only shallow, low-turbidity canals support beds of *Potamogeton* or the exotic *Hydrilla* in midchannel. To prevent aquatic vegetation from slowing water flow, herbicides are routinely applied, eliminating fish habitat. Water quality in some canals is chronically poor because of agricultural and urban runoff. Water flows vary seasonally, with greatest flows occurring during the wet season. The channels range from 3 to 30 m (10–100 ft) wide and 2 to 7 m (7–25 ft) deep. Substrates are typically limestone with overlays of marl or organic sediments.

    Slow-flowing, deep rivers.—This category is easily the least satisfactory of those listed. No two large rivers in Florida share even a preponderance of features, and they may be notably different in very basic ways. Not all are uniformly deep, they may differ sharply with regard to clarity and water color, and some may carry large quantities of clay or silt and thus are usually turbid, whereas others may carry very low silt loads and are basically clear. The St. Johns River has areas well upstream where the salinity is actually greater than in sections down toward the mouth, a situation nearly unique among North American rivers. It is clear in many places but with fairly high color. The Escambia River is basically whitewater in character, carries a significant amount of clay and silt, and is always turbid. Many shallow bars exist where one can wade well out into the stream during periods of low water. The Suwannee River, which flows mostly through a region of calcareous bedrock overlain by sand, is deeply gouged and has very few wadable areas except in times of extremely low water or in places where bedrock sills come close to the surface. It is basically clear but with considerable dark color, although this may vary somewhat depending on the amount of rainfall and the influence of such large tributaries as the Santa Fe River, which contributes a large amount of relatively clear water. Finally, although none of the large rivers of Florida can be considered fast-flowing in the sense of many inland montane streams, neither are they exceptionally sluggish.

The large rivers of Florida have continuous flow, and during excessive rains they spread out over their floodplains. Vegetation is limited and occurs principally near the shores in protected places where the current is slow. However, masses of water hyacinths (*Eichhornia crassipes*) are very common in rivers such as the St. Johns, and side-water areas of that river also may contain much greater quantities of submergent aquatic vegetation than other large streams around the state, particularly near the headwaters.

Larger calcareous streams.—This category includes streams that are, in general, smaller than those included above and definitely basic in character (i.e., have a higher pH). Most of these streams rise from springs and form small rivers such as the Silver, Wakulla, and Santa Fe. They are clear, cool (usually 12°–13.5° C), and of moderate flow, with rather dense growths of vegetation in the stream proper. Vegetation is comprised chiefly of *Vallisneria, Sagittaria, Naias, Ludwigia*, mosses, and many algae, which in the shallower zones form dense mats that completely cover the floor of the stream. The water may be colorless if the source is confined to springs, but if swamp waters also contribute to the stream the water may be tinged with brown. Many of these rivers have sand bottoms, and there may be thick deposits of calcareous silt in the quieter shallow zones. Leaf drift and other debris become entangled in fallen trees and other catchalls, and such debris forms an important habitat for small aquatic organisms. In some of the rivers there are outcrops of limestone, and in the Santa Fe River specifically there are many loose rocks that are of great importance as habitats for such organisms. The depth of these streams varies from 1 to 6 m (3–20 ft) or more and the width from 23 to 92 m (75–300 ft). This type of stream is faunistically the richest in Florida, in numbers of both individuals and species.

Springs

Springs provide the source of water for the larger calcareous streams, and the two therefore share common hydrological and chemical features. Most of the large springs of Florida are artesian. The water flowing from them rises through deep, generally vertical limestone holes, some of which open into nearly horizontal caverns, through which flow underground rivers.

The cavity through which water ascends to an artesian spring is generally a former sink in which the direction of motion of the water has been reversed by the rise of the water table. If the water table were to fall below the mouth of the cavity, the spring would cease to flow and would revert to a sink, provided the tubular cavity leading to the spring does not penetrate an impervious stratum, which might confine the water below it under pressure.

Vegetation is very dense just below the exit of the spring, but around the spring itself is nothing but bare sand. Immediately beyond the periphery of the "boil," *Chara, Myriophyllum, Ceratophyllum, Sagittaria,* and *Ludwigia* become very abundant. The surface of the vegetation close to the spring is usually covered with a coating of calcium carbonate deposited from the water as the bicarbonate exposed to the air changes to the carbonate. The low oxygen content of the water is reflected in the small populations of truly aquatic insects in this region; however, snails of the genus *Elimia* are exceedingly numerous on the vegetation, and *Pomacea* occurs frequently on the bottom sands. Approximately 0.4 km below the head of the springs a more abundant insect fauna becomes noticeable, and in this region the plants are free of the calcium carbonate. The water of the springs is crystal clear, cool, and definitely alkaline. Because of the large quantities of phosphates emitted with the spring water, springs and spring runs are among the most productive aquatic habitats known. Rosenau et al. (1977) described all major Florida springs and their features.

Ditches and Puddles

Roadside ditches.—A common sight throughout the state, many ditches are created by removal of fill for adjacent road beds or for mosquito control. If permanent standing water is present, this may be a very rich habitat for aquatic organisms. Although the ditches are quite variable in appearance, depending on edaphic and climatic factors, the fauna may be fairly constant within a region.

Ditches in central and northern Florida differ in many ways from those in southern Florida. Water temperatures may be similar in summer, but ice may form in northern Florida ditches in winter. The pH and turbidity of the ditches depend on local geology. Waters of ditches situated in sandy or organic soils normally are acidic and often stained, whereas ditches cut in southern Florida limestome are usually clear and basic. In many locations *Pontederia*, *Typha*, and *Sagittaria* are predominant emergent plants in the shallows. Deeper sections have beds of submerged plants, and bottoms of ditches may have heavy growths of *Micranthemum, Ludwigia*, and *Polygonum*. In southern Florida the ditches are square in shape (i.e., "box cut"), so that emergent plants are sparse. Submerged beds of *Chara, Hydrilla,* or *Utricularia* are common. In sunny locations, floating mats of periphyton, *Lemna, Azolla, Salvinia, Pistia*, and/or *Eichhornia* often occur. Water depths vary from several centimeters to 2 and the width from 0.3 to 5 m.

Temporary pools.—This habitat is of little importance to fishes because of its limited duration. Pools typically form when water courses overflow their channels to flood adjacent lands or when heavy rains flood local depressions. Little or no aquatic vegetation occurs there. Pools that are flooded seasonally and for longer periods are able to develop a persistent algal and invertebrate biota, which produce resting stages that are able to survive intervening dry periods. Fishes may move into these temporary aquatic habitats when dispersing from permanent water bodies during flood periods, but they subsequently become stranded and are preyed on as the pool dries. The thousands of solution ponds that pock the limestone substrate on the edges of the Everglades may be included in this category, although the subsurface water reserves enable truly aquatic plant communities to survive there. Most solution holes range from 0.5 to 1 m in depth and 1 to 3 m across.

Ponds

The ponds of Florida may be divided into several types, but nearly all share the common characteristic of seldom having any surface streams draining in or out.

Sinkhole ponds.—These ponds are formed by the dissolution of underlying limestone. Rain water, percolating downward to the water table, dissolves vertical chimneys in the lime rock into which the surface cover may collapse gradually or suddenly, producing a steep-walled, open sink. Where the cover is thicker or less compact, a saucer- or funnel-shaped depression may result. Many of these ponds of sinkhole origin occur in Florida, particularly around the Gainesville area. Although some of them are dry, the great majority have standing water that maintains a fairly constant level because the water table is high enough to supply the ponds continually. The sides of the ponds both above and below the water level are steep, and the zone of rooted aquatic vegetation is very limited. The sides of the sinkholes above the water are usually covered with vegetation that extends from the edge of the water up to the rim of the depression. In many of the sinkholes a narrow sand beach may be formed where the slope of the sides levels off, but the shore zone extending into the water from this beach is very narrow, and the drop-off to deep water is rapid. The sinkhole ponds are usually about 30–90 m (100–300 ft) in diameter and are mostly round. Some of the larger ponds are formed by the coalition of two or more sinkholes.

There are two chief types of sinkhole ponds: those with their surfaces free of vegetation and those with their surfaces covered by vegetation. The first of these is one of the common types of sinkholes encountered in peninsular Florida. The margin of the pond has a fairly rich growth of both submergent and emergent vegetation, which extends outward to the region where the drop-off into deep water occurs. The plants are principally *Sacciolepis striata, Mayaca fluviatilis, Polygonum, Panicum,* and some *Typha,* as well as numerous species of algae. This sudden drop to deeper water begins at a depth of about 1.3 m (4 ft) and extends to a depth of about 3.3 m (10 ft); from there the drop continues more gradually to about 6 m (20 ft). In many of the ponds there may be deeper holes, such as the one found in Lake Mize, near Gainesville in Alachua County, which over a very small area reaches a depth of nearly 24 m (80 ft). In the shallower portions the bottom is sandy and is covered with patchy growths of *Utricularia.* There are only small deposits of silt in the shallower zones, but in the very deepest parts the bottom may be thickly covered with dense black silt, in which practically anaerobic conditions exist and from which larger organisms are almost entirely absent. The water varies from colorless to a strong tea color, depending on the type of region drained by the pond. Many of the ponds are rather turbid, and this turbidity, combined with strongly tinged water, allows little penetration of light to the deeper parts. The water varies in reaction from pond to pond, being acidic, circumneutral, or slightly basic.

The second type of sinkhole pond comes in two principal forms: those covered with water hyacinths, *Eichhornia crassipes*, and those covered with duckweed, *Lemna obscura*, mud-marys, *Spirodela punctata*, and *Azolla caroliniana*. The first kind of pond may have a marginal ring of open water, with the water hyacinths concentrated over most of the remaining area, or the entire surface may be covered with these plants. If there is some open water, submergent vegetation may take root and become fairly well established, but usually water hyacinths are the only plants of any importance in the ponds.

The duckweed-covered ponds seldom have any submergent vegetation growing in them, for the entire surface is covered with a single layer of the plants, which cuts off light from any vegetation that might attempt to grow on the pond bottom. When there is any wind, the duckweed piles up and leaves clear areas on the water surface, but as soon as the wind dies down, the plants again spread evenly over the surface. Amphipods living among the duckweed are exceedingly numerous in the ponds, but bottom organisms are scarce, probably because of the small amount of available oxygen. The bed of the duckweed-covered pond has rather thick accumulations of black silt, which is heavily loaded with hydrogen sulphide.

Fluctuating ponds.—These constitute one of the more frequently encountered types of Florida ponds. Water fills shallow basins, some merely depressions in the original sea-laid sands but the majority produced by solution of underlying limestone or by wind action. The water level in these hollows varies with the amount of rain and surface run-off. There may be considerable fluctuation in the area occupied by the water, inasmuch as a slight rise or fall causes marked spread or retreat of the margins; however, the depth usually does not change greatly because of the shallowness of the pond. True aquatic vegetation follows the rise and fall of the water to some extent, but it is chiefly confined to the part of the pond below the more permanent water level. The vegetation includes many true aquatics such as *Pontederia*, *Utricularia*, *Polygonum*, *Micranthemum*, and *Typha*, as well as *Hydrocotyl*, maidencane, *Panicum*, and other semiaquatics. Many of the ponds support *Nymphaea*, but very few are covered with water hyacinths. Plants are not confined to a shore zone, as in the sinkhole ponds, but may extend much farther out and, in some instances, may completely penetrate the ponds. The bottom of the fluctuating pond is mucky, but the layer of silt is not deep. The water is subject to rapid changes in temperature and is much influenced by external weather conditions. There is normally a slight tint to the water, and it is usually acidic.

Temporary woodland ponds.—These ponds are formed in depressions in hammocks and are of a more or less temporary nature; however, the vegetation present is such as to indicate its habitual occupation of the depression. In the ponds and around their margins are frequently found black gum (*Nyssa biflora*), button bush (*Cephalanthus occidentalis*), willow (*Salix nigra*), and bladderworts (*Utricularia* sp.), and, if the water remains for a sufficient length of time, other more succulent vegetation will become established. After the water has been standing in the depression long enough to allow growth of algae, many of the usual pond animals begin to migrate to, and become established in, the pond.

Sporadic ponds.—The sporadic ponds, which are rather temporary, may disappear briefly or even permanently during the dry season. The ponds are shallow and may be large or small, depending on the depression and the drainage of the region.

Alligator ponds.—In the Everglades marsh and the Big Cypress Swamp, depressions in the underlying limestone are deepened and cleared of soil by the American alligator (*Alligator mississippiensis*) to create open-water ponds. Ponds are usually from 25 to 30 m² in area, from 1 to 2 m deep during the wet season. During severe droughts ponds may dry completely, but in most years they retain water year-round, providing important dry-season refugia for aquatic species. Submerged vegetation is sparse, consisting mainly of *Utricularia*; emergent species bordering the ponds include *Pontederia*, *Sagittaria*, *Thalia*, and *Cephalanthus*. Some ponds, called willow ponds, are edged by *Salix caroliniana*, *Annona glabra*, and sometimes by *Taxodium*.

Lakes

Nearly all lakes in Florida result from the solution of underlying limestone; however, such lakes as Lake Okeechobee seem to occupy basins that are natural depressions in the surface formed as the land rose during the last geologic period. Many solution lakes are simply sinks that have always been tributary to the groundwater supply and never have had a surface outlet. Others at one time or another formed part of the surface drainage and therefore were connected with a particular river. Their histories are complicated, for the fluctuations of sea level and the consequent fall or rise of the water table provided opportunities to alternately deepen or flood their respective basins. Some of them appear to have been estuaries during higher stages of the sea, for the sand-covered terraces around them stand within the limits of altitude of the coastal terraces.

Lake Okeechobee, Lake Istokpoga, Lake Kissimmee, Crescent Lake, Lake George, and others apparently originated as hollows in the sea bottom.

Sand-bottomed lakes.—The sand-bottomed lakes, by far the most common type of lake found in Florida, form the most conspicuous bodies of water in the Central Highlands. There are literally thousands of these lakes in this region, and they are particularly numerous in Lake County. The lakes vary in size from 0.4 to 16 km (.25 to 9 or 10 mi) in width, but the depth is not correspondingly great and most of them are shallow, not more than 12–14 m (40–45 ft) deep at their deepest spots. There is little vegetation except at the margin, and this is chiefly *Sacciolepis striata*, *Utricularia*, and algae. Wave action is slight, but it is probably sufficient to prevent the growth of other aquatic vegetation along the sandy shore. *Sacciolepis* extends out into the lakes to a depth of 1.5–1.8 m (5–6 ft), and beyond this zone vegetation is limited to submergent plants such as *Utricularia*, which lies on the sand bottom as far out as there is sufficient light penetration for normal photosynthetic processes to take place. In this region, some silt is intermingled with the sand, but much of the sand is bare. Beyond a depth of about 6 m (20 ft), silt accumulates and covers the bottom sand with a layer several inches deep; with increase in depth of the lake there is a direct increase in the amount of silt. In the deepest parts of the lakes the silt may reach a depth of 0.3 m (1 ft) or more, and in this region it is a very thick, black, fine, and oozy mud in which few organisms live. Along the shore some debris collects, but it is not abundant; this debris provides habitat for many insects that in Florida are normally found in streams. Probably the wave action in this region is sufficient to oxygenate the water and produce conditions that simulate those found in the moderately flowing streams of the state. The water of the lakes varies from very clear to strongly colored, and the turbidity is also variable according to the lake. Most of the lakes are circumneutral, ranging not much more than 0.5 on either side of a pH of 7.0.

Silt-bottomed lakes.—This type is typified by Newnan's Lake, near Gainesville. The lake is large, about 16 km (10 mi) in length and about 5 km (3 mi) wide. It is bordered by a ring of cypress trees that extend from dry land into the water. Also lining the lake are water hyacinths that form dense growths between the bases of the cypress trees and extend out into the lake as far as there is a protected zone. With every shift in direction of the wind, water hyacinth plants break free and float across the lake, pushed onward by the wind. Frequently, during a period of sustained moderate winds, the lake is dotted with numerous floating "rafts" of water hyacinths; eventually the plants pile up along one shore until the wind again changes and sends them sailing back to the opposite side. The continual rain of dead water hyacinths onto the bottom of the lake gives rise to a thick layer of loose flocculent silt that completely covers the bottom to a depth of nearly one meter. Organisms are rare in these bottom deposits since conditions are not conducive to life. The lake is shallow; in the middle it is not much more than 3 m (10 ft) deep, and over most of its area it is shallower than this. The water has a definite brownish tinge and is rather turbid.

Numerous other lakes in the Central Highlands also belong in this same category. Orange Lake, one of the larger lakes in the region, is similar to Newnan's Lake in its type of bottom but is deeper, has much rooted vegetation in the form of water bonnets (*Brasenia schreberi*), and is somewhat exceptional in having numerous floating islands of vegetation. Some of the floating islands are large enough to support trees, but the great majority are composed of small clumps of vegetation that float about, changing location with each change in direction of the wind.

These lakes show great variations in their aquatic vegetation; in many, the succession is directly toward swamp conditions, with extensive development of cypress along the muddy shores; in others there is a distinct development and zonation of marsh vegetation before the shallow water is invaded by cypress or hardwood swamps.

Disappearing lakes.—Certain large lakes in the northern part of Florida become dry during periods of drought. Lake Iamonia, which went completely dry in 1938, is an ideal example of a disappearing lake. There is a lake near Lake City that is said to go dry "once every seven years." These lakes are shallow and in most respects similar to the silt-bottomed lakes in supporting an abundant growth of water hyacinths and in being ringed by cypress. Although the disappearing lakes are fairly large at their maximum extent, they vary greatly in size, with notable seasonal fluctuations in depth.

Marshes

Marshes are very common in peninsular Florida, particularly in the south. They may be very limited in extent or quite large, according to the size of the original basin. Many ponds and lakes have become converted into marshes, and many others are in the process of transition. The water is shallow, and profuse vegetation grows throughout. The predominant plants are emergent and include cattail, pickerelweed, maidencane, saw-grass, water lilies, smartweed, and various grasses. Submergent plants are prominent, and include *Ludwigia, Micranthemum, Myriophyllum*, and many algae. The water is rather warm during the summer and in northern Florida may freeze over during prolonged periods of cold. The filling of lake and pond basins is rapid, and the great amount of decaying vegetation quickly builds up deposits of peat, which finally replace the water of the marshes. The level of the water is subject to great fluctuations according to the amount of rainfall, and at times the marshes go completely dry; however, during the greater part of the year they contain some water. The marshes of central and northern Florida are definitely acidic. Some may have a pH below 3.6, but this condition is local, and at different places in the same marsh the pH may range from 3.6 to 6.0 or higher. The organisms found in the marshes are essentially the same as those occupying similar habitats in ponds and lakes, for conditions in the marshes are very similar to those of the pond or lake margins. The principal differences relate to (1) the occurrence of emergent vegetation throughout the water rather than its confinement to a shore zone and (2) shallowness of the marshes, which are not much more than three feet deep at their deepest point.

Another type of marsh found in the central part of Florida is very similar to the above, except that vegetation consists principally of *Polygonum* and sawgrass (*Cladium jamaicensis*), with *Pontederia* much more limited in extent and with no *Nymphaea* present; however, the organisms inhabiting these marshes are identical to those found in the other types.

The Everglades occupies a nearly level plain, which slopes from 4.5 m (15 ft) above sea level at the south shore of Lake Okeechobee to sea level at the tip of the peninsula, a distance of more than 160 km (100 mi). To the west the Everglades merges into the Big Cypress Swamp, which presumably is slightly higher in elevation. To the south and southwest the Everglades is bounded by mangrove swamps, which separate it from the open waters of Florida Bay and the Gulf of Mexico.

The Everglades is a vast marsh system that is seasonally inundated by a thin sheet of water. The general direction of water flow is slowly to the south and southwest. Water depths to one meter are typical during the wet season; in the winter–spring dry period, large areas of marsh become dry. Davis (1943) has provided the best description of the vegetation communities of the historical Everglades. Dense stands of monotypic sawgrass once blanketed the northern Everglades, but these have now been replaced by farm crops. Tree islands of tropical hardwoods and bayheads (see next section) are common in the eastern and southern segments of the marsh. Open wet prairies of *Eleocharis, Panicum*, and *Sagittaria* are interspersed among the sawgrass strands in the southern Everglades and are usually shaded by a floating mat of *Utricularia* and periphyton. Alligator ponds are scattered throughout the marsh system. Soils in the central trough of the Everglades consist of organic mucks formed by centuries of aquatic plant decomposition. When drained, as in the Everglades Agricultural Area south of Lake Okeechobee, these mucks support vegetable, sod, and sugarcane industries. The edges of the Everglades rise gently and thus are inundated for shorter periods of time than the central marshes. Vegetation and soils are different there, with *Muhlenbergia filipes* and other grasses and sedges dominating on the marl and limestone substrates. True aquatic plant communities exist mainly in the numerous small solution holes along the edges. Many of the short-hydroperiod marshes on the eastern side of the Everglades have been lost by conversion to agriculture and urbanization.

The hydrology of the historical Everglades is poorly understood; that of today's marsh is very complex and is made so by the intensive management of its waters. The source of the region's water is rainfall. The limestone bedrock underlying the Everglades results in most marshes having neutral to basic waters, usually of low turbidity. Water temperatures range from a minimum of 5°–7°C after winter cold fronts to 40°–42°C in shallow waters during late spring. The supply of water is augmented by water delivery or diminished by drainage by the extensive canal system. Canals affect regional ecology by delivering nutrient-rich agricultural waters to the marshes, thereby causing vegetation patterns to shift. Although canals offer dry-season refuge for aquatic species, they conversely make those species unavailable to avian predators that feed in the marshes. To the west, the Everglades intergrades with the swamps, prairies, and sloughs of the Big Cypress Swamp ecosystem. The faunas of the two systems are very similar, and many species move seasonally from one to the other. At the southern terminus of the Everglades, the marshes merge with the complex of mangrove swamps, creeks, rivers, and pools that borders the Gulf of Mexico and Florida Bay.

Swamps

Cypress swamps.—These heavily wooded aquatic habitats are very common in the state. The largest is Big Cypress Swamp in southern Florida, which was best described by Duever et al. (1986); other cypress swamps may be small, isolated heads growing in topographical depressions or lining the channels of stream headwaters and channels. Ewel and Odum (1984) discussed the ecological processes and relationships of these systems. In many swamps, waters are stained by humic and fulvic acids, decreasing light penetration and producing low pH's. Submerged plants are uncommon in deeper areas but may grow well in the shallows. The depth of water varies greatly but seldom exceeds 1 to 1.5 m. Other trees in the cypress swamp include black and sweet gums, pop ash, willows, and red maple.

Big Cypress Swamp is not a monotypic cypress forest but rather is a complex of intermingled plant communities. Cypress occurs along linear topographic depressions, creating formations called cypress strands, which often have deep, open ponds within. Cypress domes occupy circular depressions. Prairies of grasses and sedges, which are inundated seasonally, are common in the system. Smaller areas of pineland, hardwood hammock, and bayheads grow on slightly elevated sites. As in the Everglades, water from rainfall is critical to the system's survival. Water levels vary seasonally, and the water is usually neutral to alkaline (Duever et al. 1986).

Bayheads.—In central and northern Florida, bayheads consisting of sweet bay, titi, black gum, wax myrtle, loblolly bay, red maple, willow, and dahoon holly often form at the headwaters of small creeks. The growth of the shrubs is so dense that it is almost impenetrable. Water stands in these bayheads for most of the year and disappears only in the driest periods.

Bayheads in the Everglades region are composed of many of the same tree species mentioned above with the addition of cocoplum (*Chrysobalanus*). This community grows on slightly elevated sites in the marsh, is inundated only seasonally, and usually occurs over organic soils. Fires often affect this community in dry years.

Coastal Habitats

Coastal Freshwater and Oligohaline Tributaries

Tidal rivers.—This habitat consists of the lower reaches of all riverine systems in Florida that flow into the Atlantic Ocean or Gulf of Mexico and associated estuaries (e.g., Tampa Bay, Pensacola Bay, Charlotte Harbor, and Indian River lagoon). The major hydrological character governing this habitat is the mixing of tidal saline water and fresh water. Tidal saline waters may extend below surface fresh water for considerable distances upstream, depending on river topography and flow rates. Water flow in the St. Johns River may become reversed; tides may extend as far as 145 miles upstream, with considerable mixing of fresh and salt waters between about 32 to 80 km (20–50 miles) upstream (McLane 1955).

Tidal riverine habitats offer various vegetative communities around the Florida peninsula, as the character of these communities changes radically with both latitude and salinity gradient. Upstream vegetation may be similar throughout much of the Florida peninsula (e.g., *Taxodium distichum, Acer* spp., *Salix* spp., *Acrostichum* spp., *Sagittaria* spp., *Pontederia lanceolata, Panicum* spp.). North of 28°00′N latitude, the mouths of these tributaries are normally associated with broad salt-marsh meadows, which typically consist of *Spartina* spp. and *Juncus roemerianus*. South of 28°00′N, mangrove swamps consisting of *Rhizophora mangle, Avicennia germinans*, and *Laguncularia racemosa* are more likely to develop around river mouths, along with an association of halophyte prairies vegetated with *Juncus roemerianus, Spartina* spp., *Salicornia virginiana, Salicornia bigelovii*, and *Batis maritima*. In the disturbed tidal streams draining the Everglades/Big Cypress Swamp complex, red mangrove (*R. mangle*) and pond apple (*Annona glabra*) form a narrow border along their courses, which penetrate freshwater habitats 30–40 km (19–25 mi) from the Gulf of Mexico. Submerged aquatic vegetation is generally absent, except in cases where the river flow is reversed by clear tidal ocean waters often and long enough for sea grasses to grow, such as at the mouths of the St. Lucie and Loxahatchee rivers. Tidal rivers with red mangrove associations are also host to epiphytic proproot algal communities.

The fish fauna of this habitat is typically diverse, with both euryhaline freshwater and marine species represented. A unique group of tropical peripheral fishes reproduce in this habitat in the Loxahatchee and St. Lucie rivers and in Sebastian Creek, along the southeastern coast of Florida (*Awaous tajasica, Gobiomorus dormitor, Gobionellus pseudofasciatus*, and

Microphis brachyurus lineatus). This represents the only persistent, tropical peripheral fish community in the state and perhaps throughout the United States, with the possible exception of the Rio Grande, in southern Texas. The community's existence depends on the fortuitous combination of moderate climate, suitable and relatively undisturbed hydrology, vegetation and channel physiography, and the proximity of the warm Gulf Stream. The Gulf Stream is undoubtedly responsible for transportation of the original fish stocks from the Caribbean area and is probably a source of continuous recruitment from there. The annual movement of millions of gobioid fish larvae into tributaries of the Indian River lagoon greatly resembles the *tismiche* and *seti* migrations of the Caribbean and the *ipon* migrations of the Philippines and is one of the most impressive predictable ichthyological displays in the state. The habitat of these fishes and their reproducing populations are considered threatened. The same southeastern Florida streams also support other rare tropical fishes, such as *Agonostomus monticola, Pomadasys crocro, Diapterus rhombeus, Centropomus ensiferus,* and *Gobionellus fasciatus,* which are sporadically captured in routine stream surveys; however, there is no documentation of breeding activity in Florida waters for these particular species.

Human impacts on this habitat vary from damming (e.g., the Miami, Loxahatchee, Caloosahatchee, St. Lucie, and Hillsborough rivers) and channelization (Miami, St. Lucie, Alafia, and Peace rivers) to gross pollution (St. Johns, Miami, Hillsborough, Alafia, and Peace rivers). Major urbanization has virtually eliminated viable fish habitat along portions of these rivers in Miami, Tampa, and Jacksonville. As the human population of coastal Florida continues to grow rapidly, it is highly likely that downstream, coastal riverine habitats will continue to lose their viability and capability of supporting fishes unique to these ecosystems, particularly in southeastern Florida.

Tidal creeks, ditches and canals.—These are small though common coastal tributaries found throughout the state. Canal and ditch habitats are most abundant along the southeastern coast of Florida, where extensive flood-control systems have been constructed to drain freshwater wetlands for human habitation or agricultural purposes. Because these tributaries typically are more shallow than riverine habitats, vertical stratification between saline and fresh waters does not always occur. Downstream reaches may become oligohaline or even mesohaline during drought periods. The same system may be completely fresh during periods of maximum rainfall, particularly in flood-control canals where large volumes of water are released rapidly, creating flow rates between 1.0 and 2.0 m/sec.

Floral and faunal associations in tidal creek, ditch, and canal habitats are identical to those of coastal riverine systems. However, these small water bodies, particularly canal and ditch tributaries, are more subject to disturbance and removal of native botanical communities. The fish communities are also similar to tidal riverine systems, with all the tropical peripheral species listed for the tidal riverine systems also occurring in the smaller southeastern tributaries.

These habitats are particularly susceptible to anthropogenic disturbances and are often dredged, drained, flooded, dammed, and treated with herbicides, in addition to acting as conduits for a variety of agricultural and urban waste products. As human populations continue to expand around the Florida coast, many of the natural and seminatural streams will undoubtedly be disturbed to the point that they will no longer support an indigenous fish community. Native ichthyofaunas are supplemented and disrupted by introduced species that are better adapted to altered aquatic habitats. There are many examples of this destruction available for study throughout southeastern Florida today.

Salt Marshes

Herbaceous salt marshes are found throughout coastal Florida. The greatest acreage occurs in estuaries north from Charlotte Harbor on the Gulf Coast and the Indian River lagoon on the Atlantic coast. Salt-marsh communities are extensive along the southern tip of the peninsula, although they are separated from direct contact with the Gulf of Mexico by a wide band of mangrove forest. The most conspicuous vegetation types are *Spartina* spp., *Juncus roemerianus, Distichlis spicata, Paspalum* spp., *Salicornia* spp. *Sesuvium* spp., *Limonium carolinianum*, and *Batis maritima*. The distribution and zonation of these plants are dictated by the topography and hydrology of the marsh, which vary significantly around the Florida peninsula. Very small tidal amplitudes in isolated portions of the Indian River lagoon and in certain estuaries of the lower Gulf Coast result in vegetative associations that differ significantly from those in higher energy systems at the mouth of the St. Johns and St. Marys rivers, along the northeast coast.

The fish fauna associated with salt marshes is typically one that can withstand a wide range of environmental conditions, because of the peripheral nature of the habitat. Despite their tolerance of considerable environmental variation, some fishes occur principally in this habitat; however, none is listed as endangered or threatened in this volume.

Mangrove Swamps

Coastal salt marshes broadly intergrade with mangrove forest communities from north to south along both coasts of Florida. South of 28° 00'N latitude, mangrove forests become the dominant, marginal estuarine vegetation, although they are always in association with a subtropical marine herbaceous prairie. These mangrove forests are most extensive in southwestern Florida, forming basin communities several kilometers wide. The mangrove swamps are comprised of *Rhizophora mangle, Avicennia germinans,* and *Laguncularia racemosa,* whereas the associated marine prairies consist of *Batis maritima, Salicornia* spp., *Distichlis spicata, Juncus roemerianus* and *Spartina* spp.

Tidal amplitudes are generally low throughout the range of mangrove forests on the Florida peninsula. Net primary productivity is high, and this condition, along with high detrital production and deposition, results in a high biological oxygen demand.

Fish associated with mangrove forest communities are usually adapted to the harsh environmental conditions typically found there, particularly highly variable water levels and very low oxygen levels. A species indigenous to this habitat, *Rivulus marmoratus* (an account of which is presented in this volume), has adapted remarkably well to a very limited microhabitat and anoxic conditions within the mangrove swamp.

Human impact on the mangrove forest ecosystem has varied widely, from complete removal, filling, and burning to drowning. Between 1950 and 1970 the majority of indigenous black mangrove forest habitats on the central east coast of Florida was destroyed through flooding associated with the construction of impoundments for mosquito control. These impounded wetlands are still of considerable value since, with renewed tidal access, they have been found to perform many of the same functions as preimpoundment wetlands. The rapid growth of human populations in Florida has completely eradicated mangrove communities along a major portion of the Florida coast. Considerable mangrove habitat in Palm Beach, Broward, Dade, Collier, Pinellas, and Hillsborough counties was destroyed as a result of urban development long before the value of mangrove ecosystems was realized. Plans to lease portions of the southern coastline for offshore oil exploration open the potential for oil spills, which would result in pollution of fringing mangrove swamps, with disastrous consequences to the associated biota.

Sea-grass Meadows

Submerged, shallow-water sea grass meadows are conspicuous features of most coastal estuaries throughout Florida. There are also major sea-grass communities in the northeastern Gulf of Mexico. The most conspicuous spermatophyte species are *Thalassia testudinum*, *Syringodium filiforme*, *Halodule wrightii*, *Ruppia maritima*, *Halophyla baillonis*, *Halophyla engelmannii*, and *Halophyla johnsonii*. The numerically dominant sea-grass species vary from estuary to estuary and from season to season. A wide variety of marine algae is associated with the sea-grass community, as are very diverse sessile and mobile invertebrate faunas.

The great diversity and productivity of sea-grass communities attract a wide variety of fishes, and consequently sea-grass fish communities are the richest fish communities in Florida estuaries. Not only is there an indigenous resident ichthyofauna associated with sea-grass meadows, but there is also a transient fauna consisting primarily of juveniles of larger species that may depend on other habitats as adults. The principal sea-grass inhabitant listed in this volume, *Gobionellus stigmaturus*, is considered a species of special concern.

Human impact on sea-grass communities has been more insidious and less obvious than for most other aquatic habitats. Hundreds of acres of sea grasses have been eradicated by filling for coastal developments and road causeways (e.g., Biscayne Bay, Indian and Banana River lagoons, Boca Ciega Bay, and Sarasota Bay). However, water quality declines are responsible for reduction in sea grasses over a wide range of Florida estuaries. Tampa Bay has lost the majority of its historic sea-grass meadow habitat through changes in water quality. There have been reductions in sea-grass cover in nearly all major estuaries throughout Florida. With this reduction, available habitat has declined for hundreds of species that depend on sea grasses for survival.

Rock-algal Reef Formations

Exposed bedrock formations offer habitat for coastal neritic and benthic marine invertebrate and vertebrate faunas around the state. These consist primarily of surface limestone from various Cenozoic formations. Limestone origins vary from lithifications of shell fragments (Anastasia formation) to lithification of oolite (Miami oolite) or Key Largo limestone derived from tropical coral reef communities. Erosion of these rock formations forms undercuts ledges and vertical holes, offering a variety of locations for faunal access and cover on otherwise featureless open sand or shell bottoms.

These rock substrates provide attachment sites for a wide variety of algal species, thus forming both cover and food source for a very rich fauna. The rock substrate also allows settlement of sessile, attached invertebrates (e.g., polychaete worms, sea anemones, gorgonians, and hermatypic corals). The rock-algal reef and coral reef habitats harbor the most diverse fish assemblages in Florida waters, which in turn are the richest in the United States. Various fishes are unique to this habitat, such as the striped croaker, *Bairdiella sanctaeluciae*, which is listed in this volume as a species of special concern. Other species that are dependent on this habitat may also be listed if future life-history studies demonstrate the need.

Human impact on this habitat and its fauna is manifested through direct consumption of organisms, by means of fishery or aquarist harvest, burial, or siltation from beach renourishment projects, and overuse by divers. Since little emphasis has been placed on noncoralline reef formations, the rock-algal reef habitat has received little recognition or protection, particularly the nearshore reef habitats. Millions of public dollars are spent annually on beachfront dredge-and-fill projects, which directly affect the flora and fauna of reef-algal habitats. Recent attempts by the U.S. Department of the Interior to lease sections of the Florida coastline for oil exploration create the potential for oil spills, which could adversely affect reef habitats around the state and devastate fishes with limited distributions.

Coral Reef Formations

Florida is fortunate to possess a coral reef tract, which is most extensively developed from Virginia Key to the Dry Tortugas. Shallow-water (depths < 20 m) hermatypic corals extend as far north as St. Lucie Inlet on the east and to the Florida Middle Ground reefs in the northeastern Gulf of Mexico, whereas deep reef (70–100-m depths) colonial corals (*Oculina*) occur on the continental shelf along the length of the Florida east coast and follow the Gulf Stream as far north as North Carolina.

The deep and shallow coral reef formations support basically different invertebrate and vertebrate faunas, but, like the rock-algal reef formations, which harbor a similar hard-bottom community, they support the richest aquatic communities in Florida waters. A wide variety of fishes are unique to these coral reef habitats, one of which (the key blenny, *Starksia starcki*) is so far known only from one locality in the Florida Keys (Looe Key) and from one locality off the coast of Honduras.

Human impacts on coral reef habitats range from collection of corals and the associated fauna to fisheries consumption and dredge-and-fill operations. Many of the same disturbances affecting the rock-algal reef habitats also affect coral habitats. Deep reef corals are quite brittle and are very susceptible to destruction by deep-water trawls. Of considerable concern for future preservation of these habitats are human activities that may influence water quality from adjacent urban areas or from oil-drilling operations. Many substances originating from urban, agricultural, and petroleum-based activities may prove to be quite deleterious to this fragile tropical ecosystem.

Literature Cited

Beck, W. M., Jr. 1965. The streams of Florida. Bull. Fl. St. Mus. Biol. Sci. 10(3): 91–126.

Berner, L. 1950. The mayflies of Florida. Univ. Fl. Stud. Biol. Sci. Ser. 4(4): vii–xii, 1–267.

Berner, L., and M. L. Pescador. 1988. The mayflies of Florida. Rev. ed. University Presses of Florida, Gainesville.

Carr, A. F. 1940. A contribution to the herpetology of Florida. Univ. Fl. Stud. Biol. Sci. Ser. 3:1–118.

Davis, J. H., Jr. 1943. The natural features of southern Florida. Fl. Geol. Surv. Bull. 15:1–311.

Duever, M. J., J. E. Carlson, J. R. Meeder, L. C. Duever, L. H. Gunderson, L. A. Riopelle, T. R. Alexander, R. L. Myers, and D. P. Spangler. 1986. The Big Cypress National Preserve. National Audubon Society Research Report 8. New York.

Ewel, K. C., and H. T. Odum, eds. 1984. Cypress swamps. University Presses of Florida, Gainesville.

Gilmore, R. G., Jr. 1977. Fishes of the Indian River lagoon and adjacent waters. Bull. Fl. St. Mus. Biol. Sci. 22(3): 101–148.

Herring, J. L. 1951. The aquatic and semi-aquatic Hemiptera of northern Florida. Pt. 4. Classification of habitats and keys to the species. Fl. Entomol. 34: 141–146.

Hobbs, H. H., Jr. 1942. The crayfishes of Florida. Univ. Fl. Stud. Biol. Sci. Ser. 3:1–179.

Livingston, R. J. ed. 1991. The rivers of Florida. Springer-Verlag, Inc., New York. x+289 pp.

Loftus, W. F., and J. A. Kushlan. 1987. Freshwater fishes of southern Florida. Bull. Fl. St. Mus. Biol. Sci. 31(4): 137–344.

McLane, W. M. 1955. The fishes of the St. Johns River system. Ph.D. diss., University of Florida, Gainesville.

Rogers, J. S. 1933. The ecological distribution of craneflies of northern Florida. Ecol. Monogr. 3:1–74.

Rosenau, J. C., G. L. Faulkner, C. W. Hendry, Jr., and R. W. Hall. 1977. Springs of Florida. Rev. ed. Florida Department of Natural Resources Bureau of Geology, Bulletin 31. 461 pp.

Schomer, N. S., and R. D. Drew. 1982. An ecological characterization of the lower Everglades, Florida Bay, and the Florida Keys. U.S. Fish and Wildlife Service FWS/OBS-82/58.1.

Seaman, W., Jr. ed. 1985. Florida aquatic habitat and fishery resources. Florida Chapter, American Fisheries Society, Kissimmee. xiv + 543 pp.

Introduction

Since appearance of the first FCREPA publication in 1978, few startling new developments or surprises have occurred with regard to the Florida fish fauna. We now know more about a number of species included in the original volume, although in some cases our level of knowledge remains basically the same. This new information has usually resulted from continued survey work or directed studies, which have helped to clarify questions of distribution and abundance, whereas in other cases it has been a by-product of studies not specifically aimed at fish. Life-history studies of individual species have been initiated, often in response to concern about their status and well-being. In most cases this increased knowledge has been of a positive nature, from the standpoint that certain species thought to be rare and/or localized in the state are now known to be more widespread and common than first believed. In the case of the endangered Okaloosa darter, however, indications are that the species is still losing ground to the introduced brown darter; nevertheless, healthy populations of the Okaloosa darter remain, and assuming maintenance of the *status quo*, that species should be in no immediate danger of extinction.

A number of new freshwater species have been added to the state list, most of them exotics from Africa, South America, or Asia. Many are members of the family Cichlidae, some of which were deliberately introduced (e.g., the peacock bass, *Cichla ocellaris*), but most of which are aquarium releases. Four native freshwater species have been added to the state list. One of these, the southern starhead topminnow (*Fundulus dispar blairae*), limited in Florida to the Escambia River drainage, presumably has been a long-term resident of the state; specimens collected over the years are present in museum fish collections but had escaped detection because of the fish's close physical resemblance to the russetfin topminnow (*Fundulus escambiae*), with which it sometimes occurs. The slashcheek goby (*Gobionellus pseudofasciatus*) is a Caribbean species recently discovered in a limited area of the southeast Florida coast (Hastings 1978). Recent research has revealed that the banded topminnow (*Fundulus cingulatus*) is now known to comprise two species, as is the Okefenokee pygmy sunfish (*Elassoma okefenokee*). Conversely, one species, the creek chubsucker (*Erimyzon oblongus*) has been eliminated from the state list;

1

the specimens on which the one record was based (Bailey, Winn, and Smith 1954) were shown to be misidentified individuals of the sharpfin chubsucker, *Erimyzon tenuis* (Gilbert and Wall 1985).

New Florida records for marine fishes occur with regularity, with most involving species living in deeper waters along the outer edges of the continental shelf. Some records from Florida are based on single specimens of species, for example, the slendertail cardinalfish (*Apogon leptocaulus*) and threeline basslet (*Lipogramma trilineata*), both of which are restricted to deep offshore reefs. Some species overall are represented by only a tiny number of specimens in museum collections. The above-mentioned slendertail cardinalfish is known from a total of four specimens from four geographically widely separated localities (Gilbert 1972; Dale 1977), plus one individual that was photographed but not collected (Colin 1974). The key blenny (*Starksia starcki*) is still represented from the state by the six specimens from Looe Key that formed the basis for the original description (Gilbert 1971) and is otherwise known from eight additional specimens (from Belize) taken in only six of 230 total collections made between 1970 and 1978 (Greenfield and Johnson 1981). Looe Key is now a preserve that is off-limits to biological collecting or commercial exploitation. Although the key blenny and slendertail cardinalfish obviously are not common, the problem we face is determining the degree to which the apparent rarity of these and other species is real or an artifact of collecting. Nothing is known regarding these species' ecologies and life histories, other than the conditions surrounding their captures, and there is no evidence to indicate that they have been adversely affected by human impact. The key blenny was included in the 1978 FCREPA volume, but are we justified in providing a separate account for this species while excluding others of equal rarity for which our level of knowledge is comparable? We conclude that under the circumstances it is probably better to omit all such species from this volume and instead include them all under an "umbrella" call for continued vigilance and protection of inshore marine environments, particularly the fragile coral reef ecosystems in Florida and elsewhere.

This is not to say that all marine fish species should be categorically eliminated from the revised FCREPA list. The two sturgeon species occurring in Florida spend much of their lives in the ocean or in estuaries, as do several other species largely or entirely restricted to a limited area of southeastern Florida. Collections from fresh and inshore marine waters around the state are sufficiently complete that we are reasonably confident of these fishes' distribution and abundance. The striped croaker (*Bairdiella sanctaeluciae*) is entirely marine but, in contrast to the species mentioned in the preceding paragraph, has been adequately enough sampled and studied that its abundance and geographic range in the state are well known. Based on these factors, we feel justified in continuing to include this species in the new FCREPA list.

Although numerous introductions have resulted in localized displacement of native freshwater fishes from certain areas in the southern half of peninsular Florida, in no case (to our knowledge) has this caused extermination of any native forms. To a large degree this is a reflection of the natural impoverishment of the native freshwater fish fauna of peninsular Florida. Probably the main cause for concern is the reduction in numbers, and perhaps even the eventual elimination through habitat modification, of certain diadromous species that in Florida are limited to a few tributaries of the Indian River lagoon. For example, the rare opossum pipefish (*Microphis brachyurus lineatus*), nearly all records of which are from this area, is apparently closely associated with growths of the aquatic plants *Polygonum* and *Panicum*, which are systematically sprayed with herbicides as a flood control measure. This situation is discussed further in the account of that species, as well as in a new section on marine and estuarine habitats that appear elsewhere in this volume.

In general, Florida fishes appear to be faced with fewer problems than those of certain adjacent states. Stream channelization, lock and dam construction on large rivers, and various forms of water pollution are problems seen in other states that are less pervasive in Florida and overall have been less devastating to the fish fauna. This difference has resulted not so much from increased environmental awareness in the state as from fortuitous circumstances. Florida has no coal deposits, and its oil resources (if any) have yet to be developed. The state is largely devoid of the types of industry most likely to cause severe pollution problems, and where exceptions exist (e.g., pulp and paper mills, phosphate mining) the affected streams fortunately do not have particularly distinctive faunas, as for example, the Fenholloway River which has been extensively polluted by pulpwood mills around Perry. Despite a recent drought, which has caused the water table to be significantly lowered, an adequate water supply has historically existed in the northern part of the state. Not only has this reduced the need for water-storage impoundments, but the low topographic relief results in a paucity of suitable dam sites. Very few streams in Florida are suitable for navigation by large, shallow-draft barges. The one notable exception is the St. Johns River (which actually is an ocean estuary throughout much of its lower reaches), and its major tributary, the Oklawaha River, the site of construction for the first phase of the now-defunct cross-Florida barge canal. Dams on the Oklawaha and

Apalachicola rivers are known to have severely restricted the abilities of certain anadromous fishes (such as striped bass, Atlantic sturgeon, and various species of shads) to reach spawning sites. It is also possible that the endangered shortnose sturgeon may once have spawned in the Okla- waha River prior to the construction of Rodman Dam, although there are no substantiating records. The use of agricultural pesticides undoubt- edly has had localized detrimental effects on Florida fishes and on the en- vironment in general, but its overall impact has yet to be determined completely. Although there is no evidence that any Florida freshwater fish species has been extirpated from the state, such a possibility always re- mains, and it is in the large rivers of the western panhandle where this could most likely occur. Several Florida fishes are largely confined to the Escambia River proper (most notably the crystal darter, *Crystallaria asprella*, and river redhorse, *Moxostoma carinatum*) and thus are especially vulnerable to the accidental or intentional release of agricultural or other types of chemicals into the river (particularly during times of low water) or to extreme physical manipulation of the habitat.

It should be noted that the relatively favorable situation described above does not necessarily hold true for other elements of the biota, and in fact the fishes overall may have suffered less than almost any other tax- onomic group. For example, in the Florida Keys and elsewhere in south- ern Florida there exist highly localized and numerically small populations of various land plants, as well as vertebrate and invertebrate animals. Some of these have already been exterminated, and the status of others is tenuous. No marine fish species is known to have been extirpated from the Keys (although this would be impossible to prove), and no strictly freshwater fish species is native there. At one time, it was believed that the key silverside (*Menidia conchorum*), a marine/euryhaline species, was very close to extinction (Gilbert 1978). Partly as a result of the recom- mendations of the FCREPA subcommittee on fishes, this fish was even- tually declared an endangered species by the state of Florida. Further investigation, however, has revealed that the key silverside is geographi- cally more widespread and numerically more common than first thought and that its apparent scarcity is mostly the result of the largely inaccessi- ble habitat to which the species is restricted (Duggins et al. 1986). Furthermore, the population shows a strong south-to-north clinal varia- tion, and in the upper Keys the fish morphologically approaches the tidewater silverside (*Menidia peninsulae*), to which it is obviously closely related. Some have suggested, in fact, that the key silverside should no longer be considered a distinct species. Regardless of its ultimate taxo- nomic status, this fish is both morphologically distinct and geographically isolated from its closest phylogenetic relatives, and it should be accorded some level of protection, although we now feel that endangered status is no longer appropriate.

In general, the present FCREPA committee has adopted a more conservative attitude from that seen in the 1978 volume. To some degree this change reflects a philosophical shift; there are populations of certain fishes living in the Florida Keys (mostly killifishes) for which there is now general agreement that their original listing was simply not warranted. In other cases, the absence of any detectable changes in the situations for individual species from those existing during the late 1970s suggests that we may have been unduly pessimistic regarding their situation. More important, however, is the knowledge that has accumulated in the intervening years (often involving directed research); some of the outstanding examples are the key silverside, mangrove rivulus, blackmouth shiner, and bannerfin shiner, all of which were found to be more common and widespread than previously realized. At first glance this declaration of conservatism would appear to be contradicted by the facts, inasmuch as (1) the total number of species on the present list (39) is only four less than that appearing on the 1978 list (43), (2) the combined number of endangered and threatened species is only two less (19) than the number appearing on the 1978 list (21), and (3) nine new species have been added to the present list. A more accurate indication, however, may be seen from the fact that 21 species appearing in the earlier list have either been downgraded from a higher category (e.g., threatened to rare, rare to special concern) or eliminated altogether, compared to only two species (the river goby [*Awaous tajasica*] and opossum pipefish [*M. brachyurus lineatus*]) whose status has been upgraded, in both cases from rare to threatened. One species listed as endangered in the 1978 FCREPA list (the key silverside, *M. conchorum*) has been downgraded to a species of special concern. Of the original 17 species earlier listed as threatened, three have been downgraded to rare (the Florida chub [*Extrarius* n. sp. cf *aestivalis*], cypress darter [*Etheostoma proeliare*], and goldstripe darter [*Etheostoma parvipinne*]); two have been downgraded to special concern (the mangrove rivulus [*Rivulus marmoratus*] and Lake Eustis pupfish [*Cyprinodon variegatus hubbsi*]); and one eliminated entirely (the key blenny [*S. starcki*]). Of the 13 species included in the rare category, six have been eliminated and one has been downgraded to special concern; of the nine listed in the category of special concern, seven have been eliminated. Of the nine species added to the FCREPA list, four (the alligator gar [*Atractosteus spatula*], Florida logperch [*Percina* n. sp. cf *caprodes*], blacktip shiner [*Lythrurus atrapiculus*], and bigmouth sleeper

[*Gobiomorus dormitor*]) should, in retrospect, have been included earlier. Three others (the rough shiner, [*Notropis baileyi*], southern striped shiner [*Luxilus chrysocephalus isolepis*], and southern bluehead chub [*Nocomis leptocephalus bellicus*]) were first discovered in the state shortly before publication of the first FCREPA volume, and their status as permanent residents had not yet been evaluated. In addition, it had not yet been determined whether these species were introduced (an issue still in doubt, although indications are that introductions were involved). The southern starhead topminnow (*Fundulus dispar blairae*) and slashcheek goby (*Gobionellus pseudofasciatus*) were not known to occur in the state until after the 1978 FCREPA volume had been published. *Fundulus dispar blairae* falls in that group of species restricted in Florida to the Escambia River drainage, and is thus accorded threatened status. *Gobionellus pseudofasciatus* is a Caribbean species known nowhere else in the United States, and it in turn belongs to a group of four species whose distribution in Florida is largely, or entirely, restricted to a series of small freshwater streams emptying into the Indian River lagoon; the other three species are the bigmouth sleeper (*G. dormitor*), a new addition to the FCREPA list, river goby (*A. tajasica*), and opossum pipefish (*M. brachyurus lineatus*). This area is under environmental pressure from various sources, and all four species are therefore regarded as threatened.

One FCREPA committee member has suggested that three of the four species of the snook genus *Centropomus* known to occur in Florida (all except *Centropomus undecimalis*) should be considered for inclusion in the present list. No action was taken on these, but they may be considered for future listing.

Several nomenclatural changes have occurred since publication of the 1978 FCREPA volume. Change of the generic and scientific names for the opossum pipefish (formerly *Oostethus lineatus*, now *Microphis brachyurus lineatus*) results from Dawson's (1984) revisionary study. The species name *Percina ouachitae* was recently changed to *Percina vigil* (Suttkus 1985), and the blackmouth shiner (earlier listed as *Notropis* n. sp.) was formally described by Bortone (1989) as *Notropis melanostomus*. The following generic name changes result from Mayden's (1989) study on cyprinid classification: *Extrarius* n. sp. cf *aestivalis* was formerly placed in the genus *Hybopsis*; and *Cyprinella callitaenia*, *Pteronotropis welaka*, *Lythrurus atrapiculus*, *Luxilus zonistius*, and *Luxilus chrysocephalus isolepis* were formerly included in the genus *Notropis*. Placement of the crystal darter (formerly *Ammocrypta asprella*) in the monotypic genus *Crystallaria* results from Simons' study (in press). With three exceptions, the above changes are also reflected in the new revised American Fisheries Society checklist of common and scientific names of North American fishes (Robins et al. 1991): *Macrhybopsis* is used instead of *Extrarius, Pteronotropis welaka* remains in *Notropis*, and *Crystallaria asprella* remains in *Ammocrypta*. Another place where the generic nomenclature used here differs from Robins et al. (1991) pertains to our employment of the generic name *Atractosteus* (rather than *Lepisosteus*) for the alligator gar, as discussed in our account of that species.

Species that are known to have been introduced are not considered in this volume, the only possible exceptions being the three minnows (rough shiner [*Notropis baileyi*], southern striped shiner [*Luxilus chrysocephalus isolepis*], and southern bluehead chub [*Nocomis leptocephalus bellicus*]) whose presence in Florida is suspected, but not confirmed, to have resulted from introductions.

We regret that a "vulnerable" category is not available to us, since we feel an important distinction exists between the terms "vulnerable" and "threatened." Briefly, "threatened" implies a more active situation. For example, those fish species that in Florida are essentially confined to the main channels of major rivers could be wiped out by a devastating pollution spill from upstream, as happened during the chemical spill from a large industrial plant on the upper Rhine River (in Europe) several years ago. When such a source of pollution is present, the affected species would be considered "threatened." If a more passive situation exists (i.e., no immediately identifiable threat), the species would more properly be classed as "vulnerable."

Dots appearing on the Florida distribution map accompanying the account of each species indicate collections or confirmed sightings of that species. In some cases a dot may indicate multiple collections or sightings from the same or closely adjacent localities, since the mapping procedure decided upon did not allow for overlapping dots. In constructing spot-distribution maps for individual fish species in state ichthyological publications, it is frequently necessary to include several different symbols on a map. These may denote such things as two or more subspecies (of a single species) within the state, known or suspected introductions of a species already native to Florida outside its natural range in the state, or changes in natural distributions (usually reductions) through time. Of the 39 species considered here, however, only in one case has it been found necessary to use more than one symbol (i.e., a solid dot) on a map. The lone exception is the Atlantic sturgeon (*Acipenser oxyrinchus*), which comprises two distinct allopatric subspecies in Florida, one on the Atlantic coast and the other on the Gulf coast. Records for the Gulf of Mexico subspecies are indicated by open circles.

The acronyms TL and SL, which accompany indications of specimen size throughout the text, indicate total and standard lengths, respectively. Total length is measured to tip of tail; standard length is measured to base of tail. Fork length (FL) is used occasionally and indicates tip of snout to fork of tail.

Museum acronyms from which specimens were examined or illustrated, and to which reference is made at various places in the text, include the Florida Museum of Natural History (UF), University of West Florida (UWF) (illustration of *Fundulus jenkinsi*), Field Museum of Natural History (Chicago) (FMNH) (account of *Acipenser oxyrinchus*), and Tulane University (TU) (account of *Etheostoma proeliare*).

Authorship of individual species accounts is indicated at the end of each account. In those cases in which this was written by a different person than in 1978, both individuals are listed as authors, with the one responsible for the revised account appearing first. Volume editor Carter R. Gilbert wrote the Introduction; William F. Loftus, Everglades National Park, Homestead, Florida, is responsible for the revised section on freshwater aquatic ecosystems; and R. Grant Gilmore, Harbor Branch Oceanographic Institution, Ft. Pierce, Florida, authored the new section on coastal habitats.

Most of the illustrations (31) were prepared by Ms. Wendy Zomlefer, staff artist of the Florida Museum of Natural History, University of Florida. The following six were prepared by Mr. Merald Clark, University of Florida: alligator gar, key silverside, striped croaker, bigmouth sleeper, slashcheek goby, and spottail goby. Mr. Noel Burkhead, National Fisheries Research Laboratory, Gainesville, Florida, took the underwater photograph of spawning Okaloosa darters that appears on the front cover. These individuals are hereby acknowledged and thanked for their outstanding efforts.

All but three of the specimens used for the illustrations are from the fish collection of the Florida Museum of Natural History (University of Florida). The illustration of *Fundulus jenkinsi* is based on a specimen from the University of West Florida, and illustrations for the two species of sturgeons (genus *Acipenser*) are the same ones that appeared in the previous FCREPA volume (1978). We wish to acknowledge and thank the Sears Foundation for Marine Research, Yale University, for permission to use the last two illustrations, which appear on pages 37 and 47 of part 3 of their published series, *Fishes of the Western North Atlantic*.

Literature Cited

Bailey, R. M., H. E. Winn, and C. L. Smith. 1954. Fishes from the Escambia River, Alabama and Florida, with ecologic and taxonomic notes. Proc. Acad. Nat. Sci. Phila. 106:109–164.

Bortone, S. A. 1989. *Notropis melanostomus*, a new species of cyprinid fish from the Blackwater–Yellow River drainage of northwest Florida. Copeia 1989(3): 737–741.

Colin, P. L. 1974. Mini-prowlers of the night reef. Sea Frontiers 20(3):139–145.

Dale, G. 1977. *Apogon mosavi*, a new western Atlantic cardinalfish, and a note on the occurrence of *Apogon leptocaulus* in the Bahamas. Proc. Biol. Soc. Wash. 90(1):19–29.

Dawson, C. E. 1984. Revision of the genus *Microphis* Kaup (Pisces: Syngnathidae). Bull. Mar. Sci. 35(2):117–181.

Duggins, C. F., Jr., A. A. Karlin, K. Relyea, and R. W. Yerger. 1986. Systematics of the key silverside, *Menidia conchorum*, with comments on other *Menidia* species (Pisces: Atherinidae). Tulane Stud. Zool. Bot. 25(2):133–150.

Gilbert, C. R. 1971. Two new Atlantic clinid fishes of the genus *Starksia* Q. J. Fl. Acad. Sci. (1970) 33(3):193–206.

———. 1972. *Apogon leptocaulus*, a new cardinalfish from Florida and the western Caribbean Sea. Proc. Biol. Soc. Wash. 85(36):419–425.

———. 1978. Key silverside, *Menidia conchorum* Hildebrand and Ginsburg. Pp. 1–2 *in* Carter R. Gilbert, ed., *Rare and endangered biota of Florida*. Vol. 4. Fishes. University Presses of Florida, Gainesville. 58 pp.

Gilbert, C. R., and B. R. Wall, Jr. 1985. Status of the catostomid fish *Erimyzon oblongus* from eastern Gulf slope drainages in Florida and Alabama. Fla. Sci. 48(3):202–207.

Greenfield, D. W., and R. K. Johnson. 1981. The blennioid fishes of Belize and Honduras, Central America, with comments on their systematics, ecology, and distribution (Blenniidae, Chaenopsidae, Labrisomidae, Tripterygiidae). Fieldiana Zool. (n. ser.) 8:v–viii, 1–106.

Hastings, P. A. 1978. First North American continental record of *Gobionellus pseudofaciatus* (Pisces: Gobiidae). Northeast Gulf Science 2(2):140–144.

Mayden, R. L. 1989. Phylogenetic studies of North American minnows, with emphasis on the genus *Cyprinella* (Teleostei: Cypriniformes). Misc. Publ. Mus. Nat. Hist. Univ. Kans. 80:1–189.

Simons, A. M. The phylogenetic relationships of the crystal darter, *Crystallaria asprella*. Copeia (in press).

Suttkus, R. D. 1985. Identification of the percid, *Ioa vigil* Hay. Copeia 1985(1): 225–227.

Designations of Status

The following are the Florida fish species included in present and previous (1978) FCREPA lists, with official federal and state classifications and unofficial FCREPA designations. UR2 indicates a species is formerly under review for listing, but substantial evidence of biological vulnerability of threat is lacking.

Family and Species	Federal	State	1978 FCREPA	Current FCREPA
Family Petromyzontidae (lampreys)				
Sea lamprey (*Petromyzon marinus*)	N	N	R	R
Family Acipenseridae (sturgeons)				
Shortnose sturgeon (*Acipenser brevirostrum*)	E	E	E	E
Atlantic sturgeon (*Acipenser oxyrinchus*)[a]	UR[2]	SSC	T	T
Family Lepisosteidae (gars)				
Alligator gar (*Atractosteus spatula*)[b]	N	N	N	R
Family Catostomidae (suckers)				
River redhorse (*Moxostoma carinatum*)	N	N	T	T
Grayfin redhorse (*Moxostoma* n. sp. cf *poecilurum*)	N	N	T	T
Family Cyprinidae (minnows and carps)				
Bluestripe shiner (*Cyprinella callitaenia*)[d]	UR[2]	N	T	T
Bannerfin shiner (*Cyprinella leedsi*)[d]	N	N	R	Elim.

E=endangered, T=threatened, R=rare, SSC=species of special concern, Elim.=eliminated, N=no status, UR[2]=under review-level 2.

Family and Species	Federal	State	1978 FCREPA	Current FCREPA
Florida chub (*Extrarius* n. sp. cf *aestivalis*)[c]	N	N	T	R
Cypress minnow (*Hybognathus hayi*)	N	N	T	T
Southern striped shiner (*Luxilus chrysocephalus isolepis*)[f]	N	N	N	R
Bandfin shiner (*Luxilus zonistius*)[f]	N	N	R	R
Blacktip shiner (*Lythrurus atrapiculus*)[g]	N	N	N	R
Southern bluehead chub (*Nocomis leptocephalus bellicus*)	N	N	N	R
Rough shiner (*Notropis baileyi*)	N	N	N	R
Dusky shiner (*Notropis cummingsae*)	N	N	SSC	Elim.
Blackmouth shiner (*Notropis melanostomus*)[h]	UR^2	E	T	T
Bluenose shiner (*Pteronotropis welaka*)[i]	N	SSC	SSC	SSC
Family Ictaluridae (bullhead catfishes)				
Snail bullhead (*Ameiurus brunneus*)[j]	N	N	R	Elim.
Spotted bullhead (*Ameiurus serracanthus*)[j]	N	N	R	Elim.
Family Umbridae (mudminnows)				
Eastern mudminnow (*Umbra pygmaea*)	N	N	R	Elim.
Family Cyprinodontidae (killifishes and topminnows)				
Sheepshead minnow (Keys) (*Cyprinodon* cf *variegatus*)	N	N	SSC	Elim.

E=endangered, T=threatened, R=rare, SSC=species of special concern, Elim.=eliminated, N=no status, UR^2=under review-level 2.

Family and Species	Federal	State	1978 FCREPA	Current FCREPA
Lake Eustis pupfish (*Cyprinodon variegatus hubbsi*)	N	SSC	T	SSC
Southern starhead topminnow (*Fundulus dispar blairae*)[c]	N	N	N	T
Southern Gulf killifish (*Fundulus grandis saguanus*)	N	N	SSC	Elim.
Saltmarsh topminnow (*Fundulus jenkinsi*)	N	SSC	T	T
Longnose killifish (Keys) (*Fundulus similis* n. subsp.)	N	N	SSC	Elim.
Rainwater killifish (Keys) (*Lucania* cf *parva*)	N	N	SSC	Elim.
Family Aplocheilidae (rivulines)				
Mangrove rivulus (*Rivulus marmoratus*)[k]	N	SSC	T	SSC
Family Poeciliidae (livebearers)				
Mangrove gambusia (*Gambusia rhizophorae*)	N	N	SSC	SSC
Sailfin molly (Keys) (*Poecilia* cf *latipinna*)	N	N	SSC	Elim.
Family Syngnathidae (pipefishes and seahorses)				
Opossum pipefish (*Microphis brachyurus lineatus*)[l]	N	N	R	T
Family Atherinidae (silversides)				
Key silverside (*Menidia conchorum*)	N	T	E	SSC
Family Mugilidae (mullets)				
Mountain mullet (*Agonostomus monticola*)	N	N	R	R

E=endangered, T=threatened, R=rare, SSC=species of special concern, Elim.=eliminated, N=no status, UR[2]=under review-level 2.

Family and Species	Federal	State	1978 FCREPA	Current FCREPA
Family Percidae (perches and darters)				
Crystal darter (*Crystallaria asprella*)[m]	UR^2	T	T	T
Harlequin darter (*Etheostoma histrio*)	N	SSC	T	T
Okaloosa darter (*Etheostoma okaloosae*)	E	E	E	E
Southern tessellated darter (*Etheostoma olmstedi maculaticeps*)	N	SSC	T	T
Goldstripe darter (*Etheostoma parvipinne*)	N	N	T	R
Cypress darter (*Etheostoma proeliare*)	N	N	T	R
Florida logperch (*Percina* n. sp. cf *caprodes*)	N	N	N	R
Saddleback darter (*Percina vigil*)[n]	N	N	T	T
Family Centrarchidae (sunfishes and black basses)				
Mud sunfish (*Acantharchus pomotis*)	N	N	R	Elim.
Blackbanded sunfish (*Enneacanthus chaetodon*)	N	N	R	R
Shoal bass (*Micropterus* n. sp. cf *coosae*)	N	SSC	T	T
Suwannee bass (*Micropterus notius*)	N	SSC	R	Elim.
Family Centropomidae (snooks)				
Common snook (*Centropomus undecimalis*)	N	SSC	N	N
Family Sciaenidae (croakers)				
Striped croaker (*Bairdiella sanctaeluciae*)	N	N	R	SSC
Family Eleotrididae (sleepers)				
Bigmouth sleeper (*Gobiomorus dormitor*)	N	N	N	T

E=endangered, T=threatened, R=rare, SSC=species of special concern, Elim.=eliminated, N=no status, UR^2=under review-level 2.

Family and Species	Federal	State	1978 FCREPA	Current FCREPA
Family Gobiidae (gobies)				
River goby (*Awaous tajasica*)	N	N	R	T
Slashcheek goby (*Gobionellus pseudofasciatus*)[c]	N	N	N	T
Spottail goby (*Gobionellus stigmaturus*)	N	N	SSC	SSC
Family Labrisomidae (clinids)				
Key blenny (*Starksia starcki*)[o]	N	SSC	T	Elim.

Notes

a. Atlantic sturgeon comprises two distinct allopatric subspecies in Florida

b. *Atractosteus spatula* (often placed in genus *Lepisosteus*)

c. *Fundulus dispar blairae* (southern starhead topminnow) and *Gobionellus pseudofasciatus* (slashcheek goby) only recently found to occur in Florida; former previously called *Fundulus blairae*

f. *Luxilus chrysocephalus isolepis* and *L. zonistius* (both formerly in genus *Notropis*)

g. *Lythrurus atrapiculus* (formerly in genus *Notropis*)

h. *Notropis melanostomus* (formerly *Notropis* n. sp. cf *ortenburgeri*)

i. *Pteronotropis welaka* (formerly in genus *Notropis*)

j. *Ameiurus brunneus* and *A. serracanthus* (both formerly in genus *Ictalurus*)

k. *Rivulus marmoratus* (previously included in family Cyprinodontidae)

l. *Microphis brachyurus lineatus* (formerly *Oostethus lineatus*)

m. *Crystallaria asprella* (formerly *Ammocrypta asprella*)

n. *Percina vigil* (saddleback darter) (formerly *Percina ouachitae* [stargazing darter])

o. *Starksia starcki* (previously included in family Clinidae)

Nomenclatural or classification changes since 1978 FCREPA volume

d. *Cyprinella callitaenia* and *C. leedsi* (both formerly in genus *Notropis*)

e. *Extrarius* n. sp. cf *aestivalis* (formerly *Hybopsis aestivalis*)

E=endangered, T=threatened, R=rare, SSC=species of special concern, Elim.=eliminated, N=no status, UR[2]=under review-level 2.

Endangered

Shortnose Sturgeon

Acipenser brevirostrum

FAMILY ACIPENSERIDAE

Order Acipenseriformes

Shortnose sturgeon, *Acipenser brevirostrum* Lesueur, 1818. Spawning female, 580 mm TL. Hudson River near Kingston, New York (from *Fishes of the Western North Atlantic*).

OTHER NAMES: Pinkster (young, New York); Esturgeon à museau court (Quebec); Little sturgeon (St. John River, New Brunswick); Roundnoser (Hudson River); Bottlenose (Delaware River); Mammose (Delaware River); Salmon sturgeon (North and South Carolina); Softshell (Altamaha River, Georgia); Lake sturgeon (Altamaha River, Georgia).

DESCRIPTION: *Acipenser brevirostrum* is distinguished from the other Florida species of *Acipenser* (*Acipenser oxyrinchus*) by (1) a shorter and more rounded snout at comparable body length (snout shorter than postorbital distance in individuals of all sizes vs. longer than postorbital distance in individuals less than 95 cm total length); (2) a wider mouth, the width inside lips more (vs. less) than 3/5 of bony interorbital width; (3) absence of pupil-sized bony plates (vs. two to six such plates) between anal base and lateral row of scutes; (4) total number of gillrakers in outer gill arch averaging 25–26 (range 22–29) (vs. 21–22 [range 17–27]); (5) pigmentation of lateral scutes much paler than background (vs. same shade as background); (6) intestine darkly pigmented (vs. lightly pigmented); and (7) much smaller maximum size (56 in total length [TL] and 93 lbs vs. 14 ft TL and 811 lbs).

15

RANGE: Atlantic coast of North America, from St. John River, New Brunswick, south to St. Johns River, Florida. An old record from Indian River, Florida (Evermann and Bean 1898), requires confirmation and thus has not been plotted on the spot-distribution map. The specimen on which this record is based could not be located at the National Museum of Natural History (Jeffrey T. Williams, personal communication), and we think it is likely based on a misidentified individual of *A. oxyrinchus*, which regularly ranges south to the Indian River area during winter months.

The range of *A. brevirostrum* may not be continuous but may comprise a series of disjunct populations. This is suggested by the fact that there

Distribution map of *Acipenser brevirostrum*.

are extensive sections of coast from which the species has never been re-corded, combined with the fact that the species seldom, if ever, enters full-strength sea water. A spot-distribution map appears in Gruchy and Parker (1980).

Although a few shortnose sturgeon are caught in the St. Johns River, Florida, by commercial fishermen each year, the overall number of indi-viduals involved is very small and the fish is considered to be extremely rare. Only four Florida specimens have been added to the Florida Mu-seum of Natural History collection during the past 40 years, one of which (UF 5714) is now lost. Other records, with years of collection, in-clude UF 7106 (1949), UF 35745 (1977), and UF 31480 (ca 1979). Sev-eral other records (accompanied by photographs and associated collection data) of specimens caught and subsequently released by commercial fish-ermen were provided to the museum by personnel of the Florida Game and Fresh Water Fish Commission between 1979 and 1981.

There is no direct evidence that the shortnose sturgeon has ever spawned in Florida. It is possible that individuals that are occasionally caught in the St. Johns River represent strays that have worked their way down the coast, perhaps from as far away as the Altamaha River, in Georgia. It is also possible that both this species and the Atlantic stur-geon may have spawned in the St. Johns drainage at one time but no longer do so today. Good spawning substrate appears to be very limited in this drainage but at one time may have existed in the Oklawaha River. Black Creek, which enters the St. Johns River above Palatka, appears to be the only other area that might offer marginal spawning habitat. As a result of the construction of Rodman Dam, the Oklawaha is no longer available as a spawning area for anadromous species. The striped bass (*Morone saxatilis*) is one fish known to have been so affected. Although no sturgeon eggs or larvae have ever been collected in the St. Johns River, this does not comprise conclusive evidence that reproduction did not occur there at one time. Because of their strongly benthic nature, early life stages of sturgeon are seldom collected, even in areas where spawning is known to occur.

HABITAT: The shortnose sturgeon is an anadromous species that spends much of its life in brackish water and migrates up coastal rivers to spawn. The maximum recorded salinity at which the species has been found is 30–31 ppt (Holland and Yelverton 1973; Dadswell et al. 1984), or slightly less than full-strength sea water. In the St. John River estuary (New Brunswick), large juveniles of *A. brevirostrum* and *A. oxyrinchus* were found to be ecologically segregated on the basis of salinity, the former predominating in water of <3 ppt and the latter predominating in water of >3 ppt (Appy and Dadswell 1978; Dadswell 1979). Substrate preference of *A. brevirostrum* varies according to time and circumstances. While living in estuaries, the shortnose sturgeon occurs in areas with little or no current over a bottom comprised primarily of mud and silt. During spawning migration the fish is almost continually exposed to currents of varying velocities, and the substrate of the rivers is cleaner and firmer on the average than in the estuaries. Dadswell (1979) and Dovel (1979) reported adult shortnose sturgeon in shallow water (2–10 m) in summer and in deeper water (10–30 m) in winter. Dadswell et al. (1984) found juveniles at depths greater than 9 m in river channels. Higher aquatic vegetation is usually absent.

LIFE HISTORY AND ECOLOGY: Partly because of its status as a federally endangered species, a considerable amount of basic research has been done on *A. brevirostrum* over the past 10–15 years. This information has been summarized by Dadswell et al. (1984) and Gilbert (1989).

As indicated above, the shortnose sturgeon is anadromous but is more closely restricted to fresh water than is the Atlantic sturgeon. In two places (Holyoke Pool, Massachusetts, and Lake Marion, South Carolina), landlocked populations have continued to survive and reproduce in fresh water after access to the sea was blocked by dam construction. In contrast to the Atlantic sturgeon, which is known to make oceanic excursions as great as 900 miles (Magnin and Beaulieu 1963), coastal movements of the shortnose sturgeon are much more restricted, a circumstance brought about by the species' apparent avoidance of full-strength sea water.

The shortnose sturgeon undergoes earlier migration and spawning than the Atlantic sturgeon at comparable latitudes. Migration may begin during the fall or winter, and spawning has been reported to occur as early as January in South Carolina and Georgia and as late as mid-May in the St. John River, New Brunswick (Dadswell et al. 1984). Those populations beginning their migration during the fall may remain at the upstream spawning grounds for several months before reproductive activities begin. Taubert (1980) found the species spawning in relatively fast-flowing sections of Holyoke Pool over a mixture of gravel, rubble, and large boulders, with little sand or silt. Large numbers of eggs are produced, and Heidt and Gilbert (1978) reported between 79,000–90,000 in individuals 75–87 cm fork length (FL). Eggs are broadcast into the water, with no evidence of parental care, and are demersal and adhesive, becoming attached to rocks, weeds, and other submerged objects. Length of incubation depends on water temperature, with hatching occurring in 8 days at 17° C and 13 days at 10° C (Dadswell et al. 1984). It is uncertain exactly how long juveniles remain in upstream areas before moving down into the estuaries, but in the Hudson River, New York, Smith (1985) indicated this might be anywhere from two to six years. Age at first spawning varies latitudinally and also varies widely individually. Earliest spawning in females occurs at about 6 years of age in the Altamaha River but not until 15 years in the St. John River, New Brunswick. Taubert (1980) concluded that female shortnose sturgeon in Holyoke Pool spawned for the first time between 8–12 years of age. Individuals do not spawn annually, and Taubert (1980) found a range of 4–12 years between first and second spawnings.

Aging of sturgeons is complicated by the above-mentioned circumstance of nonannual spawning. Feeding is greatly reduced or eliminated during upstream spawning migrations, resulting in an annulus that is much better defined than those laid down during years when migration does not occur and when reduction in feeding is largely a function of reduced water temperatures. This problem may be especially acute in aging individuals from southern populations, where shorter winters and generally warmer water temperatures would mean fewer and less prolonged cessations of feeding. The oldest recorded female from the St. John River (New Brunswick) was calculated to be 67 years old, whereas the oldest female recorded from the Altamaha River was only 10 years (Dadswell et al. 1984). The oldest male examined by Dadswell (1979) was calculated to be 32 years of age.

The relative kinds and percentages of food eaten by shortnose sturgeon change between the juvenile and adult stages (Dadswell et al. 1984). Juveniles feed mostly on benthic crustaceans and insect larvae (Dadswell 1979), and individuals of 20–30 cm FL often feed extensively on cladocerans (Dadswell et al. 1984). Adults feed largely on molluscs, which are sometimes supplemented by polychaetes and small benthic fish in estuarine areas. Sturgeons characteristically feed by rooting along the bottom with their snouts, using their barbels as organs of touch and "vacuuming" the bottom with their protrusible mouths. Large quantities of mud and detritus are also consumed. Fish foraging in muddy backwater areas containing abundant aquatic vegetation have been observed feeding on small gastropods living on the undersides of lily pads and on the stems and leaves of submerged macrophytes (Dadswell et al. 1984), which suggests that feeding is occasionally selective. Dadswell et al. (1984) found an inverse relationship between light intensity and feeding, with nearly all feeding activity occurring at night. It also has been found that feeding activity in shortnose sturgeon is greatly reduced with reduction in water temperature, with feeding in estuaries during the winter about half the summer level.

Shortnose sturgeons in northern parts of their range are seldom found where water temperatures exceed 22° C, and in the St. John River (New Brunswick) surface temperatures above 21° C appear to stimulate movement into deeper water. In the Connecticut River, however, this species was frequently captured at temperatures of 27°–30° C (Dadswell et al. 1984), and, in the Altamaha River, shortnose sturgeons were found at water temperatures as high as 34° C. Dadswell (1979) and Marchette and Smiley (1982) reported that a 2°–3° C decline in temperature during fall stimulated downstream movement of this species. Temperatures at overwintering sites ranged from 0°–13° C in the St. John River and from 5°–10° C in Winyah Bay, South Carolina (Marchette and Smiley 1982; Dadswell et al. 1984). As indicated earlier, shortnose sturgeon migrate upstream and spawn earlier than Atlantic sturgeon, indicating a preference for lower temperatures.

BASIS OF STATUS CLASSIFICATION: *Acipenser brevirostrum* was declared a federally "endangered" species in 1967 and is at present also on the state of Florida endangered list. Partly for these reasons it is accorded the same status here, as it was in the first FCREPA volume (Gilbert 1978). The species has unquestionably suffered a pronounced overall decline in numbers, especially in the middle parts of its range. Contributing factors, as with all sturgeon species, are (1) the unusual length of time required for *A. brevirostrum* to reach maturity and (2) the several years that may elapse between times of spawning. For these reasons, the shortnose sturgeon cannot recover from population declines nearly as rapidly as most fishes. Despite these factors, stable populations remain in the northern and southern parts of its range, especially in northern New England and the St. John River, New Brunswick, as well as in South Carolina and Georgia. All things considered, the shortnose sturgeon is overall probably less critically endangered than are certain other fish species.

RECOMMENDATIONS: Continue to monitor this species in the St. Johns River. It is possible that the individuals occasionally taken in this river were originally spawned there. If so, most or all suitable spawning habitat would have been eliminated after construction of Rodman Dam, and since the species does not appear to undergo extensive coastal migrations the St. Johns population of this species may be expected to eventually disappear. Removal of Rodman Dam and restoration of the Oklawaha

River to its natural state are probably necessary to the continued survival of this and certain other anadromous fishes in the area.

Literature Cited

Published Information

Appy, R. G., and M. J. Dadswell. 1978. Parasites of *Acipenser brevirostrum* Lesueur and *Acipenser oxyrhynchus* Mitchill (Osteichthyes: Acipenseridae) in the St. John River estuary, N.B., with a description of *Caballeronema pseudoargumentosus* sp. n. (Nematoda: Spirurida). Can. J. Zool. 56:1382–1391.

Dadswell, M. J. 1979. Biology and population characteristics of the shortnose sturgeon, *Acipenser brevirostrum* LeSueur 1818 (Osteichthyes: Acipenseridae), in the Saint John River Estuary, New Brunswick, Canada. Can. J. Zool. 57: 2186–2210.

Dadswell, M. J., B. D. Taubert, T. S. Squiers, D. Marchette, and J. Buckley. 1984. Synopsis of biological data on shortnose sturgeon, *Acipenser brevirostrum* LeSueur 1818. NOAA Technical Report NMFS 14 (FAO Fish. Synopsis 140). U.S. Department of Commerce. iv+45 pp.

Dovel, W. L. 1979. The biology and management of the shortnose and Atlantic sturgeon of the Hudson River. New York State Department of Environmental Conservation, Final Rept. Proj. AFS-9-R, Albany. 54 pp.

Evermann, B. W., and B. A. Bean. 1898. Indian River and its fishes. Rept. U.S. Comm. Fish and Fish. (1896) 22:227–262.

Gilbert, C. R. 1978. Shortnose sturgeon, *Acipenser brevirostrum* Lesueur. Pages 4–5 *in* Carter R. Gilbert, ed., Rare and endangered biota of Florida. Vol. 4. Fishes. University Presses of Florida, Gainesville. 58 pp.

———. 1989. Species profiles: life histories and environmental requirements of coastal fishes and invertebrates (Mid-Atlantic Bight)—Atlantic and shortnose sturgeons. U.S. Fish Wildl. Serv. Biol. Rept. 82(11.122). U.S. Army Corps of Engineers, TR EL-82-4. 28 pp.

Gruchy, C. G., and B. Parker. 1980. *Acipenser brevirostrum* Lesueur, Shortnose sturgeon. Page 38 *in* D. S. Lee et al., eds. Atlas of North American freshwater fishes. North Carolina State Museum of Natural History, Raleigh. i–x+854 pp.

Heidt, A. R., and R. J. Gilbert. 1978. The shortnose sturgeon in the Altamaha River drainage, Georgia. Proc. Rare Endangered Wildlife Symp. Ga. Dept. Nat. Res.: 54–60.

Holland, B. F., Jr., and G. F. Yelverton. 1973. Distribution and biological studies of anadromous fishes from offshore North Carolina. N. C. Dept. Nat. Econ. Res. Spec. Sci. Rept. 24. 132 pp.

Magnin, E., and G. Beaulieu. 1963. Etude morphometrique comparée de l'*Acipenser oxyrhynchus* Mitchill du Saint-Laurent et de l'*Acipenser sturio* Linné de la Gironde. Nat. Can. 90:5–38.

Smith, C. L. 1985. The inland fishes of New York state. New York State Department of Environmental Conservation, Albany. xi+522 pp.

Taubert, B. D. 1980. Reproduction of the shortnose sturgeon (*Acipenser brevirostrum*) in Holyoke Pool, Connecticut River, Massachusetts. Copeia 1980(1): 114–117.

Unpublished information

Marchette, D. E., and R. Smiley. 1982. Biology and life history of incidentally captured shortnose sturgeon, *Acipenser brevirostrum* in South Carolina. S. C. Wildl. Mar. Res. (unpubl. report).

Prepared by: Carter R. Gilbert, *Florida Museum of Natural History, University of Florida, Gainesville, Florida 32611.*

Okaloosa Darter

Etheostoma okaloosae

FAMILY PERCIDAE

Order Perciformes

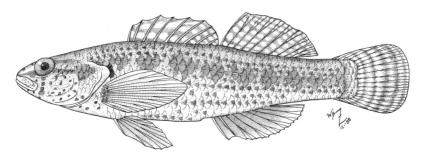

Okaloosa darter, *Etheostoma okaloosae* (Fowler, 1941). UF 74516. Adult female, 45.0 mm SL. Long Creek (tributary to Rocky Bayou), Eglin Air Force Base, Okaloosa County, Florida. 17 January 1973.

OTHER NAMES: None.

DESCRIPTION: *Etheostoma okaloosae* is a darter of relatively small to moderate size (maximum 49 mm standard length [SL]), which is characterized by the following features: a well-developed humeral blotch; body color in life red-brown to yellow-brown dorsally, lighter ventrally, the pigment broken up into small dots arranged in 5 to 8 rows along sides of body; midside of body with 9 to 10 dark dashes or blotches, which vary in degree of prominence; suborbital bar present but thin and not particularly prominent; cheeks and prepectoral area with well-developed spotting, but latter without a prominent bar; both sexes without red spots on body, but dorsal fin with a thin orange-red submarginal stripe; lateral line very slightly arched anteriorly (nearly straight), separated from origin of dorsal fin by 3 to 4 scale rows; lateral line complete or nearly complete, the total number of scales ranging from 32 to 37 (usually 34 to 36), with no more than 4 unpored scales; cheeks, opercle, belly, and nape fully scaled, the breast fully or partly scaled; premaxillary frenum present and well developed; branchiostegal membranes narrowly connected, the apex forming a broad "V" and located at a point below posterior part of cheek; dorsal-fin rays VIII–X, 10–13 (usually IX, 11–12); pectoral-fin rays, 12–14 (usually 13); anal-fin rays II, 6–8 (usually II, 7).

TAXONOMIC REMARKS: Collette and Yerger (1962) believed that *E. okaloosae* was most closely related to *Etheostoma edwini*, the brown darter (a species whose geographic range surrounds that of the Okaloosa darter), and that these two species were the sole representatives of the subgenus *Villora*. Page (1981) subsequently decided that the relationships of *E. okaloosae* are actually closer to *Etheostoma mariae* and *Etheostoma fricksium*,

Distribution map of *Etheostoma okaloosae*.

two geographically disjunct species occurring on the lower Atlantic slope from Georgia to southeastern North Carolina and that these three species comprise the subgenus *Belophlox*.

RANGE: The Okaloosa darter is endemic to the panhandle of northwestern Florida. It is confined to two bayou systems, Boggy and Rocky bayous, of the Choctawhatchee Bay drainage in Okaloosa and Walton counties. The principal tributary watersheds are Toms, Turkey, and Mill creeks of Boggy Bayou (90.9 total stream miles), and Swift, Turkey, and Rocky creeks of Rocky Bayou (151.9 stream miles). The vast majority of the darter's range is in streams draining approximately 115,000 acres of Eglin Air Force Base and about 12,000 acres outside the base (Mettee et al. 1976). This region is notable for its relatively high endemism of other plants and animals (Yerger 1978; Moler 1985).

HABITAT: *Etheostoma okaloosae* inhabits small- to moderate-sized streams (4–40 ft wide) of generally low gradient but with persistent discharge. Because of consistent groundwater discharge, most streams are clear and cool and exhibit only minimal diel temperature fluctuation throughout the season. During February, when the air temperature was 0° C, the lowest observed water temperature was 12.0° C, whereas in midsummer (when daytime air temperatures range from about 32° to 37° C), the highest water temperature was 24.5° C (mean = 22.0° C).

Most streams inhabited by the species drain sandhill terrain with managed mixed deciduous or coniferous forests and typically have a sand bottom with clear to slightly tea-colored water. In the Turkey Creek watershed of Boggy Bayou, many stream reaches are moderately incised (50–100 ft) in the surrounding terrain. The streams are fairly soft, with reported pH extremes ranging from 5.6 (Crews et al. 1977) to 8.4 (Bortone 1989). The latter extreme is considered exceptional and perhaps erroneous; typical pH extremes are in the subneutral range. Detritus is usually present along stream margins, in backwaters, macrophyte beds, and in the bottoms of slow-flowing pools. The Okaloosa darter is typically associated with cover, principally submerged macrophytes in open sunlit stream sections and with detritus in well-canopied areas. *Etheostoma okaloosae* may sometimes occur over open sand or nonsheltering detritus, but if so sheltered areas are usually nearby.

Some stream reaches are heavily silted by sediment runoff from road crossings, sand and clay pits, old railroad beds, and other sources of disturbance. *Etheostoma okaloosae* seems to be intolerant of extensive siltation, as it is observably less abundant in extensively silted sections of stream.

LIFE HISTORY AND ECOLOGY: Life history and ecological data have not previously been published but are available in state and federal reports by Mettee and Crittenden (1979) and Ogilvie (1980).

Stomach analyses of 325 specimens revealed that chironomid midges (70.3% of total food items), ephemeropteran larvae (17.4%), and tricopteran larvae (7.6%) dominate the diet. Miscellaneous food items included oligochaetes, copepods, ostracods, gastropods, odonates, plecopterans, and dipterans (simulids, ceratopogonids, and culicids) (Ogilvie 1980).

The duration of the spawning period greatly exceeds reproductive quiescence. Spawning extends from March into October, with most activity in April but with a minor peak in October (Ogilvie 1980). Spawning observations were reported on by Collette and Yerger (1962) and Mettee and Crittenden (1979). Detailed observations of spawning were videorecorded by Burkhead and Williams (1989, 1990) in June and July between 0845–1215 hours, with none noted after midday. Water temperature during the spawning observations ranged from 20° to 21.5° C. Reproductive behavior is presently being studied in the laboratory.

During spawning courtship, a male follows a single female as she slowly moves over and through fine-stemmed algae or macrophytes, including *Nitella* sp. (stonewort), *Myriophyllum heterophyllum* (variable-leaf milfoil), and *Eleocharis* sp. (spike rush). At fairly regular intervals, the male will mount the female dorsolaterally, sometimes curving his peduncle downward and at other times keeping it relatively straight. Very subtle to overt lateral vibrations by one or both sexes attend this activity, after which the female again moves a short distance away. The area covered by the darters during the series of spawning acts tends to be fairly linear. Mettee and Crittenden (1979) observed males spawning with several females.

Fecundity is low, as is true of darters in general. Ogilvie (1980) reported the mean total number of ova to be 79 and the mean number of mature ova as 29. *Etheostoma okaloosae* is probably a fractional spawner (i.e., eggs develop and mature over an extended period), and thus ovarian egg counts indicated above may be less than actual total seasonal fecundity. The mature ova are large for darters (2.0-mm diameter [Ogilvie 1980]), as are the water-hardened ova (2.9-mm diameter [Mettee and Crittenden 1979]). Larval development is poorly known, the only reference being a brief description by Mettee and Crittenden (1979). A newly hatched prolarva measured 4.9 mm TL.

Egg deposition is by attachment, although the female genital papilla is not pendulous. In the laboratory, only one egg shed per spawning act has been observed. Based on the number of spawning acts per day and the low fecundity of the species, it is probable that only one egg is shed at a time in the wild as well.

Based on our interpretation of length-frequency data (Mettee and Crittenden 1979; Ogilvie 1980), individuals typically live to be two years old, and occasionally may live three years. Average adult size is about 28–38 mm SL (Ogilvie 1980), with the smallest mature female observed at 27 mm SL; although there are no data regarding the smallest mature male, the length is likely comparable. Because of the small size at maturation, it is possible that young spawned during the early spring may themselves spawn by late fall.

BASIS OF STATUS CLASSIFICATION: The Okaloosa darter was nationally listed as "endangered" by the U.S. Fish and Wildlife Service on 4 June 1973 (Federal Register, vol. 38, no. 106). The principal reason for listing this species was its extremely small geographic range. Within this limited range, *E. okaloosae* is persistently present in most reaches of stream, and in some cases it is fairly abundant. Density is very low in the wooded, well-canopied stream sections that represent the vast majority of occupied stream miles, but it can be relatively high in open sunlit reaches. Although rigorous population estimates have not been made, educated guesses range between 1,500 and 10,000 individuals (Yerger 1978). Based on our recent (1988–present) survey efforts, the total population probably numbers in the thousands.

Several abiotic and biotic factors appear to be negatively affecting Okaloosa darter populations. As noted, the majority of the home range of *E. okaloosae* occurs on Eglin Air Force Base (AFB), a situation that might normally be viewed positively. Unfortunately, Air Force stewardship has not been entirely benign. Poor land-use practices on Eglin AFB have resulted in extensive siltation in localized stream reaches, including Florida Route 285 crossing on Little Rocky Creek (near the type locality). At some of the worst erosion sites, probably several tons of sediment have been deposited. In middle and upper Mill Creek, Okaloosa darters were fairly common at the state Route 190 bridge until this section of the stream was extensively silted. The silt originated from steep-banked golf course fairways that sloughed into Mill Creek during heavy rains. The large amount of sediment entering Mill Creek coincided with a population crash of *E. okaloosae* at this site and probably caused direct and indirect mortality in this population.

Stream sections extralimital to Eglin AFB are also silt impacted or have the potential to receive extensive sediment runoff. For example, Mill Creek, at and just above its mouth below the state Route 20 crossing in

Niceville, is heavily silted by deposits up to three feet deep. No Okaloosa darters now occur there, although they are known from the mouth of nearby Turkey Creek. Two sewage sprayfields for the city of Niceville are located in the headwater reaches of Swift and Turkey creeks, in the Rocky Bayou system. The headwater tributaries of Swift Creek receiving spray-field runoff are Shaw Still and Sanders Branch. *Etheostoma okaloosae* is not known from either of these headwater tributary streams, but persists in Turkey Creek above a tiny, swampy impoundment. The darter's absence in tributaries of Swift Creek may result from the presence of the brown darter in that system (see below).

The last major, and possibly most insidious, threat to *E. okaloosae* is the introduced brown darter, *Etheostoma edwini*. *Etheostoma edwini* was first recorded in the home range of *E. okaloosae* in 1964 in the Rocky Bayou system at the state Route 20 bridge in Niceville; until recently, this was the only system believed to have been so "contaminated." Compilation of all known collection records from this system reveals a pattern of re-placement of Okaloosa darters by brown darters in certain sections of stream, whereas in other sections they are currently sympatric. It is un-known at present whether this replacement results from ecological or be-havioral interactions or perhaps is due to other factors, particularly habitat degradation. However, present data point to some form of competitive interaction.

Generally speaking, *E. okaloosae* is found in the greatest numbers in areas of moderate current in beds of submerged fine-stemmed macro-phytes. Similarly, *E. edwini* is also strongly associated with cover, but in stream sections of reduced current which tend to have larger depositions of detritus. This ecological segregation is reinforced by the fact that in downstream areas with a reduced flow and bottom detritus, *E. edwini* has been found to the exclusion of *E. okaloosae*, whereas in headwater areas with stronger flow and clean bottom the reverse has been true. In many areas, the two species occur sympatrically, but in such cases *E. edwini* usu-ally is the more common. On the other hand, in some places where habi-tat apparently suitable for *E. okaloosae* is present, only *E. edwini* has been found (Burkhead and Williams, personal observation). It seems clear from the above that, although competition between the two species is clearly indicated, the situation is more complex than it initially appears.

Although one specimen of brown darter was collected in 1971 from Turkey Creek in the Boggy Bayou system, subsequent collections have failed to reveal additional specimens. A brown darter population does not appear to be established in the Boggy Bayou system.

It seems obvious that the presence of the brown darter in areas inhabited by the Okaloosa darter is not a natural occurrence. Yerger (1978) suggested that baitbucket introduction was the underlying cause and that this may have occurred independently in several tributaries of the Rocky Bayou system. Bait-bucket introduction does appear to be the most likely explanation for the single Boggy Bayou system record and is probably the mode by which the brown darter entered the system. Another possible mode of introduction relates to U.S. Fish and Wildlife Service stream reclamation efforts in the late 1950s and early 1960s. Certain sections of stream in the Rocky Creek system were treated with the ichthyocide rotenone and "reclaimed" for stocking with nonnative rainbow trout and smallmouth bass, as well as with native largemouth bass. Stock of the last species was shipped from the federal fish hatchery in Welaka, Florida, which is within the range of *E. edwini*, and it is possible that brown darters were accidentally included in the shipment.

RECOMMENDATIONS: Yerger (1978) concluded that studies on the life history, population dynamics, and nature of interaction of *E. okaloosae* and *E. edwini* were needed. The National Fisheries Research Center in Gainesville has initiated a multiyear study, the primary objectives of which are to conduct a thorough distributional survey of the Okaloosa and brown darters and to study and compare their respective microhabitats, reproduction, and behavior. Information resulting from this work is summarized in this account.

The Service is working with personnel of Eglin AFB to abate the numerous point-source siltation sites on the base. It is hoped that these research and cooperative efforts will produce meaningful management recommendations for the protection of the Okaloosa darter.

Literature Cited

Published Information

Collette, B. B., and R. W. Yerger. 1962. The American percid fishes of the subgenus *Villora*. Tulane Stud. Zool. 9:213–230.

Mettee, M. F., Jr., R. W. Yerger, and E. Crittenden. 1976. A status report on the Okaloosa darter in northwest Florida. Southeast. Fishes Counc. Proc. 1(2):1–3.

Moler, P. E. 1985. A new species of frog (Ranidae: *Rana*) from northwestern Florida. Copeia 1985(2):379–383.

Page, L. M. 1981. The genera and subgenera of darters (Percidae: Etheostomatini). Occ. Pap. Mus. Nat. Hist. Univ. Kans. 90:1–69.

Yerger, R. W. 1978. Okaloosa darter, *Etheostoma okaloosae* (Fowler). Pages 2–4 *in*

Carter R. Gilbert, ed., Rare and endangered biota of Florida. Vol. 4. Fishes. University Presses of Florida, Gainesville. 58 pp.

Unpublished information

Bortone, S. A. 1989. The status of the Okaloosa darter (*Etheostoma okaloosae*) regarding increases in sprayfield loading. Report to Polyscience Engineering, Dothan, Ala.

Crews, R. C., S. M. Lefstad, G. G. Wyman, and C. I. Miller. 1977. Water quality: streams and ponds on selected test areas on Eglin Air Force Base, Florida. Air Force Armament Laboratory, AFATL-TR-76-4, Eglin Air Force Base, Fla.

Mettee, M. F., and E. Crittenden. 1979. A study on *Etheostoma okaloosae* (Fowler) and *E. edwini* (Hubbs and Cannon) in northwestern Florida, 1975–78. Report to U.S. Fish and Wildlife Service, Atlanta, Ga.

Ogilvie, V. E. 1980. Endangered wildlife project E-1, Study I-J: Okaloosa darter investigation. Completion report, October 1, 1977–June 30, 1980. Florida Game and Fresh Water Fish Commission, Tallahassee.

Prepared by: Noel M. Burkhead and James D. Williams, *National Fisheries Research Center, 7920 N.W. 71st Street, Gainesville, Florida 32606*; and Ralph W. Yerger (retired), *Department of Biological Sciences, Florida State University, Tallahassee, Florida 32306.*

Atlantic Sturgeon

Acipenser oxyrinchus

FAMILY ACIPENSERIDAE

Order Acipenseriformes

Atlantic sturgeon, *Acipenser oxyrinchus oxyrinchus* Mitchill, 1815. Immature male, 581 mm TL. St. Lawrence River near St. Vallier, Quebec (from *Fishes of the Western North Atlantic*).

OTHER NAMES: Sea sturgeon, Common sturgeon, Big sturgeon (adults, Hudson River), Sharpnose sturgeon (young, Hudson River) (*Acipenser oxyrinchus oxyrinchus*); Common sturgeon, Gulf of Mexico sturgeon, Gulf sturgeon (*Acipenser oxyrinchus desotoi*).

DESCRIPTION: *Acipenser oxyrinchus* is distinguished from the other Florida species of *Acipenser* (*Acipenser brevirostrum*) by (1) a longer and more pointed snout at comparable body length (snout longer than postorbital distance in individuals of all sizes vs. shorter than postorbital distance in individuals less than 95 mm TL); (2) a narrower mouth, the width inside lips less than 3/5 of bony interorbital width; (3) two to six pupil-sized bony plates (vs. absence of plates) between anal base and lateral row of scutes; (4) total number of gill rakers in outer gill arch averaging 21–22 (range 17–27) (vs. average of 25–26 [range 22–29]); (5) pigmentation of lateral scutes same shade as background (vs. much paler than background); (6) intestine lightly pigmented (vs. darkly pigmented); and (7) a much larger maximum size (14 ft TL and 811 lbs vs. 56 in TL and 93 lbs).

Florida populations of *A. oxyrinchus* are separable into two distinct, geographically disjunct subspecies, *A. oxyrinchus oxyrinchus* and *A. oxyrinchus desotoi* (Vladykov 1955), which are restricted to the Atlantic and Gulf coasts, respectively. According to Wooley (1985), the only distinguishing character showing no overlap at any size is length of the spleen, which comprises 5.7%–6.0% of fork length in the Atlantic subspecies, versus 12.7%–17.5% of fork length in the Gulf subspecies. Other characters showing statistically significant differences between the two forms (Wooley 1985) include pectoral-fin length/fork length ratio (mean of 13.6% in *oxyrinchus* vs. 29.4% in *desotoi*); head length/fork length ratio (mean of 27.4% in *oxyrinchus* vs. 29.4% in *desotoi*); and length/width ratio of 5th and 6th dorsal scutes (mean of 0.89 and 0.87%, respectively, in *oxyrinchus* vs. 1.11% and 1.16%, respectively, in *desotoi*). (Although only the fifth

Distribution map of *Acipenser oxyrinchus*. Solid dots indicate subspecies *A. oxyrinchus oxyrinchus*; open dots refer to subspecies *A. oxyrinchus desotoi*. Northern part of total range for subspecies *oxyrinchus* extends beyond limits of inset.

and sixth scutes were analyzed, differences presumably exist for other dorsal scutes as well.)

NOMENCLATURAL REMARKS: It was recently discovered that the species name for the Atlantic sturgeon has been consistently misspelled for over a hundred years. Reference to Mitchill's (1815) description indicates that the name originally appeared as *oxyrinchus* instead of *oxyrhynchus*, the spelling that has long been used for this species. Since the rules of zoological nomenclature clearly state that the spelling of a scientific name must conform to that appearing in the original description (i.e., rule of original orthography), the species name is accordingly modified.

RANGE: *Acipenser oxyrinchus oxyrinchus* ranges along the Atlantic coast of Canada and the United States from Ungava Bay, Labrador, south to the east coast of Florida (Gruchy and Parker 1980; Wooley 1985). *Acipenser oxyrinchus desotoi* is essentially restricted to the eastern Gulf of Mexico, from the lower Mississippi River eastward to the west coast of peninsular Florida. However, there is a recent (1991) reliable sight record from the Rio Grande above the mouth of the Pecos River along the Texas-Mexico boundary (S. P. Platania and B. M. Burr, personal communication). A spot-distribution map of the species appears in Gruchy and Parker (1980).

In Florida, the subspecies *oxyrinchus* apparently enters the state only sporadically. We have seen only five museum specimens, two from the St. Johns River (FMNH 35376 [collected in January 1900] and UF 30956 [January 1981]), one from the Port Canaveral area, in Brevard County (UF 30903 [January 1981]), and two (represented by heads in the Harbor Branch Foundation fish collection) from off Ft. Pierce Inlet and off Hutchinson Island in St. Lucie County (January and March 1980). In addition, R. Grant Gilmore has provided a photograph and collection information for a specimen, which was not saved, taken either during December 1977 or January 1978 off Hutchinson Island. Six records were provided by personnel of the Florida Game and Fresh Water Fish Commission of specimens collected by commercial fishermen in the St. Johns River, all from northern Putnam County near the Clay County line, between 1979 and 1981. Two of the St. Johns collections (both specimens released) were made in April, whereas the others were made during January.

Although there is no evidence that the subspecies *oxyrinchus* breeds in Florida today, it possibly did so at one time, most likely in the Oklawaha River. Although this situation closely parallels that described for *Acipenser brevirostrum* (see discussion of that species in this volume), the stronger marine orientation of the Atlantic sturgeon increases the possibility that individuals appearing in the St. Johns River are winter migrants from the north. This receives strong confirmation from the fact that all Atlantic records of *A. oxyrinchus oxyrinchus* in Florida are from the winter or early spring months (January to April).

Acipenser oxyrinchus desotoi (hereafter called the Gulf sturgeon) maintains, or once maintained, breeding populations in most large tributaries to the eastern Gulf of Mexico east to the Suwannee River, Florida. These populations have been eliminated or greatly reduced in size in many places, with the largest and most stable population today occurring in the Suwannee. As is true also for the typical subspecies, individuals occasionally range farther south during winter, with one taken in Charlotte Harbor in Lee County (UF 35332) on 1 February 1982. During exceptionally cold winters (e.g., 1957, 1959, 1962), individuals have been seen as far south as Florida Bay (Wooley and Crateau 1985). The Gulf sturgeon at one time (1886–1889) occurred in sufficiently large numbers in Tampa Bay to support a winter commercial fishery (Wooley 1985).

HABITAT: *Acipenser oxyrinchus* is an anadromous species, spending most of its adult life in salt or brackish water and during certain years moving into fresh water to spawn. It frequently enters the ocean, where it may make extensive coastal migrations, and has been found in water as deep as 46 m (Bigelow and Schroeder 1953). It is less closely restricted to fresh water than *A. brevirostrum*, and in the St. John River estuary (New Brunswick) large juveniles of the two species were found to be ecologically separated on the basis of salinity, *A. oxyrinchus* predominating in water of >3 ppt and *A. brevirostrum* predominating in water of <3 ppt (Appy and Dadswell 1978; Dadswell 1979). As a result of its movements in the ocean and into fresh water, the Atlantic sturgeon encounters a broad range of substrates (ranging from soft mud to hard rock) and may occur in water of widely varying clarity. The species usually is found in areas devoid of submergent aquatic vegetation. Little or no current is usually present, except when the species enters rivers and moves upstream to spawn. Spawning occurs in areas with strong water movement, and the early life stages are spent under these conditions.

LIFE HISTORY AND ECOLOGY: Although a considerable amount of literature exists for *A. oxyrinchus*, the depth and detail of knowledge is surprisingly less than for *A. brevirostrum*. The most recent summary is by Gilbert (1989).

As indicated above, the Atlantic sturgeon, although anadromous, is less closely restricted to fresh water than the shortnose sturgeon. In contrast to *A. brevirostrum*, there are no reproducing landlocked populations of this species. Spawning occurs later than for the shortnose sturgeon at comparable latitudes, and in addition the Atlantic sturgeon appears usually to spawn farther downstream. Spawning migrations of Atlantic sturgeon may occur as early as mid-February in southern parts of its range (Florida to South Carolina) (Huff 1975; T. Smith et al. 1982), and as late as mid-June or even July in tributaries to the Gulf of Maine and in the St. Lawrence River (Bigelow and Schroeder 1953; Vladykov and Greeley 1963; Scott and Crossman 1973). Males begin to migrate earlier than females, with migration in New York beginning when water temperatures reach 5.6°–6.1° C (C. Smith 1985). By the time females appear at the spawning sites, water temperatures are 12.2°–12.8° C. Spawning follows within a few weeks, when temperatures have risen still further (13.3°–17.8° C) (Borodin 1925; Vladykov and Greeley 1963). Huff (1975) found *A. oxyrinchus desotoi* spawning from March through May in the Suwannee River, with peak activity in April.

Sturgeons lay large numbers of eggs. The ovary of a ripe 8 3/4-ft TL, 352-lb Atlantic sturgeon weighed 91 lbs and contained an estimated 3,750,000 eggs (Vladykov and Greeley 1963). Spawning occurs over a rock, rubble, or hard-clay bottom where a constant flow of water is present. Although this may take place in relatively shallow water, it seems to occur more often in deep holes or channels of rivers, where direct observations cannot be made; C. Smith (1985) reported this to take place just above the salt front in the Hudson River, New York, but in the Suwannee River, at least, this apparently occurs farther upstream well above tidal influence. Eggs are broadcast over the bottom in areas where current is present, with little evidence of either prenatal or postnatal care. The eggs are demersal, become strongly adhesive very soon after being laid, and thus become readily attached to rocks, weeds, and other submerged objects. Length of incubation is dependent on water temperature, with hatching being reported within 94 hours at about 20° C (Dean 1895), from 121–140 hours at about 18° C (T. Smith et al. 1980), and 168 hours at 17.8° C (Vladykov and Greeley 1963). Development proceeds in fresh water, and the young individuals may remain there from two to six years (C. Smith 1985).

Spent Atlantic sturgeons gradually return to salt water. According to C. Smith (1985), females move downstream and out of the Hudson River soon after spawning (which occurs from May to early June), but males may remain until the fall, when cold weather sets in. Huff (1975) reported that Gulf sturgeon in Florida migrate downstream from October through December.

Age at which individuals become sexually mature also appears to be related to temperature. In New York, males were calculated to be 12 years of age and females 18–19 years of age at time of first spawning, whereas, in the Suwannee River, Huff (1975) found the youngest ripe specimens of male and female Gulf sturgeon to be 9 and 12 years old, respectively.

Although Scott and Crossman (1973) indicated that spawning may occur yearly in some female Atlantic sturgeons, the weight of evidence suggests otherwise. Vladykov and Greeley (1963) suggested that females of this species spawn only once every 2 or 3 years. In South Carolina, T. Smith et al. (1982) indicated that on the average 5.4 and 3.5 years elapsed between the first and second and second and third spawnings, respectively, in female *A. oxyrinchus*. In males, these same respective figures were 4.5 and 1.6 years.

Longevity may vary with latitude, although no estimates of average life expectancy have been made. The oldest reported age for *A. oxyrinchus* is 60 years, based on an individual from the St. Lawrence River (Magnin 1964; Murawski and Pacheco 1977), whereas the next oldest reported age (42 years) is based on a specimen of Gulf sturgeon from the Suwannee River (Huff 1975). Elsewhere, maximum reported ages are about 30 years for the Pee Dee, St. John, and Hudson rivers (in South Carolina, New Brunswick, and New York, respectively) (Magnin 1964; Dovel 1979; T. Smith 1985). The above inconsistencies likely result in part at least from inherent difficulties in aging sturgeons, as discussed in the account of *A. brevirostrum*.

The Atlantic sturgeon may undergo extensive latitudinal oceanic migrations, which may be as great as 900 miles (Magnin and Beaulieu 1963). Individuals tend to move southward as temperatures decrease (late fall and winter) and northward again as temperatures increase (late winter and spring). They appear not to wander very far offshore, however; the greatest depth at which an individual has been recorded is only 46 m (Bigelow and Schroeder 1953).

The relative kinds and percentages of food consumed by Atlantic sturgeon change between the juvenile and adult stages. Although food consumed by larvae in natural settings has not yet been documented, reared individuals thrive on various items, including live brine shrimp, insect larvae, worms, zooplankton, and prepared foods. Juveniles feed mostly on benthic crustaceans and insect larvae, whereas adults feed largely on molluscs (both pelecypods and gastropods), which may be extensively supplemented by polychaetes, shrimps, isopods, amphipods, and small benthic fishes in saltwater areas. Although larvae and postlarval individuals feed in fresh water, there are indications that subadults and adults feed little if at all while in fresh water.

All sturgeons characteristically feed by rooting along the bottom with their snouts, using their barbels as organs of touch, and "vacuuming" the bottom with their protrusible mouths. All reports so far indicate that the Atlantic sturgeon feeds indiscriminately throughout life (Bigelow and Schroeder 1953; Vladykov and Greeley 1963). There appears to be no information on the effects of light and temperature on Atlantic sturgeon; however, one may assume that the inverse and direct correlations of light and water temperature, respectively, with feeding activity reported for the shortnose sturgeon (Dadswell et al. 1984) hold true for the Atlantic sturgeon as well.

BASIS OF STATUS CLASSIFICATION: The Atlantic sturgeon was accorded "threatened" status in the 1978 FCREPA report and is presently officially listed as a species "of special concern" by the state of Florida. It has no listing nationally. Resolution of its status here presents certain complications not encountered with other "threatened" species on the present FCREPA list. One centers around the fact that two distinct allopatric subspecies are involved, each of which presents very different problems. The Atlantic sturgeon (*A. oxyrinchus oxyrinchus*) may have bred in the St. Johns River drainage at one time, although this has never been proved. In any event, reproduction almost certainly does not occur there today. At the same time, individuals of this subspecies migrate into the state from farther north during the winter months, and there is no reason to think that this will not continue in the future. The Gulf sturgeon, by contrast, has always maintained breeding populations in Florida. Barkuloo (1988) reviewed the occurrence of *A. oxyrinchus desotoi* throughout its range, and although recent catches or sightings (i.e., since 1987) are known from all major rivers from Lake Pontchartrain east to the Apalachicola River, population size has been reduced in all cases from what it was in the past. Only in the Suwannee River do population levels appear to remain close to those reported previously. Added complications are the unusually long maturation time and the fact that sturgeons do not spawn annually. These serve to increase their vulnerability since populations cannot recover as rapidly as those of most fishes.

In contrast to other species listed as "threatened" in Florida, *A. oxyrinchus* has a wide range and is not subject to extirpation from the state by a single massive environmental disaster. Nevertheless, the species has several unique features that serve to increase its vulnerability. It is therefore considered "threatened," as it was also in the earlier FCREPA list (Gilbert 1978). Barkuloo (1988) also recommended that the Gulf sturgeon be accorded "threatened" status nationally.

RECOMMENDATIONS: Continue to monitor this species in the St. Johns River. Maintain the ecological and physical integrity of the Suwannee River, which remains the last good spawning area for the Gulf subspecies.

Literature Cited

Appy, R. G., and M. J. Dadswell. 1978. Parasites of *Acipenser brevirostrum* LeSueur and *Acipenser oxyrhynchus* Mitchill (Osteichthyes: Acipenseridae) in the St. John River estuary, N.B., with a description of *Caballeronema pseudoargumentosus* sp. n. (Nematoda: Spirurida). Can. J. Zool. 56:1382–1391.

Barkuloo, J. M. 1988. Report on the conservation status of the Gulf of Mexico sturgeon, *Acipenser oxyrhynchus desotoi*. Rept. U.S. Fish Wildl. Serv., Panama City, Fla. 32 pp.

Bigelow, H. B., and W. C. Schroeder. 1953. Fishes of the Gulf of Maine. Fish. Bull. 74 U.S. Fish Wildl. Serv. 53. 577 pp.

Borodin, N. 1925. Biological observations on the Atlantic sturgeon (*Acipenser sturio*). Trans. Amer. Fish. Soc. 55:184–190.

Dadswell, M. J. 1979. Biology and population characteristics of the shortnose sturgeon, *Acipenser brevirostrum* LeSueur 1818 (Osteichthyes: Acipenseridae), in the Saint John River Estuary, New Brunswick, Canada. Can. J. Zool. 57:2186–2210.

Dadswell, M. J., B. D. Taubert, T. S. Squiers, D. Marchette, and J. Buckley. 1984. Synopsis of biological data on shortnose sturgeon, *Acipenser brevirostrum* LeSueur 1818. NOAA Technical Report NMFS 14 (FAO Fish. Synopsis 140). U.S. Department of Commerce. iv+45 pp.

Dean, B. 1895. The early development of gar-pike and sturgeon. J. Morphol. 11:1–62.

Dovel, W. L. 1979. The biology and management of shortnose and Atlantic sturgeon of the Hudson River. New York State Department Environmental Conservation, Final Rept. Proj. AFS-9-R, Albany. 54 pp.

Gilbert, C. R. 1978. Atlantic sturgeon, *Acipenser oxyrhynchus* Mitchill. Pages 5–8 *in* C. R. Gilbert, ed., Rare and endangered biota of Florida. Vol. 4. Fishes. University Presses of Florida, Gainesville. 58 pp.

————. 1989. Species profiles: life histories and environmental requirements of coastal fishes and invertebrates (Mid-Atlantic Bight)—Atlantic and shortnose sturgeons. U.S. Fish Wildl. Serv. Biol. Rept. 82(11.122). U.S. Army Corps of Engineers, TR EL-82-4. 28 pp.

Gruchy, C. G., and B. Parker. 1980. *Acipenser oxyrhynchus* Mitchill, Atlantic sturgeon. Page 41 *in* D. S. Lee et al., eds., Atlas of North American freshwater fishes. North Carolina State Museum of Natural History, Raleigh. i–x+854 pp.

Huff, J. A. 1975. Life history of Gulf of Mexico sturgeon, *Acipenser oxyrhynchus desotoi*, in Suwannee River, Florida. Florida Mar. Res. Publ. 16:1–32.

Magnin, E. 1964. Crossance en longueur de trois esturgeons d'Amerique du Nord: *Acipenser oxyrhynchus* Mitchill, *Acipenser fulvescens* Rafinesque, et *Acipenser brevirostris* LeSueur. Verh. Int. Ver. Limnol. 15:968–974.

Magnin, E., and G. Beaulieu. 1963. Etude morphometrique comparée de l'*Acipenser oxyrhynchus* Mitchill du Saint-Laurent et de l'*Acipenser sturio* Linne de la Gironde. Nat. Can. 90:5–38.

Murawski, S. A., and A. L. Pacheco. 1977. Biological and fisheries data on Atlantic sturgeon, *Acipenser oxyrhynchus* (Mitchill). U.S. Department Commerce National Marine Fisheries Service, Northeast Fisheries Center Technical Services Report 10. 69 pp.

Scott, W. B., and E. J. Crossman. 1973. Freshwater fishes of Canada. Bull. Fish. Res. Board Can. 184:1–966.

Smith, C. L. 1985. The inland fishes of New York state. New York State Department of Environmental Conservation, Albany. xi+522 pp.

Smith, T. I. J. 1985. The fishery, biology, and management of Atlantic sturgeon, *Acipenser oxyrhynchus*, in North America. Pages 61–72 *in* F. P. Binkowski and S. I. Doroshov, eds., North American sturgeons: biology and aquaculture potential. Developments in Environmental Biology of Fishes 6. Junk, Dordrecht, Netherlands. 163 pp.

Smith, T. I. J., E. K. Dingley, and D. E. Marchette. 1980. Induced spawning culture of the Atlantic sturgeon, *Acipenser oxyrhynchus* in the U.S.A. J. World Maricult. Soc. 12:78–87.

Smith, T. I. J., D. E. Marchette, and R. A. Smiley. 1982. Life history, ecology, culture and management of the Atlantic sturgeon, *Acipenser oxyrhynchus oxyrhynchus* Mitchill, in South Carolina. S.C. Wildl. Mar. Res. Comm. Tech. Rept. AFS-9. 75 pp.

Vladykov, V. M., and J. R. Greeley. 1963. Order Acipenseroidei. Pages 24–60 *in* Fishes of the western North Atlantic. Mem. Sears Found. Mar. Res. 1(3). xxi+630 pp.

Wooley, C. M. 1985. Evaluation of morphometric characters used in taxonomic separation of Gulf of Mexico sturgeon, *Acipenser oxyrhynchus desotoi*. Pages 97–103 *in* F. P. Binkowski and S. I. Doroshov, eds., North American sturgeons: biology and aquaculture potential. Developments in Environmental Biology of Fishes 6. Junk, Dordrecht, The Netherlands. 163 pp.

Wooley, C. M., and E. J. Crateau. 1985. Movement, microhabitat, exploitation and management of Gulf of Mexico sturgeon, Apalachicola River, Florida. N. Amer. J. Fish. Management. 590–605.

Prepared by: Carter R. Gilbert, *Florida Museum of Natural History, University of Florida, Gainesville, Florida 32611.*

River Redhorse

Moxostoma carinatum

FAMILY CATOSTOMIDAE

Order Cypriniformes

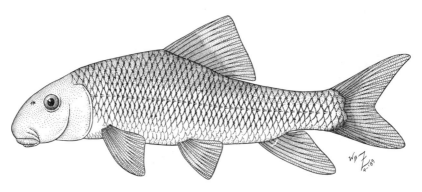

River redhorse, *Moxostoma carinatum* (Cope, 1870). UF 14216. Adult, 340 mm SL. Little Tennessee River, Macon County, North Carolina. 19 April 1967.

OTHER NAMES: None.

DESCRIPTION: *Moxostoma carinatum* is the largest species of redhorse sucker, reaching a length of 30 inches and a weight of 10 pounds. Redhorses as a group are distinguished by relatively coarse scales (usually 39–48 in lateral line, either 12 or 16 rows of scales in the caudal-peduncle series) and a short dorsal fin (12–16 rays). The river redhorse usually has 42–44 lateral-line scales, 12 rows of scales in the caudal-peduncle series, 12–13 dorsal rays, a straight-edged dorsal fin, and a large and plicate lower lip; but it is most readily distinguished from other southern species of *Moxostoma* by its pharyngeal teeth, which are enlarged and molariform (Jenkins 1970). Like many other redhorse species, its body coloration varies from uniform gray to brassy yellow, and the caudal and paired fins are reddish. The lips are large and plicate, and there are 12 scale rows around the caudal peduncle (Jenkins 1970).

RANGE: A spot-distribution map of *M. carinatum* appears in Jenkins (1980). This species is widespread throughout the east-central United States and southern Canada, where it is exclusively confined to large rivers. Because of its restriction to large bodies of water, as well as its specialized diet, it has become extirpated throughout much of its natural range. Its range includes the Great Lakes basin (lower Lake Michigan and western Lake Erie drainages only), the middle and upper Mississippi River drainage (there are no records from the Mississippi River proper from Tennessee southward), and the various river drainages of the eastern Gulf slope (Pearl, Alabama, and Escambia). There is also a disjunct

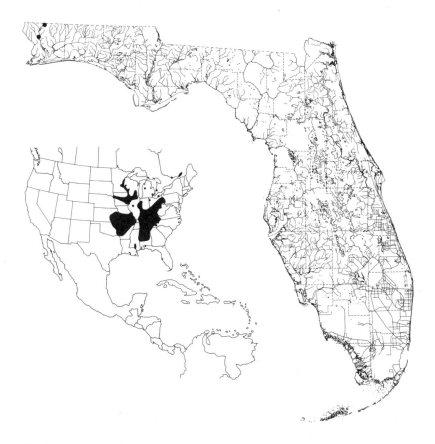

Distribution map of *Moxostoma carinatum*.

population in the vicinity of Montreal, Canada. It was first reported from Florida by Yerger and Suttkus (1962).

HABITAT: As implied by its common name, the river redhorse is normally confined to large rivers, primarily those with substantial flow or current. Young and juvenile individuals may rarely enter the lower reaches of smaller tributary streams. Although occasionally captured in impoundments and lakes, standing-water habitats appear to be largely unsuitable. Throughout its range this species typically is found only in relatively clean, unpolluted, unmodified streams with sand and/or gravel bottoms.

LIFE HISTORY AND ECOLOGY: Knowledge of the life history of this species is based primarily on studies conducted in Alabama. Stomach analyses indicate that *M. carinatum* feeds primarily on bivalve molluscs and aquatic insect larvae. The enlarged and modified pharyngeal teeth are apparently adaptations for crushing mussel shells. The introduced Asiatic clam (*Corbicula*) appears to be a preferred food item in Alabama.

The river redhorse spawns later than other redhorse species. Although spawning time varies with latitude, in the southern part of its range this species appears to reproduce in mid-April at water temperatures of 71°–76° F. An upriver spawning migration has been reported, and spawning adults concentrate in shallows, a phenomenon known locally as "shoaling." The male constructs a redd (nest) in a riffle area with a clean gravel bottom. As a female approaches the redd, the resident male begins a series of short, vigorous swims. A second male usually joins the pair at this time. The act is consummated when the female takes a position between the two males, and eggs and milt are deposited over the redd.

Adult females carry between 6,000 and 23,000 eggs, depending on the size of the individual. The eggs are large (3–4 mm in diameter) and hatch in 3–4 d at a temperature of 72° F. Growth of the young fish is rapid.

The natural longevity of the river redhorse in southern waters is 5–7 yr. Females are, on the average, slightly smaller than males of the same age. Both sexes become sexually mature at age three at a size of about 16 in TL.

This species supports a minor sport fishery in some parts of its range. Adult fish are captured during the spawning period, when they are "shoaling." The two methods most often employed to catch redhorse are snaring with a wire loop and snagging with an unbaited treble hook. A limited amount of gigging is also utilized. The meat is said to be palatable but bony. At current limited levels, the sport fishery is thought to be of no significance in the overall well-being of this species (Hackney et al. 1968; Tatum and Hackney 1970).

BASIS OF STATUS CLASSIFICATION: Because of its large size, swimming ability, and predilection for riverine habitats, it is difficult to make precise comments regarding the distribution and abundance of this fish. It has been characterized as a common species in certain regions where streams are clean and undisturbed. However, in many parts of its range this species appears to be declining or to have already become extirpated. This trend has been most noticeable in polluted or disturbed areas near metropolitan centers or in heavily farmed regions. Pollution and siltation apparently have a marked effect on the ability of this species to survive. Adverse effects may relate to a reduction of food supply and/or a reduction of spawning areas. Insect larvae and especially molluscs, the major food item of this fish, require clean gravel-sand stream bottoms and are very susceptible to reduction or extirpation through excessive siltation. As previously noted, this species requires a clean gravel substrate for spawning. Many such stream sections have been physically eliminated through channelization projects, and siltation can effectively destroy the suitable areas that remain.

In Florida, the species is known only from the main Escambia River, between Pine Barren and Century, with three specimens (two lots) being deposited in the Florida Museum of Natural History collection (UF 9337 [2], UF 75227 [1]). Seven other specimens from just over the state line in Alabama were listed by Yerger and Suttkus (1962). The river redhorse specimen appearing (with no accompanying locality data) in the photograph on the front cover of the 1978 FCREPA volume on fishes unfortunately was not placed in a museum collection. Based on collector's name and related information, however, the specimen in all likelihood was also from the Escambia River in Florida. We are not aware of any collections of this species from this river during the 1980s.

The paucity of Escambia River specimens of *M. carinatum* in museum fish collections may reflect in part the difficulties involved in sampling big-river habitats. At the same time, sufficient collecting effort has been expended in the Escambia River in recent years that were this species at all common additional material should have been collected. This is particularly true when one considers that H. A. Beecher made numerous collections from this area during the 1970s in conjunction with his research on the biology of two other big-river suckers (*Carpiodes cyprinus* and *Carpiodes velifer*) (Beecher 1979). Because of the susceptibility of a river such as the Escambia to environmental pollution and modification, as well as the specialized diet of *M. carinatum*, the future of this species in Florida remains tenuous. For this reason, we once again recommend a "threatened" classification for this species.

RECOMMENDATIONS: Protect the Escambia River proper against pollution, siltation, or other types of habitat modification. Encourage and support efforts to monitor the species to determine its presence status and abundance in Florida.

Literature Cited

Published Information

Hackney, P. A., W. M. Tatum, and S. K. Spencer. 1968. Life history study of the river redhorse, *Moxostoma carinatum* (Cope), in the Cahaba River, Alabama, with notes on the management of the species as a sport fish. Proc. 21st Ann. Conf. Southeast. Assoc. Game Fish Comm. (1967):324–332.

Jenkins, R. E. 1980. *Moxostoma carinatum* (Cope), River redhorse. Pages 415–416 *in* D. S. Lee et al., eds., Atlas of North American freshwater fishes. North Carolina State Museum of Natural History, Raleigh. i–x+854 pp.

Tatum, W. M., and P. A. Hackney. 1970. Age and growth of River redhorse, *Moxostoma carinatum* (Cope) from the Cahaba River, Alabama. Proc. 23rd Ann. Conf. Southeast. Assoc. Game Fish Comm. (1969):255–261.

Yerger, R. W., and R. D. Suttkus. 1962. Records of freshwater fishes in Florida. Tulane Stud. Zool. 9(5):323–330.

Unpublished information

Beecher, H. A. 1979. Comparative functional morphology and ecological isolating mechanisms in sympatric fishes of the genus *Carpiodes* in northwestern Florida. Ph.D. diss., Florida State University, Tallahassee.

Jenkins, R. E. 1970. Systematic studies of the catostomid fish tribe Moxostomatini. Ph.D. diss., Cornell University, Ithaca, N.Y.

Prepared by: Carter R. Gilbert, *Florida Museum of Natural History, University of Florida, Gainesville, Florida 32611*; and Franklin F. Snelson, Jr., *Department of Biological Sciences, University of Central Florida, Orlando, Florida 32816*

Grayfin Redhorse

Moxostoma n. sp. cf *poecilurum*

FAMILY CATOSTOMIDAE

Order Cypriniformes

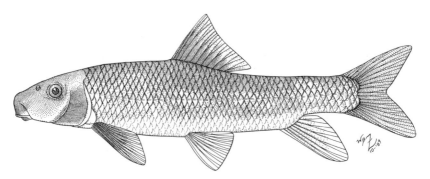

Grayfin redhorse, *Moxostoma* n. sp. cf *poecilurum*. UF 79965. Adult, 264 mm SL. Chipola River, Jackson County, Florida. 8 May 1989.

OTHER NAMES: Referred to as *Moxostoma duquesnei* (Black redhorse) in some of the scientific literature (Yerger and Suttkus 1962).

DESCRIPTION: The species of redhorse suckers are difficult to identify, and most diagnostic characters are technical in nature. This as yet undescribed species possesses alternating light and dark stripes down the sides of the body. It is distinguished from most other striped redhorse species by having 12 (rather than 16) scales around the caudal peduncle. The lips are plicate, and the pharyngeal teeth are not enlarged (Jenkins 1970). It also is distinguished from many other redhorse suckers in lacking bright red or orange color on the fins. Although sometimes called *Moxostoma duquesnei* in the scientific literature, its closest relative actually is *Moxostoma poecilurum* (the blacktail redhorse), from which it is distinguished by having the lowermost caudal-fin rays uniformly dusky rather than immaculate in large juveniles to adults. Only in small juveniles of the grayfin redhorse are the lowermost caudal rays depigmented.

A formal description of this species is being prepared by Robert E. Jenkins, Roanoke College.

RANGE: A spot-distribution map of *Moxostoma* new species appears in Jenkins (1970, p. 783). The grayfin redhorse is endemic to the Apalachicola River basin in Alabama, Georgia, and Florida. The species is present in the upper half of the Flint River system in Georgia and formerly was widely distributed throughout the Chattahoochee River and its larger tributaries in Georgia and Alabama. Much of its habitat in the lower and middle sections of the Chattahoochee (on the Alabama-Georgia line) has been eliminated as a result of dam construction, but good populations

Distribution map of *Moxostoma* n. sp. cf *poecilurum.*

exist in the upper reaches of the system, as well as in the Flint River. Florida is at the southern limits of its range, and in general the species is less widely distributed and more localized here than elsewhere. It was first reported in the state by Yerger and Suttkus (1962).

HABITAT: This sucker inhabits a wide range of stream types in the Apalachicola basin, but it appears to be most common in the larger tributaries and rivers. It is very rare in impoundments and reservoirs, suggesting that standing-water habitats are unsuitable. This species never enters brackish or salt water.

LIFE HISTORY AND ECOLOGY: The life history of this fish has been studied by personnel of the Georgia Game and Fish Division (McSwain and Pasch 1972). Males mature when between 13 and 15 inches long; females mature between 15 and 18 inches. Spawning takes place in late winter and spring, usually between February and April. On the basis of reports on other *Moxostoma* species, spawning is presumed to take place over clean sand or gravel bottoms in shallow areas where there is substantial current. A mature female carries between 7,000 and 8,000 eggs, depending on her size.

The major food items of the grayfin redhorse are aquatic insect larvae (flies, mayflies, and caddisflies) and bivalve molluscs. Large quantities of organic detritus are also ingested.

The species reaches a total length of about 20 inches and a weight of about 3 pounds. Maximum age under natural conditions is about 6 years (McSwain and Pasch 1972).

BASIS OF STATUS CLASSIFICATION: Where habitat is suitable, the grayfin redhorse is a common species. Electrofishing capture rate for the species was 6.14 fish per hour in sections of the Flint River in Georgia, where it was the most common species of *Moxostoma* taken. Despite an overall reduction in population size throughout its range, the species is in no serious danger. In Florida the species is present in the Apalachicola River below Jim Woodruff Dam and (like *Cyprinella callitaenia*) is afforded some degree of protection by the dam's presence (which serves to intercept much of the silt and pollution), even though the dam has resulted in habitat destruction upstream. In Florida, however, the species is regarded as "threatened" because of its restriction to the Apalachicola River and the lower half of the Chipola River, which makes the fish vulnerable to massive influxes of pollutants. It should be noted, however, that such an event is less likely to occur in the Chipola River than in the

Apalachicola, and in addition the Chipola would probably only be marginally affected by pollutants in the Apalachicola River itself. Despite its present classification, it should be emphasized that the grayfin redhorse is in a less vulnerable position than would be true for some other Florida fishes placed in this category. The distribution and abundance of this species in Florida does not appear to have changed since publication of the first FCREPA volume.

RECOMMENDATIONS: Continued preservation of the habitat where the grayfin redhorse occurs in the lower Apalachicola River basin should ensure the continued survival of the species in the state. The possibilities that this will occur are enhanced for reasons discussed in the preceding section.

Literature Cited

Published Information

Yerger, R. W., and R. D. Suttkus. 1962. Records of freshwater fishes in Florida. Tulane Stud. Zool. 9(5):323–330.

Unpublished information

Jenkins, R. E. 1970. Systematic studies of the catostomid fish tribe Moxostomatini. Ph.D. diss., Cornell University, Ithaca, N.Y.

McSwain, L. E., and R. W. Pasch. 1972. Life history studies of stream fishes: age and growth, reproduction, food habits, and abundance and distribution of the grayfin redhorse. Federal Aid (Dingell-Johnson) Progress Report, Georgia: Proj. F-21-4 (mimeograph).

Prepared by: Carter R. Gilbert, *Florida Museum of Natural History, University of Florida, Gainesville, Florida 32611*; and Franklin F. Snelson, Jr., *Department of Biological Sciences, University of Central Florida, Orlando, Florida 32816.*

Bluestripe Shiner

Cyprinella callitaenia

FAMILY CYPRINIDAE

Order Cypriniformes

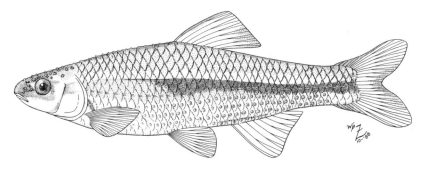

Bluestripe shiner, *Cyprinella callitaenia* (Bailey and Gibbs, 1956). UF 16353. Adult tuberculate male, 72.3 mm SL. Apalachicola River below Jim Woodruff Dam, Gadsden County, Florida. 12 May 1968.

OTHER NAMES: None.

DESCRIPTION: *Cyprinella callitaenia* is characterized by 1,4–4,1 pharyngeal teeth and 8 anal rays. It shares with the closely related *Cyprinella callisema* and *Cyprinella leedsi* (of which only the latter occurs in Florida) the characters of an acutely pointed snout with a distinctly inferior mouth; nuptial tubercles in three linear rows on top of head in adult males; a relatively large and rounded dorsal fin (in adults), which contains a distinct dark blotch of pigment on the anteriormost ray and membrane and which lacks the distinct blotch of dark pigment on the next-to-last dorsal membrane that is characteristic of many other species in the subgenus; and a prominent steel-blue midlateral stripe (lead colored to black in preservation), with a dark basicaudal spot that is slightly wider than the stripe. It differs from its closest congener, *C. callisema*, in having 1,4–4,1 (vs. 4–4) pharyngeal teeth; a dark, crescent-shaped line of melanophores between eye and angle of gape (vs. no such line in this area); and usually a darker basicaudal spot. Both species differ from *C. leedsi* in having scales that are pigmented near the margin to form a regular lateral pattern of oblique dark lines (resulting in a diamond-shaped appearance); usually 36 or 37 (vs. 38 or 39) lateral-line scales; and a less concentrated, wider and usually shorter lateral stripe.

TAXONOMIC REMARKS: Until recently, the bluestripe shiner was included in the genus *Notropis*, of which *Cyprinella* was regarded as a subgenus. Elevation of *Cyprinella* to generic status follows the recommendation of Mayden (1989).

Distribution map of *Cyprinella callitaenia*.

RANGE: A spot-distribution map of *C. callitaenia* appears in Gilbert (1980). The species is endemic to the Apalachicola River basin (including the Flint and Chattahoochee river drainages) in Florida, Georgia, and Alabama. The single record from the Escambia River drainage, reported by Bailey and Gibbs (1956), was considered by Gilbert (1978) to have resulted from the mixing of collections; no subsequent information has appeared that might change this assessment. The bluestripe shiner now appears to have a somewhat disjunct range within the Apalachicola basin, having been recorded in four widely separated areas: the upper Chattahoochee River in northern Georgia, the middle Chattahoochee drainage in Georgia and Alabama, the middle Flint River in southwestern Georgia, and the Apalachicola River near Jim Woodruff Dam in Florida. Although this may result in part from inadequate collecting in the big-river habitat to which the species is confined, there is little doubt that *C. callitaenia* has become greatly depleted throughout much of its range during the past 50 years, primarily because of the destruction of its preferred habitat by dam construction.

HABITAT: *Cyprinella callitaenia* is restricted to the largest rivers and their major tributaries of the Apalachicola River basin. Bottom type in such areas usually consists of sand, possibly mixed with gravel or small rubble at localities above the Fall Line. It appears not to inhabit small creeks or places containing a soft bottom.

LIFE HISTORY AND ECOLOGY: Wallace and Ramsey (1981) published on the reproductive behavior and biology of this species in Uchee Creek, a large tributary of the middle Chattahoochee River in eastern Alabama. They reported that spawning occurs mostly from April to August, at water temperatures between 21°–25° C and that there was indirect evidence that the species is a fractional spawner (i.e., not all eggs laid at once). Thus, the spawning period of individual fish is probably extended over a fairly long period of time. As is true of other species of *Cyprinella*, the bluestripe shiner spawns in crevices, with eggs being extruded into crevices of large rocks, where they are immediately fertilized by the male. Crevices are naturally limited in size and can accommodate relatively few eggs, which is probably a major reason why fractional spawning has developed in *C. callitaenia* and in other species of *Cyprinella*. Between 88 and 230 ripe eggs were counted in the females examined, but the total number of eggs spawned during the entire breeding season is probably much greater. Wallace and Ramsey (1981) did not investigate other aspects of the species' biology, such as feeding habits or age and growth.

SPECIALIZED OR UNIQUE CHARACTERISTICS: The bluestripe shiner is one of six fish species (four cyprinids and two catostomids) that are endemic or nearly endemic to the Apalachicola River basin.

BASIS OF STATUS CLASSIFICATION: *Cyprinella callitaenia* has a very limited range in Florida and has been recorded only in that section of the Apalachicola River from just below Jim Woodruff Dam downstream to Bristol at the state Route 20 bridge. It is apparently common in this stretch of river, however, and has been consistently collected there over many years. Twenty-seven cataloged lots are present in the Florida Museum of Natural History collection, ranging in size from 1 to 57 specimens. Of these, all but four are from the area just below Jim Woodruff Dam. Although Jim Woodruff Dam has resulted in the elimination of much favorable habitat in the now-impounded area upstream, it actually serves to protect that segment of the population living below the dam since it intercepts much of the silt and pollutants coming down from above. Conversely, the shoal area below Jim Woodruff Dam, which is the main spawning area for the bluestripe shiner, is the site of a large gravel-removal operation. In addition, water is released through the dam only at certain intervals so that water levels below undergo considerable fluctuation. Until now, neither factor seems to have adversely affected the bluestripe shiner population living below, but there is no guarantee this situation might not change in the future. In this regard, the more extended spawning season of this and other southern species probably serves as a safeguard in comparison to the much more restricted spawning seasons normally seen in fish species farther north. Nevertheless, the factors discussed above, coupled with the restricted range of the bluestripe shiner in Florida, serve to place this species in a vulnerable position. Consequently, it is accorded "threatened" status as was the case in the 1978 FCREPA report.

RECOMMENDATIONS: Continue to monitor the Apalachicola River to determine size and status of the population. Also limit gravel removal and water releases from the dam as much as possible to those times when spawning is less likely to occur.

Literature Cited

Bailey, R. M., and R. H. Gibbs. 1956. *Notropis callitaenia*, a new cyprinid fish from Alabama, Florida, and Georgia. Occ. Pap. Mus. Zool. Univ. Mich. 576:1–14.

Gilbert, C. R. 1978. *Notropis callitaenia* Bailey and Gibbs, Bluestripe shiner. Pages 13–14 *in* Carter R. Gilbert, ed., Rare and endangered biota of Florida. Vol. 4. Fishes. University Presses of Florida, Gainesville. 58 pp.

———. 1980. *Notropis callitaenia* Bailey and Gibbs, Bluestripe shiner. Page 247 *in* D. S. Lee et al., eds., Atlas of North American freshwater fishes. North Carolina State Museum of Natural History, Raleigh. i–x+854 pp.

Mayden, R. L. 1989. Phylogenetic studies of North American minnows, with emphasis on the genus *Cyprinella* (Teleostei: Cypriniformes). Misc. Publ. Mus. Nat. Hist. Univ. Kans. 80:1–189.

Wallace, R. K., Jr., and J. S. Ramsey. 1981. Reproductive behavior and biology of the bluestripe shiner (*Notropis callitaenia*) in Uchee Creek, Alabama. Amer. Midl. Nat. 106(1):198–200.

Prepared by: Carter R. Gilbert, *Florida Museum of Natural History, University of Florida, Gainesville, Florida 32611.*

Cypress Minnow
Hybognathus hayi

FAMILY CYPRINIDAE

Order Cypriniformes

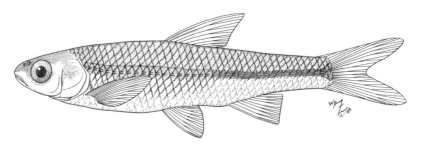

Cypress minnow, *Hybognathus hayi* Jordan, 1885. UF 14584. Adult, 48.7 mm SL. Backwater pool of Escambia River, Escambia County, Florida. 28 October–2 November 1952.

OTHER NAMES: None.

DESCRIPTION: The cypress minnow is a species of the cyprinid fish genus *Hybognathus*, which is distinguished from all other Florida cyprinid species by the combination of dorsal-fin origin slightly in advance of pelvic-fin insertion; 4–4 pharyngeal teeth (without hooks); 8 anal rays, and a long, coiled intestine. It is also characterized by 9–13 body-circumference scale rows above the lateral line (average 11–12) and 10–15 body-circumference scale rows below the lateral line (average 12–13). It occasionally occurs sympatrically with *Hybognathus nuchalis* (which is not found in Florida), from which it is distinguished by having a more compressed (vs. a subterete) body; an angular (vs. a rounded) profile; a more distinctly diamond-shaped pigmentary pattern to the scales; melanophores on the anterior part of the lateral stripe small (vs. large) and only slightly larger (vs. noticeably larger) than those on the upper parts of the sides and back; the median dorsal stripe in front of dorsal fin wider and darker; a relatively much shorter intestine in proportion to the standard length; and a more broadly rounded snout that does not project anteriorly beyond the upper lip. A detailed comparison of *Hybognathus hayi* and the very similar *H. nuchalis*, based on specimens from the Pearl River in Mississippi, was published by Fingerman and Suttkus (1961).

RANGE: A spot-distribution map of *H. hayi* appears in Gilbert (1980). The species occurs in lowland areas of the Gulf Coast and lower Mississippi Valley, from extreme western Florida (Escambia drainage) (Bailey et al. 1954) to the lower Mississippi River basin of Louisiana and Mississippi (but not in the extreme coastal bayou areas). It occurs in the upper half of the Sabine River drainage bordering Louisiana and Texas and in

Distribution map of *Hybognathus hayi*.

the Red River drainage of Louisiana, Arkansas, and extreme northeastern Texas, but surprisingly has not yet been recorded from Oklahoma (Miller and Robison 1973). It occurs (or has recently occurred) in lowland areas of those other states bordering the Mississippi and lower Ohio rivers northward to extreme southern Illinois and extreme southwestern Indiana.

HABITAT: The cypress minnow usually occurs in sluggish backwaters of streams (frequently in areas where cypress trees abound) and is often taken together with its congener, *H. nuchalis*. The bottom type generally consists of sand overlain with silt and detritus. *Hybognathus hayi* is less wide-ranging than *H. nuchalis*, which may indicate a somewhat lower tolerance of turbidity and low extremes of temperature.

LIFE HISTORY AND ECOLOGY: Little is known of the life history or ecology of this species other than it is a herbivorous feeder. Cook (1959) reported that females collected during May in Mississippi contained well-developed eggs, indicating that spawning occurs in midspring in that region.

BASIS OF STATUS CLASSIFICATION: *Hybognathus hayi* is one of nine species (six of which are definitely native) whose distribution in Florida is confined to the Escambia River drainage. It is neither very common nor widespread in this area, as evidenced by the presence of only four lots (totaling 13 specimens) (UF 14584 [10], UF 73656 [1], UF 75327 [1], UF 75373 [1]) in the Florida Museum of Natural History collection, collected in 1952, 1975, and 1976. Specimens have been taken periodically in this area by other collectors during subsequent years, and there is no indication that the level of abundance or distribution of this species has changed in any way since preparation of the earlier FCREPA report. We continue to accord it "threatened" status, although it probably is slightly less vulnerable to pollution or other types of environmental disturbance than are other species living largely or entirely in the main Escambia River, such as *Crystallaria asprella* and *Moxostoma carinatum*.

RECOMMENDATIONS: Continue to monitor suitable looking areas in an attempt to find other localities for this species in the state. Preserve backwater habitats where the species is known to occur or might likely occur in extreme western Florida.

Literature Cited

Bailey, R. M., H. E. Winn, and C. L. Smith. 1954. Fishes from the Escambia River, Alabama and Florida, with ecologic and taxonomic notes. Proc. Acad. Nat. Sci. Phila. 106:109–164.

Cook, F. A. 1959. Freshwater fishes in Mississippi. Mississippi Game and Fish Commission, Jackson. 239 pp.

Fingerman, S. W., and R. D. Suttkus. 1961. Comparison of *Hybognathus hayi* Jordan and *Hybognathus nuchalis* Agassiz. Copeia 1961(4):462–467.

Gilbert, C. R. 1978. Cypress minnow, *Hybognathus hayi* Jordan. Page 11 *in* Carter R. Gilbert, ed., Rare and endangered biota of Florida. Vol. 4. Fishes. University Presses of Florida, Gainesville. 58 pp.

———. 1980. *Hybognathus hayi* Jordan, Cypress minnow. Page 176 *in* D. S. Lee et al., eds., Atlas of North American freshwater fishes. North Carolina State Museum of Natural History, Raleigh. i–x+854 pp.

Miller, R. J., and H. W. Robison. 1973. The fishes of Oklahoma. Oklahoma State University Press, Stillwater. 246 pp.

Prepared by: Carter R. Gilbert, *Florida Museum of Natural History, University of Florida, Gainesville, Florida 32611.*

Blackmouth Shiner

Notropis melanostomus

FAMILY CYPRINIDAE

Order Cypriniformes

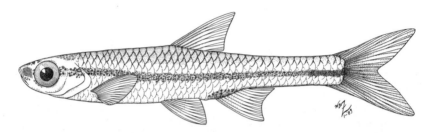

Blackmouth shiner, *Notropis melanostomus* Bortone, 1989. UF 78305. Adult, 32.0 mm SL. Pond Creek, upstream of confluence with Blackwater River, Santa Rosa County, Florida. 6 September 1988.

OTHER NAMES: Pond Creek shiner.

DESCRIPTION: *Notropis melanostomus* is a small, rather slender species of *Notropis*, with a small, very oblique mouth; 4–4 pharyngeal teeth, with the posterior 3 teeth in each arch serrated; 10–12 anal rays; 8 dorsal rays; numerous (12–14) long gill rakers on lower limb of first gill arch; black peritoneum; a black lateral stripe that passes through the eye and onto the snout; and numerous black melanophores on lips and chin. Most individuals are less than 30-mm standard length, with the largest known specimen 38-mm SL (Suttkus and Bailey 1990).

TAXONOMIC REMARKS: Two errors have been noted in the description of this species appearing in the first FCREPA volume (Gilbert 1978): (1) maximum standard length is only 38 mm, not 45 mm as indicated earlier; (2) the usual number of dorsal rays is 8 (typical of all but two of the 120+ species of *Notropis*) rather than 9 as previously indicated.

Although the taxonomic relationships of the species were indicated as being uncertain (Gilbert 1978), the blackmouth shiner in fact appears to

58

be intimately related to *Notropis ortenburgeri*, a species restricted to clear upland streams of western Arkansas and eastern Oklahoma. In addition to a striking similarity in basic physiognomy, the two species share a unique combination of pharyngeal teeth and anal-ray counts, an unusually high number of long, slender gill rakers, and a similar pigmentation pattern.

RANGE: At the time of the 1978 FCREPA report, the blackmouth shiner was known to occur only in Pond Creek, at the U.S. Highway 90 bridge near Milton, Florida. It has since been taken in adjacent areas of Pond Creek, from localities in the Blackwater and Shoal rivers as far east as

Distribution map of *Notropis melanostomus.*

Walton County, and from the Pascagoula River drainage in Perry County, Mississippi (Suttkus and Bailey 1990). Although the species is now known to have a much broader range than previously believed, its high habitat specificity (see following discussion) indicates that its distribution is highly fragmented.

HABITAT: *Notropis melanostomus* has a narrow range of habitat to which it is apparently confined at all times. It is found in rather shallow backwater pools (typically less than 1 m deep) connected with the main stream, where no flow is present. The substrate consists of soft mud and detritus, and the water is usually clear but tannin stained. The species occurs within 1–5 m of a rather steeply sloping shore (where cypress and juniper are usually present) and is found in clearings or openings of submerged aquatic vegetation in tightly packed schools of 25 to 200 individuals. The group typically lives about 0.5 m below the surface, often beneath a school of brook silversides (*Labidesthes sicculus vanhyningi*). The specificity of this habitat allows one to predict with a high degree of accuracy localities where the species is likely to be found (Bortone 1989).

LIFE HISTORY AND ECOLOGY: Until now, life-history information on this species has been limited to brief remarks in the first FCREPA account (Gilbert 1978) and comments in subsequent papers by Bortone (1989) and Suttkus and Bailey (1990). The life history is currently being investigated by Stephen A. Bortone, aided by a grant from the Florida nongame research program.

The blackmouth shiner is short-lived (probably less than 1.5 years), and visual inspection of size frequencies in specimen samples indicates that few two-year-old individuals are present. It apparently spawns from early spring to midsummer, tuberculate males and gravid females having been collected from the end of April to the end of July during several different years. Although spawning has not yet been observed, the species presumably is a substrate spawner, as evidenced by the rather elongated genital papilla present in both males and females. Although nothing has yet been published regarding food habits, the presence of numerous long gill rakers, serrations on the pharyngeal teeth, and the strongly oblique mouth, coupled with its habit of living in communal groups in the upper part of the water column, suggests that it feeds on planktonic crustaceans.

SPECIALIZED OR UNIQUE CHARACTERISTICS: *Notropis melanostomus* is one of the most enigmatic species of North American freshwater fishes. After its initial capture in 1939 by Reeve M. Bailey, it was not found again until 1975 (Southeastern Fishes Council Proceedings 1977), despite numerous attempts by ichthyologists to collect it at the Pond Creek locality. Most attempts, however, were made in the flowing waters of Pond Creek itself rather than in the adjacent backwaters to which it is now known to be closely confined. All localities of occurrence but one are from the Blackwater Bay drainage of Florida. Although the Blackwater Bay drainage is not known for endemism of its fish fauna, William L. Peters of Florida A&M University points out that several aquatic invertebrate species are believed to be endemic to Pond Creek. The widely disjunct distribution of *N. melanostomus* and its closest relative, *Notropis ortenburgeri*, coupled with their marked difference in habitat preference, cannot be satisfactorily explained.

BASIS OF STATUS CLASSIFICATION: *Notropis melanostomus* was recommended for "threatened" status in the 1978 FCREPA publication, and partly because of this recommendation the state subsequently listed it as "endangered" (one of only three Florida fish species to be so designated). Collections by other ichthyologists subsequent to the first FCREPA report (1978), as well as ongoing studies of the species by Dr. Bortone, have revealed that the blackmouth shiner has a wider range than first believed. Although recent commercial development along Pond Creek (including the area where the species was first discovered) poses a serious threat to its existence there, the species is apparently doing well in areas along the adjacent lower Blackwater River, where there are no immediate prospects for development (S. A. Bortone, personal observation). Considering these factors, we feel that, despite its present official status as a state endangered species, a "threatened" status is more appropriate.

RECOMMENDATIONS: The intensive ecological and distributional study called for in the original FCREPA account has now been initiated. Inasmuch as possible, the areas along Pond Creek, where the species was first discovered, should be left in their natural state, particularly the backwater area at the U.S. Highway 90 bridge near Milton.

Literature Cited

Bortone, S. A. 1989. *Notropis melanostomus*, a new species of cyprinid fish from the Blackwater-Yellow River drainage of northwest Florida. Copeia 1989 (3):737–741.

Gilbert, C. R. 1978. Blackmouth shiner, *Notropis* new species. Pages 14–15 *in*

Carter R. Gilbert, ed., Rare and endangered biota of Florida. Vol. 4. Fishes. University Presses of Florida, Gainesville. 58 pp.

Southeastern Fishes Council Proceedings. 1977. News notes: Pond Creek shiner lives. Southeast. Fishes Counc. Proc. 1(4):3.

Suttkus, R. D., and R. M. Bailey. 1990. Characters, relationship, distribution, and biology of *Notropis melanostomus*, a recently named cyprinid fish from southeastern United States. Occ. Pap. Mus. Zool. Univ. Mich. 722:1–15.

Prepared by: Stephen A. Bortone, *Biology Department, University of West Florida, Pensacola, Florida 32514*; and Carter R. Gilbert, *Florida Museum of Natural History, University of Florida, Gainesville, Florida 32611.*

Southern Starhead Topminnow

Fundulus dispar blairae

FAMILY CYPRINODONTIDAE

Order Atheriniformes

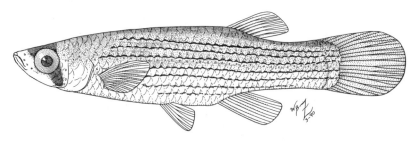

Southern starhead topminnow, *Fundulus dispar blairae* Wiley and Hall, 1975. UF 45709. Adult male, 41.5 mm SL. Canoe Creek, Escambia County, Florida. 19 April 1975.

OTHER NAMES: Blair's starhead topminnow; Northern starhead topminnow (vernacular name applied to *Fundulus dispar*).

DESCRIPTION: A moderate-sized species of *Fundulus*, the southern starhead topminnow usually measures 50-mm SL maximum, occasionally ranging up to 65-mm SL. It is characterized by the origin of dorsal fin which is slightly posterior to origin of anal fin; a broad, distinct blotch of pigment (teardrop) situated below eye; overall pigmentation on body light; about 10 parallel rows of spots on sides of body in both sexes (the spots joining to form wavy lines in females, always separate and tending to be less regular in males); both sexes without any vertical bars on body; anal-fin rays 10–11; dorsal rays usually eight (sometimes seven or nine); lateral-line scales 32–33; and pores 4a and 4b of supraorbital sensory pore series on top of head widely separated.

Fundulus dispar blairae is superficially similar to *Fundulus escambiae*, with which it occurs sympatrically in several parts of the Escambia River drainage in western Florida and with which it had previously been confused. The two species are distinguished by the positions of pores 4a and b in the supraorbital series on top of the head (widely separated in *F. dispar blairae*, fused in *F. escambiae*); absence of vertical bars in males of *F. dispar blairae* (present in *F. escambiae*); presence of a clear, iridescent yellow spot immediately in front of dorsal fin in living specimens only (vs. spot absent in living specimens of *F. escambiae*); presence of small faint spots on inner half of caudal fin and on anal fin in male *F. dispar blairae* down to 22-mm SL (vs. spots always absent in *F. escambiae*); anal-fin rays usually 10 (range 9–11) in *F. dispar blairae* (vs. usually 9 [range 8–10] in *F. escambiae*).

Distribution map of *Fundulus dispar blairae*. Open areas on inset indicate distribution of *F. dispar dispar*; blacked-in area indicates distribution of *F. dispar blairae*.

TAXONOMIC COMMENTS: Until recently the southern starhead top-minnow was regarded as a distinct species, *Fundulus blairae*. Reduction to a subspecies of *F. dispar* is based on the recommendation of Robert C. Cashner, University of New Orleans, who is engaged in a systematic study of the *Fundulus nottii* species complex. *Fundulus dispar blairae* differs from the typical subspecies (*dispar*) primarily in lacking vertical bars in adult males. The problem is complex, however, and occasionally specimens from within the range of *F. dispar blairae* look more like *F. dispar dispar* (i.e., males may have a few bars present); the opposite situation also is true (i.e., some *F. dispar dispar* males may lack bars; R. C. Cashner, personal communication). Apparently few or no electrophoretic differences exist between the two subspecies, in contrast to other members of the species complex.

RANGE: A spot-distribution map appears in Wiley (1980). The species ranges from the Brazos River drainage, Texas, eastward along the Gulf slope to the Escambia River drainage in western Florida, and northward in the Red River drainage to extreme southeastern Oklahoma and southwestern Arkansas. Wiley and Hall (1975) and Wiley (1977) did not record the species from Florida, and the present report appears to be the first published indication of its presence in the state or from the Escambia drainage. Four lots of *F. dispar blairae* from Florida are present in the Florida Museum of Natural History collection, as follows: UF 45709 (1), UF 75221 (4), UF 77314 (1), UF 77315 (1). Of these, all but UF 75221 were collected together with the superficially similar *F. escambiae*. Florida collections of the southern starhead topminnow are also present at the University of Michigan Museum of Zoology, the University of West Florida, and the University of New Orleans. Wiley's (1977) statement (under the heading of Geographic Variation in his account of *F. escambiae*) that "males from the Escambia River may lack vertical bars on the side of the body or have only one or two bars when preserved" may partly result from misidentification of specimens of *F. dispar blairae*.

The southern starhead topminnow is assumed to be native to Florida, as is true for most of those Florida species restricted to the Escambia drainage. Evidence for this comes from a mixed series of *F. dispar blairae* and *F. escambiae* in the University of Michigan collection (identified by John S. Williams, formerly at the University of West Florida) that had been collected near Cantonment, Florida, in the fall of 1952, and that were reported by Bailey et al. (1954) as *F. dispar*. In contrast, several other species restricted in Florida to the Escambia drainage (*Notropis bai-*

leyi, Luxilus chrysocephalus isolepis, and *Nocomis leptocephalus bellicus*) were not present in Florida collections before 1975, and *N. baileyi* is now the dominant species at one locality where it was formerly absent. (See *Notropis baileyi* FCREPA account for further details.)

HABITAT: *Fundulus dispar blairae* occurs in relatively clear ponds, lakes, and bayous, in shoreline vegetation, and in streams where current is slow. It is also commonly found in borrow ditches that receive regular overflow from larger bodies of water (Wiley and Hall 1975). Smith (1979) reported that *F. dispar dispar* inhabits swamps, marshes, well-vegetated ponds and lakes, and small streams. Almost all Florida records of *F. dispar blairae* are from backwaters immediately adjacent to the Escambia River or from similar areas in the lower reaches of its major tributaries. Although *F. escambiae* has also been taken in the same collections, it is generally less common here than *F. dispar blairae* (R. C. Cashner, personal communication). In contrast, many of the records of *F. escambiae* from the Escambia River drainage and elsewhere in western Florida have been from tributary streams, often where there is a slight current.

LIFE HISTORY AND ECOLOGY: Nothing is known about the life history and ecology of this species, although it probably is very similar to *F. dispar dispar,* the northern starhead topminnow. Smith (1979) reported that in Illinois *F. dispar dispar* breeds during early spring in dense vegetation. Gunning and Lewis (1955) found the diet of *F. dispar dispar* to include aquatic insects, snails, crustaceans, and algae.

BASIS OF STATUS CLASSIFICATION: *Fundulus dispar blairae* is here accorded "threatened" status. Although not strictly confined to big rivers, as are *Crystallaria asprella* and *Moxostoma carinatum,* all records of *F. dispar blairae* are from the Escambia River and adjacent backwaters or from the lower portions of its major tributaries. Its habitat is closely comparable to that of *Hybognathus hayi,* which is also regarded as "threatened" in Florida. Pollution from upriver areas in Alabama constitutes the main threat to the species.

RECOMMENDATIONS: Recommendations are similar to those for the several other fish species confined to the Escambia River and closely adjacent areas. Known populations should be monitored and a search should be made for new populations, particularly in large tributary streams where the species is more likely to survive in case of a massive pollution spill.

Literature Cited

Bailey, R. M., H. E. Winn, and C. L. Smith. 1954. Fishes from the Escambia River, Alabama and Florida, with ecologic and taxonomic notes. Proc. Acad. Nat. Sci. Phila. 106:109–164.

Gunning, G. E., and W. M. Lewis. 1955. The fish population of a spring-fed swamp in the Mississippi bottoms of southern Illinois. Ecology 36(4):552–558.

Smith, P. W. 1979. The fishes of Illinois. University of Illinois Press, Urbana. 314 pp.

Wiley, E. O. 1977. The phylogeny and systematics of the *Fundulus nottii* species group (Teleostei: Cyprinodontidae). Occ. Pap. Mus. Nat. Hist. Univ. Kans. 66:1–31.

————. 1980. *Fundulus blairae* Wiley and Hall, Blair's starhead topminnow. Page 508 *in* D. S. Lee et al., eds., Atlas of North American freshwater fishes. North Carolina State Museum of Natural History, Raleigh, i–x+854 pp.

Wiley, E. O., and D. D. Hall, 1975. *Fundulus blairae*, a new species of the *Fundulus nottii* complex (Teleostei, Cyprinodontidae). Amer. Mus. Novit. 2577:1–13.

Prepared by: Carter R. Gilbert, *Florida Museum of Natural History, University of Florida, Gainesville, Florida 32611.*

Saltmarsh Topminnow

Fundulus jenkinsi

FAMILY CYPRINODONTIDAE

Order Cyprinodontiformes

Saltmarsh topminnow, *Fundulus jenkinsi* (Evermann, 1892). UWF 1650. Young adult, 22.0 mm SL. Whiteoak Bayou at entrance to Blackwater Bayou, Santa Rosa County, Florida. 3 March 1976.

OTHER NAMES: None.

DESCRIPTION: The saltmarsh topminnow is a relatively small species of *Fundulus*, attaining a maximum size of about 60-mm SL but with most adults being between 35 and 45 mm. The species' most distinctive diagnostic feature is the series of 12–30 round spots (each the size of a scale or less and sometimes coalesced into short, indistinct bars), often arranged in two rows and situated along the midside of the body from above the middle of the pectoral fin to the caudal-fin base (Jordan and Evermann 1900; Thompson 1980). Other diagnostic features include the combination of 8–9 dorsal and 11–13 anal rays, the dorsal-fin origin situated slightly behind the anal-fin origin; usually 16 rows of scales around the caudal peduncle; top of head flat or slightly concave in front of eyes and snout short and sharp; and dark cross hatching situated dorsally and dorsolaterally. The species apparently displays virtually no color in life, and there is little sexual dimorphism other than in median fin length (Thompson 1980). Simpson and Gunter (1956) found range lengths of 9 males from Texas to be 26–45 mm SL and, for 15 females, 25–60 mm SL. Although this is based on a limited sample, it does suggest that females may reach a larger size than males.

TAXONOMIC COMMENTS: Brown (1957) and Rosen (1973) included this species in the subgenus *Zygonectes*, but Thompson (1980) said that ongoing studies indicate no intimate relationships with other members of this subgenus.

RANGE: *Fundulus jenkinsi* ranges sporadically from the Galveston Bay area around Houston, Texas, eastward along the northern coast of the Gulf of Mexico to extreme western Florida. In Florida, it is known from Perdido and Escambia bays and possibly East Bay. Fowler (1945) included it in a table of fishes from the Rio Grande, but the occurrence of

Distribution map of *Fundulus jenkinsi*.

the species there cannot be confirmed and the record is presumed to be erroneous.

The vast majority of records for this species are between southeastern Louisiana and Florida, and in fact Thompson (1980) showed no collection localities between Galveston Bay and southeastern Louisiana. Although this may represent a collecting artifact, data appearing in Simpson and Gunter (1956) suggest that this distributional hiatus is real. In their ichthyological survey (involving 84 collections from 60 different sites) of Texas salt marshes from the Sabine River to the Rio Grande, *F. jenkinsi* was present in only 6 collections (representing a total of 24 specimens), all from in and around Galveston Bay. Rarity is also suggested by the small sample size of Simpson and Gunter's (1956) collections, as well as by the presence of only 7 total specimens (in 4 series) from Florida in the Florida Museum of Natural History collection (UF 44405 [2], UF 62412 [1], UF 63976 [3], and UF 64213 [1]). However, the statement by Bailey et al. (1954) that "many specimens" were present at a site in the lowermost Escambia River suggests that the species occasionally may be locally common.

HABITAT: The saltmarsh topminnow inhabits brackish water and salt marshes and seems to be most common in small, shallow tidal meanders of *Spartina* marshes, where the salinity is usually 1–4 ppt (Thompson 1980). Simpson and Gunter (1956) indicated that two of their specimens from Texas were taken at a salinity of 3.4, whereas the remaining 22 individuals were caught at salinities ranging from 11.3 to 20.6. Robins et al. (1980) listed the saltmarsh topminnow as occasionally occurring in fresh water (0.0 ppt), although no confirmatory evidence was given.

LIFE HISTORY AND ECOLOGY: Very little is known regarding the life history and ecology of *Fundulus jenkinsi*, other than a few observations by Simpson and Gunter (1956) and Thompson (1980). Simpson and Gunter (1956) found a female with eggs of less than 0.25 mm in diameter collected on 26 September 1950, and individuals with clear eggs ranging from 0.25 to 0.50 mm in diameter were taken on 28 January of the following year. Thompson (1980) reported that males collected between December and March showed no evidence of nuptial contact organs.

SPECIALIZED OR UNIQUE CHARACTERISTICS: *Fundulus jenkinsi* is one of a group of fishes whose distributions in Florida are limited to the extreme western panhandle. Unlike the other species, which apparently entered the state via one or more stream crossovers involving the adjacent Mobile Bay basin, the saltmarsh topminnow is presumed to have reached Florida as a result of movement through coastal salt marshes.

BASIS OF STATUS CLASSIFICATION: *Fundulus jenkinsi* has an extremely limited distribution in Florida, being restricted to ecologically vulnerable salt marshes in Escambia and Santa Rosa counties. It still appears to be present in this area at about the same population levels as before. It was listed as "threatened" in the 1978 FCREPA report (Relyea 1978), and nothing has occurred in the meantime to suggest that its status should be changed.

RECOMMENDATIONS: Salt-marsh habitat in extreme northwestern Florida should be preserved to ensure the survival of *Fundulus jenkinsi* in the state. Conductors of surveys and environmental studies in this part of Florida should be cognizant of the species' presence there. Investigations should be initiated on the life history of the species.

Literature Cited

Bailey, R. M., H. E. Winn, and C. L. Smith. 1954. Fishes from the Escambia River, Alabama and Florida, with ecologic and taxonomic notes. Proc. Acad. Nat. Sci. Phila. 106:109–164.

Brown, J. L. 1957. A key to the species and subspecies of the cyprinodont genus *Fundulus* in the United States and Canada east of the continental divide. J. Wash. Acad. Sci. 47(3):69–77.

Fowler, H. W. 1945. A study of the fishes of the southern Piedmont and coastal plain. Monogr. Acad. Nat. Sci. Phila. 7:1–408. 313 figs.

Jordan, D. S., and B. W. Evermann. 1900. The fishes of North and Middle America. Pt. 4. Bull. U.S. Nat. Mus. 47:xii–ci, 3137–3313, pls. 1–392.

Relyea, K. 1978. Saltmarsh topminnow, *Fundulus jenkinsi* (Evermann). Pages 17–18 *in* Carter R. Gilbert, ed., Rare and endangered biota of Florida. Vol. 4. Fishes. University Presses of Florida, Gainesville. 58 pp.

Robins, C. R., R. M. Bailey, C. E. Bond, J. R. Brooker, E. A. Lachner, R. N. Lea, and W. B. Scott. 1980. A list of common and scientific names of fishes from the United States and Canada. 4th ed. Amer. Fish. Soc. Spec. Publ. 12. 174 pp.

Rosen, D. E. 1973. Suborder Cyprinodontoidei. Pages 228–262 *in* D. M. Cohen, ed., Fishes of the western North Atlantic 1(6):vi–xix, 1–698.

Simpson, D. G., and G. Gunter. 1956. Notes on habitats, systematic characters and life histories of Texas salt water Cyprinodontes. Tulane Stud. Zool. 4(4):115–134.

Thompson, B. A. 1980. *Fundulus jenkinsi* (Evermann), Saltmarsh topminnow. Page 518 *in* D. S. Lee et al., eds., Atlas of North American freshwater fishes. North Carolina State Museum of Natural History, Raleigh. i–x+854 pp.

Prepared by: Carter R. Gilbert, *Florida Museum of Natural History, University of Florida, Gainesville, Florida 32611*; and Kenneth Relyea, *Department of Biology, Wesleyan College, Macon, Georgia 31297*.

Opossum Pipefish

Microphis brachyurus lineatus

FAMILY SYNGNATHIDAE

Order Syngnathiformes

Opossum pipefish, *Microphis brachyurus lineatus* (Valenciennes, 1856). UF 6819. Adult female, 1600 mm TL. San Carlos Creek, Duval County, Florida. 30 July 1949.

OTHER NAMES: None.

DESCRIPTION: *Microphis brachyurus lineatus (= Oostethus lineatus)* is a relatively large pipefish, reaching a SL of 194 mm (7.64 in). It is the only western Atlantic member of the group with the combination of confluent lateral trunk and inferior tail ridges, 17–23 pectoral-fin rays, and 9 caudal-fin rays; and it is also the only Florida species in which the male bears the brood pouch on the trunk rather than on the tail (subfamily Doryhamphinae). The snout is long (1.5–2.0 in head length), the trunk rings number 16–21, and the tail rings number 20–26. Fine serrations are present on the body ridges, these becoming slightly less prominent in adults.

The color of the opossum pipefish is distinctive, particularly in breeding adults: upper snout and posterior half of head and body are sienna brown, with a series of dark red blotches on each lateral trunk ring forming a red stripe between lateral and superior trunk ridges; silver stripe on midside between lateral and inferior trunk ridges and silver edge on inferior trunk ridge; lower half of snout is bright red, with a variable number of black vertical bars; and caudal fin is also red, with a central dark stripe. Juveniles are less colorful, as they are either nearly transparent or light brown with widely spaced dark vertical bars.

TAXONOMIC REMARKS: The opossum pipefish has undergone several nomenclatural changes since appearance of the 1978 FCREPA report (Gilbert 1978). It was treated as a full species (*O. lineatus*) until 1979, at which time Dawson (1979) downgraded it to a subspecies of the widespread *Oostethus brachyurus*. Dawson (1984), in his revision of the genus *Microphis*, later expanded the taxonomic limits of that group to include *Oostethus*, which was accordingly downgraded to a subgenus.

Controversy surrounds authorship of the subspecific name *lineatus*. The original description first appeared, in a publication by Kaup (1856), as

Distribution map of *Microphis brachyurus lineatus*. Southern limit of range in western Atlantic region extends beyond limits of inset. Distribution of *M. brachyurus* (but not subspecies *lineatus*) also includes portions of tropical eastern Atlantic, eastern Pacific, and Indo-West Pacific regions.

"*Doryichthys lineatus* Valenciennes MS." Some, including Dawson (1982), feel this merely indicates that Valenciennes had earlier coined the name *lineatus* and was not responsible for the description itself, in which case authorship should be credited to Kaup. Although this may well be true, absolute proof is lacking; thus, we find it preferable to credit authorship to Valenciennes, *in* Kaup.

RANGE: *Microphis brachyurus* (with four subspecies) is a nearly cosmopolitan anadromous species that occurs throughout the tropical Indo-Pacific region, as well as the eastern and western Atlantic regions (Dawson 1979, 1985). It has also been recorded in the eastern Pacific Ocean near the terminus of the Panama Canal, which it unquestionably reached via migration through the canal (Hildebrand 1939).

The subspecies *lineatus* ranges from New Jersey south to São Paulo, Brazil, including the Gulf of Mexico and West Indies and (as indicated above) has also recently reached the eastern Pacific Ocean (Dawson 1982). Breeding adults and permanent populations are apparently limited to tropical and subtropical areas (Gilmore and Hastings 1983), with extralimital northern records (e.g., New Jersey) based on seasonal waifs carried there by ocean currents. It was first recorded from Florida by McLane (1955) on the basis of two specimens taken on 30 July 1949 in San Carlos Creek, near the mouth of the St. Johns River (UF 6819); however, it has not been collected there since. In Florida, it has consistently been collected only from the Loxahatchee River drainage (Palm Beach County), St. Lucie River (Martin and St. Lucie counties), Sebastian Creek (Indian River and Brevard counties), the St. Lucie Canal at Lake Okeechobee (Gilmore and Hastings 1983), and in relief canals associated with these tributaries and the southern half of the Indian River lagoon. It is able to negotiate its way through canal locks, as evidenced by its occurrence in Lake Okeechobee, which it could only have reached by moving through locks in the St. Lucie Canal, and by its occurrence at the Pacific terminus of the Panama Canal (Hildebrand 1939).

HABITAT: In southeastern Florida, the opossum pipefish matures, mates, and releases its progeny in fresh water, where it typically inhabits dense emergent bank vegetation usually dominated by *Panicum* spp. and *Polygonum* spp. These plants are generally well dispersed and grow rapidly in freshwater tributaries to the Indian River lagoon, but are subject to seasonal treatment by herbicides (see subsequent discussion). In Mississippi, individuals have been recorded from *Spartina* marshes (Dawson 1970). Juveniles (individuals less than 90-mm SL) occur primarily in pelagic oceanic or estuarine waters, including pelagic rafts of *Sargassum* (Böhlke and Chaplin 1968; Hastings and Bortone 1976).

LIFE HISTORY AND ECOLOGY: Although a definitive life-history study of *M. brachyurus lineatus* has not been conducted, considerable information has been gathered in conjunction with other studies. Some of this was summarized by Gilbert (1978) in the earlier FCREPA report and was based partly on Dawson's (1970, 1972) observations in Mississippi. Information on specimens collected in the estuary at Tortuguero, Costa Rica, appears in Gilbert and Kelso (1971). The following information is based on data obtained from 235 specimens (64–176 mm SL), which were captured between 1972 and 1981 from freshwater tributaries to the southern Indian River lagoon during every month of the year (Gilmore 1977; Gilmore and Hastings 1983).

Since adults appear to breed only in fresh water (Dawson 1982; Gilmore and Hastings 1983), freshwater microhabitats are obviously critical to the reproductive success of this species. Gilmore (unpublished data) encountered pairs of adult males and females at densities of one pair per 100 m of linear stream bank. Distribution is patchy in such areas, however, and is limited principally by the occurrence and abundance of clumps of emergent vegetation, such as *Polygonum* spp. and *Panicum* spp. (Gilmore and Hastings 1983). As is true for all species of Syngnathidae, egg brooding is performed exclusively by the males, with the number of eggs carried being a function of size of the individual. Dawson (1982) found that eggs are rarely present in males smaller than 120 mm, but he did occasionally find eggs attached to individuals as small as 102 mm (number of eggs not indicated). Herald (1943) found a 147-mm individual to have 744 eggs, and Gilbert (1978) reported one of 158 mm to contain approximately 700 eggs. Gilmore (1977) found brooding males from eastern Florida during July and November, and Dawson (1982) reported them to occur from June to September in Mississippi. In other areas, they have been noted during all months of the year except January and February (Dawson 1982).

Individuals hatch at lengths of from 3 to 6 mm (Gilmore 1977). The juveniles subsequently move into offshore waters, where they become associated with pelagic rafts of *Sargassum* or other types of floating vegetation. There they remain for an indeterminate length of time. After reaching lengths of from approximately 60 to 90 mm, they move back inshore into fresh water, as reported by Gilbert and Kelso (1971) from Tortuguero lagoon, Costa Rica.

It is impossible to determine the overall population size of opossum pipefish in Florida because of the wide dispersal of larval and juvenile stages.

BASIS OF STATUS CLASSIFICATION: The dependence of the opossum pipefish on accessible coastal freshwater habitat along the southern portion of the Indian River lagoon limits the breeding adult population to the coastal reaches of this area. Although juvenile habitat is the open ocean, the species is dependent on specific freshwater microhabitats for successful reproduction. The human population in these same coastal areas is increasing rapidly, and concurrent demands on freshwater resources have resulted in heavy impaction by a variety of anthropogenic processes. Among these is herbicide spraying of areas used for breeding by this fish. Consequently, the adult habitat of the opossum pipefish in Florida has already been destroyed in many areas, and remaining habitat is highly vulnerable to human activities.

The opossum pipefish was accorded "rare" status in the 1978 FCREPA report. Increased knowledge of the distribution, habitat, and ecology of the species in Florida indicates that it is in a more vulnerable position than earlier realized. Consequently, it is upgraded to "threatened" status, one of only two species listed in the 1978 report for which this is true.

RECOMMENDATIONS: Human population encroachment on the coastal freshwater streams where this species occurs should be limited and a buffer area implemented. Water-management agencies should attempt to "mimic" natural stream hydrologic and vegetative conditions. The remaining natural portions of the creeks and streams where the species occurs (e.g., Sebastian Creek) should be preserved. Nonpoint and point-source pollutants should be eliminated. Herbicide spraying programs should be eliminated for critical areas in the streams and canals between the water control structures and coastal estuaries. Additional research is needed to determine spatial and temporal population dynamics, microhabitat requirements, and early life history, particularly with regard to egg, larval, and juvenile stages.

Literature Cited

Published Information

Böhlke, J. E., and C. C. G. Chaplin. 1968. Fishes of the Bahamas and adjacent tropical waters. Livingston, Wynnewood, Pa. xxiii+771 pp.

Dawson, C. E. 1970. A Mississippi population of the opossum pipefish, *Oostethus lineatus* (Syngnathidae). Copeia 1970(4):772–773.

———.1972. Nektonic pipefishes (Syngnathidae) from the Gulf of Mexico off Mississippi. Copeia 1972 (4):844–848.

———. 1979. Review of the polytypic doryhamphine pipefish *Oostethus brachyurus* (Bleeker). Bull. Mar. Sci. 29(4):465–480.

———. 1982. Family Syngnathidae. Pages 1–172 *in* C. E. Dawson and R. P. Vari, eds., Fishes of the western North Atlantic. Pt. 8. Mem. Sears Found. Mar. Res., New Haven, Conn. 198 pp.

———. 1984. Revision of the genus *Microphis* Kaup (Pisces: Syngnathidae). Bull. Mar. Sci. 35(2):117–181.

———. 1985. Indo-Pacific pipefishes (Red Sea to the Americas). Gulf Coast Research Laboratory, Ocean Springs, Mississippi. 230 pp.

Gilbert, C. R. 1978. Opossum pipefish, *Oostethus lineatus* (Valenciennes). Pages 38–39 *in* Carter R. Gilbert, ed., Rare and endangered biota of Florida. Vol. 4. Fishes. University Presses of Florida, Gainesville. 58 pp.

Gilbert, C. R., and D. P. Kelso. 1971. Fishes of the Tortuguero area, Caribbean Costa Rica. Bull. Fla. St. Mus. Biol. Sci. 16(1):1–54.

Gilmore, R. G. 1977. Notes on the opossum pipefish *Oostethus lineatus*, from the Indian River lagoon and vicinity, Florida. Copeia 1977(4):781–783.

Gilmore, R. G., and P. A. Hastings. 1983. Observations on the ecology and distribution of certain tropical peripheral fishes in Florida. Fla. Sci. 46(1):31–51.

Hastings, P. A., and S. A. Bortone. 1976. Additional notes on tropical marine fishes in the northern Gulf of Mexico. Fla. Sci. 39(2):123–125.

Hildebrand, S. F. 1939. The Panama Canal as a passageway for fishes, with lists and remarks on the fishes and invertebrates observed. Zoologica 24:15–45.

Kaup, J. J. 1856. Catalogue of Lophobranchiate fish in the collection of the British Museum, London. i–iv+80 pp.

Unpublished Information

Herald, E. S. 1943. Studies on the classification and interrelationships of the American pipefishes. Ph.D. diss., Stanford University, Palo Alto, Calif.

McLane, W. M. 1955. The fishes of the St. Johns River system. Ph.D. diss., University of Florida, Gainesville.

Prepared by: R. Grant Gilmore, *Harbor Branch Oceanographic Institution, Ft. Pierce, Florida 33450*; and Carter R. Gilbert, *Florida Museum of Natural History, University of Florida, Gainesville, Florida 32611.*

Crystal Darter

Crystallaria asprella

FAMILY PERCIDAE

Order Perciformes

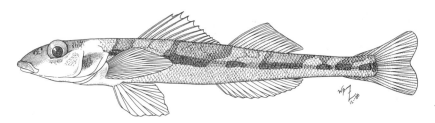

Crystal darter, *Crystallaria asprella* (Jordan, 1878). UF 73033. Adult male, 68.1 mm SL. Escambia River, Santa Rosa County, Florida. 28 November 1974.

OTHER NAMES: None.

DESCRIPTION: *Crystallaria asprella* is one of the larger darter species, reaching a maximum SL of up to 130 mm. The body is long and slender, the head bluntly pointed, with a large eye and small mouth. The scales are small (more than 80 in lateral line) and cover the entire body except for breast and belly; opercular spine is well developed. The dorsal and anal fins are high and long, caudal fin emarginate, pelvic fins well separated, and anal fin with one weak spine. The body is hyaline olive with three or four dark, broad, oblique saddle marks that project anteriorly. Distinguished from species of the subgenus *Ammocrypta* (genus *Etheostoma*), to which it was until recently referred, by a more completely scaled body; well-developed (vs. no) premaxillary frenum; higher dorsal and anal-ray counts (XII–XIV, 13–15 and I, 12–14, respectively; vs. IX–XI, 9–11 and I, 8–10); and pigmentation pattern.

TAXONOMIC REMARKS: Although long included in the genus *Ammocrypta*, Simons (in press) has shown that the crystal darter comprises a distinct monotypic genus, *Crystallaria*, and is the "sister" group to all

79

other North American darters. He further indicated that the other six species of *Ammocrypta* are most closely related to the glassy darter, *Etheostoma vitreum*, which in turn demonstrates relationships to the so-called "johnny darters" (subgenus *Boleosoma*). Simons therefore recommended that *Ammocrypta* be downgraded to a subgenus of *Etheostoma*.

The genus *Crystallaria* differs from other darters in several morphological features, some of which are shared with other percid outgroups. It is apparently unique, however, within the family Percidae in having a bifurcate (versus an undivided) supraoccipital crest on the top of the skull. It also has a single anal spine, in contrast to the two anal spines found in most species of Percidae. Although an important species-level

Distribution map of *Crystallaria asprella*.

character, this reduction in anal-spine number has occurred independently in a number of other species of darters.

James D. Williams (personal communication) has found that northern populations of the crystal darter have significantly lower meristic counts than those to the south. He further indicates that this difference does not appear to be clinal in nature, and feels that two distinct subspecies may be involved. Smith (1979) had earlier alluded to this, but was incorrect in stating that the Ozark population differed from that on the Gulf Coast.

RANGE: Spot-distribution maps for *Crystallaria asprella* appear in Page (1980, 1983). It occurs in large rivers of the Gulf coast and Mississippi Valley, from the Escambia River drainage westward to the Mississippi River basin (but excluding the Pascagoula drainage); northward in the Mississippi River and most of its major tributaries from Louisiana to southern Wisconsin and Minnesota. West of the Mississippi River, the species has been recorded from extreme southeastern Oklahoma but is not known from Texas, Kansas, or Nebraska, to the south and north. The species was first collected from Florida, as well as from the Escambia River drainage, on 7 April 1972, when one specimen (UF 71354) was collected near the state Route 4 bridge at Century. Two other specimens were collected from the same area (UF 73033, UF 73345) in November 1974. Recently, about 30 specimens (all of which were subsequently released) were collected in a single seine haul during the summer of 1988 from Big Escambia Creek (a large tributary of the Escambia) near Century. Also, a series of five specimens was collected earlier during the 1980s in the Escambia River just over the state line in Alabama.

Knowledge of the crystal darter's ecology, coupled with knowledge of its habitat (particularly substrate) throughout the main Escambia River, permits more precise predictions regarding distribution of the species in our area. The Escambia River in Alabama (which is called the Conecuh River throughout most of its length) is largely a shifting sand-bottomed stream (J. D. Williams, personal communication). This affords prime habitat for such species as the Florida sand darter, *Etheostoma bifascia*. The preference of *C. asprella* for a substrate consisting of a combination of sand and gravel (see below), however, suggests that this species likely is absent or rare throughout most of the Escambia drainage in Alabama. A sand-gravel substrate first becomes apparent along the Florida-Alabama line, in the same area where *C. asprella* has been collected. It may be predicted that the range of the crystal darter in the Escambia River probably is not much different from that already defined, except that the species may range somewhat farther downstream.

HABITAT: The crystal darter primarily occupies large sand or gravel bars and riffles, as well as flowing pools, of large rivers. Water in such areas is white and usually turbid. In general, it occurs only sparingly in areas composed entirely of shifting sand, unlike the situation in the Florida sand darter (*Etheostoma bifascia*) and its close relatives.

LIFE HISTORY AND ECOLOGY: Few details are known regarding the life history of this species. As is true of species of the subgenus *Ammocrypta*, individuals bury themselves in the substrate, where they lie in wait for passing prey. Collette (1965) reported that breeding tubercles begin to develop on the pelvic and anal fins of males from the Pearl River, Mississippi, in late November and reach maximum development by late January. A female *C. asprella* from Wisconsin, collected in July, was found to contain about 6,900 undeveloped eggs in the ovary (Lutterbie 1979). Although actual spawning has not been observed, indirect information suggests that this occurs in mid or late winter to early spring in the southern states and probably later farther north. Site of egg deposition has not been reported, but habits and habitat of the species suggest that eggs are probably buried in the substrate. Lutterbie (1979) reported that some individuals may reach four years of age, although most probably do not live that long. He also found the digestive tracts of two Wisconsin specimens to contain various insects, of which midge larvae comprised 36 percent of the total food weight.

SPECIALIZED OR UNIQUE CHARACTERISTICS: *Crystallaria asprella* is one of relatively few native North American freshwater fishes that is confined to areas having a sand or fine-gravel substrate and is also an exclusive inhabitant of big rivers. It is one of six species thought to be native to Florida whose range in the state is confined to the Escambia River drainage (another species, *Etheostoma stigmaeum*, ranges only narrowly outside of this area). Three other species (all cyprinids) whose range is limited to this drainage are suspected of having been introduced.

BASIS OF STATUS CLASSIFICATION: This species continues to be accorded "threatened" status, for reasons discussed in the 1978 FCREPA report (Gilbert 1978). Its situation is very similar to that of several other Florida species restricted to the Escambia drainage and ecologically restricted to the Escambia River itself and the lowermost portions of its major tributaries. Of these, the crystal darter and river redhorse are the most closely restricted to this type of habitat and thus are the most vulnerable to extirpation via pollution or other types of ecological perturbations.

The recent discovery of an apparently large population in Big Escambia Creek is encouraging and may mean that the apparent rarity of the species is partly the result of inadequate sampling.

RECOMMENDATIONS: Protect the Escambia River against pollution or other types of habitat modification. Encourage and support efforts to collect the species to determine more fully its present status and abundance in Florida.

Literature Cited

Collette, B. B. 1965. Systematic significance of breeding tubercles in fishes of the family Percidae. Proc. U.S. Nat. Mus. 117 (3518):567–614.

Gilbert, C. R. 1978. Crystal darter, *Ammocrypta asprella* (Jordan). Pages 19–21 *in* C. R. Gilbert, ed., Rare and endangered biota of Florida. Vol. 4. Fishes. University Presses of Florida, Gainesville. 58 pp.

Lutterbie, G. W. 1979. Reproduction and age and growth in Wisconsin darters (Osteichthyes: Percidae). Rept. Fauna and Florida Wisconsin 15. 44 pp.

Page, L. M. 1980. *Ammocrypta asprella* (Jordan), Crystal darter. Page 615 *in* D.S. Lee et al. eds., Atlas of North American freshwater fishes. North Carolina State Museum of Natural History, Raleigh. i–x+854 pp.

———. 1983. Handbook of darters. T.F.H. Publications, Inc., Neptune City, N.J. 271 pp.

Simons, A. M. The phylogenetic relationships of the crystal darter, *Crystallaria asprella*. Copeia (in press).

Smith, P. W. 1979. The fishes of Illinois. University of Illinois Press, Champaign. xxix+314 pp.

Prepared by: Carter R. Gilbert, *Florida Museum of Natural History, University of Florida, Gainesville, Florida 32611.*

Harlequin Darter

Etheostoma histrio

FAMILY PERCIDAE

Order Perciformes

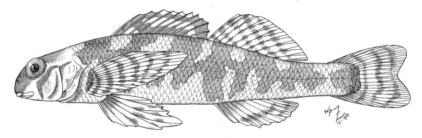

Harlequin darter, *Etheostoma histrio* Jordan and Gilbert, 1887. UF 28169. Adult male, 38.5 mm SL. Little Corney Bayou, Union Parish, Louisiana. 14 June 1980.

OTHER NAMES: None.

DESCRIPTION: *Etheostoma histrio* is a small darter with red-brown blotches that is strikingly colored black and green; second dorsal, caudal, pectoral, and pelvic fins heavily spotted; margin of first dorsal fin with a wide, wine-colored stripe; ventral areas of head and breast with many dark spots or blotches, lines, and bars; a pair of large dark blotches at base of caudal fin; and six or seven dorsal blotches or saddles. These markings are so distinctive that the harlequin darter cannot be confused with any other Florida fish.

RANGE: Spot-distribution maps of *Etheostoma histrio* appear in Tsai (1968), Hocutt (1980), and Page (1983, map 37). The harlequin darter is widely distributed in tributaries of the lower Mississippi River from Illinois and Indiana southward to eastern Texas and western Florida, primarily below the Fall Line. In Florida it has been collected at only two localities in the Escambia River proper and in a closely adjacent tributary between McDavid and the Alabama state line. This species was not reported from the Escambia drainage by Bailey et al. (1954) and was recorded from this area for the first time by Yerger and Suttkus (1962) on the basis of five specimens, four from Florida (UF 55911) and one from a closely adjacent area in Alabama. To our knowledge, the only other specimens taken in Florida are a single individual collected in 1976 (UF 75326) and another individual collected in 1988 (specimen retained in private collection). The species has also been taken in the Big Escambia Creek watershed in Alabama (Hocutt 1980). The species apparently is rare in Florida and from the Escambia River drainage in general but may be moderately common in certain other parts of its range.

Distribution map of *Etheostoma histrio*.

HABITAT: This species is found in Coastal Plain rivers and their tributaries, chiefly in shallow riffles with moderate to swift current and over rocky or gravel bottoms. However, in some areas outside of Florida it has occasionally been taken over bottoms of sand and mud and in quiet water among fine tree roots, vegetation, and organic debris. Hubbs and Pigg (1972), based on collections from Oklahoma and Texas, always found it behind obstructions in heavy detritus, and Sisk and Webb (1976) reported the species living in a deep riffle-detritus habitat with or without a sandy bottom.

LIFE HISTORY AND ECOLOGY: Pflieger (1975) reported adults in spawning condition that were collected during February in Missouri, and Kuehne and Barbour (1983) found ripe individuals in west-central Mississippi in mid-March. Other than this, no life-history information appears to be available.

SPECIALIZED OR UNIQUE CHARACTERISTICS: The harlequin darter is one of several species whose distribution in Florida is limited to the Escambia River drainage.

BASIS OF STATUS CLASSIFICATION: As indicated, very few specimens of *E. histrio* from the Escambia River drainage are extant in museum fish collections. Although a high percentage of records from throughout the species's range are from large creeks and rivers, it is less closely confined to these areas than species such as *Crystallaria asprella* and *Moxostoma carinatum*. The only new information we have on local populations of the harlequin darter since publication of the earlier FCREPA account (Yerger 1978) are records from Big Escambia Creek in Alabama (Hocutt 1980). Because of the vulnerability of big-river habitat, coupled with the rarity of *E. histrio* in Florida and in the Escambia drainage in general, this species was accorded "threatened" status in the 1978 FCREPA publication. We see no reason to change this classification.

RECOMMENDATIONS: Efforts should continue to be aimed at locating additional populations of the harlequin darter in the Escambia drainage. Investigations on the biology of the species should be initiated. The few streams in Florida where the species is known to occur should be preserved in their natural state.

Literature Cited

Bailey, R. M., H. E. Winn, and C. L. Smith. 1954. Fishes of the Escambia River, Alabama and Florida, with ecologic and taxonomic notes. Proc. Acad. Nat. Sci. Phila. 106:109–164.

Hocutt, C. H. 1980. *Etheostoma histrio* Jordan and Gilbert, Harlequin darter. Page 653 *in* D. S. Lee et al., eds., Atlas of North American freshwater fishes. North Carolina State Museum of Natural History, Raleigh, i–x+854 pp.

Hubbs, C., and J. Pigg. 1972. Habitat preferences of the harlequin darter, *Etheostoma histrio*, in Texas and Oklahoma. Copeia 1972 (1):193–194.

Kuehne, R. E., and R. W. Barbour. 1983. The American darters. University of Kentucky Press, Lexington. 177 pp.

Page, L. M. 1983. Handbook of darters. T.F.H. Publications, Inc., Neptune City, N.J. 271 pp.

Pflieger, W. L. 1975. The fishes of Missouri. Missouri Department of Conservation, Jefferson City. 343 pp.

Sisk, M. E., and D. H. Webb. 1976. Distribution and habitat preference of *Etheostoma histrio* in Kentucky. Trans. Ky. Acad. Sci. 37:33–34.

Tsai, Chu-Fa. 1968. Distribution of the harlequin darter, *Etheostoma histrio*. Copeia 1968 (1):178–181.

Yerger, R. W. 1978. *Etheostoma histrio* Jordan and Gilbert, Harlequin darter. Pages 21–22 *in* Carter R. Gilbert, ed., Rare and endangered biota of Florida. Vol. 4. Fishes. University Presses of Florida, Gainesville. 58 pp.

Yerger, R. W., and R. D. Suttkus. 1962. Records of freshwater fishes in Florida. Tulane Stud. Zool. 9 (5):323–330.

Prepared by: Carter R. Gilbert, *Florida Museum of Natural History, University of Florida, Gainesville, Florida*; and Ralph W. Yerger (retired), *Department of Biological Science, Florida State University, Tallahassee, Florida 32306.*

Southern Tessellated Darter

Etheostoma olmstedi maculaticeps

FAMILY PERCIDAE

Order Perciformes

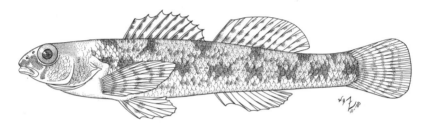

Southern tessellated darter, *Etheostoma olmstedi maculaticeps* (Cope, 1870). UF 23159. Adult female, 45.6 mm SL. Orange Creek, Putnam/Marion counties, Florida. 23 January 1976.

OTHER NAMES: Tessellated johnny darter.

DESCRIPTION: *Etheostoma olmstedi* is a moderately large, elongate, slender darter that commonly reaches a SL of 60 mm (about 2.5 in) and occasionally reaches a length of 88 mm. It is characterized by a complete lateral line, a series of 9–11 dark X- or Y-shaped brown-black markings along the midside of the body in both sexes, and the absence of chromatic pigmentation at any time of the year. It is most readily distinguished from *Etheostoma nigrum*, its closest relative (which does not occur in Florida), by the number of markings along the sides of the body (6 or 7 in *E. nigrum*), in usually having 13 (vs. 11 or 12) pectoral-fin rays and 12–14 (vs. 10–12) second dorsal-fin rays and 8 (vs. 6) infraorbital canal pores (Cole 1965). The subspecies *maculaticeps* is distinguished from other subspecies of *E. olmstedi* in usually having two (vs. one) anal spines and in a naked nape, cheek, breast, and belly (vs. scaled or else naked only in certain areas) (Cole 1967).

RANGE: Spot-distribution maps of *E. olmstedi* appear in Lee and McAllister (1980) and Page (1983, map 45), and the Florida distribution was mapped by Burgess et al. (1977). The tessellated darter ranges from eastern Ontario (Lake Ontario and St. Lawrence drainages), northern New York (Lake Champlain), and southern New Hampshire south to the St. Johns River drainage in Florida. The St. Johns population is widely disjunct from the next closest population to the north (the Altamaha River drainage in central Georgia), and the species is absent from the intervening St. Marys and Satilla river drainages. The subspecies *maculaticeps* ranges from North Carolina southward. In Florida, all known specimens have been collected from three localities: the Oklawaha River at Daven-

Distribution map of *Etheostoma olmstedi*. The Florida subspecies is *E. olmstedi maculaticeps*. The several recognized subspecies of *E. olmstedi* are not differentiated on inset.

port Landing, about seven miles upstream from its mouth in the St. Johns River and about two miles below the present site of Rodman Dam; Orange Creek at Orange Springs; and Eaton Creek at the western edge of the Ocala National Forest. The species was first collected in Florida in 1948 and 1949 at Davenport Landing (McLane 1955) but was not found again in the state until October 1975, when one specimen was taken in Orange Creek. Four additional specimens were collected in Orange Creek and one in Eaton Creek in February 1976. Efforts to collect it again at the Davenport Landing locality have been unsuccessful, but small numbers of specimens have regularly been found at the Orange Creek site in recent years.

HABITAT: *Etheostoma olmstedi* is one of the most characteristic species of small- to medium-sized streams along the eastern coast of the United States, from central Georgia northward. It usually is found in areas where the current is less than maximal (thus is not primarily a riffle form) and frequently occurs in flowing pools. Bottom type varies, but sand, mud, silt, or gravel is frequently present. The species has occasionally been found in water of very low salinity (2.23 ppt) (Hildebrand and Schroeder 1928, p. 238), although the family Percidae as a whole is considered to be intolerant of salt water.

LIFE HISTORY AND ECOLOGY: The tessellated darter is a carnivore, as are all percid species, and subsists on small items such as insects, crustaceans (principally *Gammarus*), insect larvae, and small fish. The species spawns during the spring along the mid-Atlantic coast; spawning females have been collected during May in Maryland; the ovary of a 62-mm female contained 340 eggs of uniform size. Specimens become sexually mature at sizes of at least 40-mm SL. Although spawning times have not been precisely determined for the Florida population, data from other fish species having broad latitudinal distributions suggest that in Florida reproductive activities probably begin in January or February.

SPECIALIZED OR UNIQUE CHARACTERISTICS: This species is remarkable in that it has been found at only three places in Florida, over 300 km from the next closest locality. It always has been found in small numbers and has been consistently absent in collections from closely adjacent areas in Florida where apparently favorable habitat exists. This is all the more remarkable in view of the wide distribution and abundance of the species elsewhere throughout its range. Its isolated occurrence in the St. Johns drainage is paralleled by the distributions of *Pteronotropis welaka*, *Notropis cummingsae*, and *Ameiurus brunneus*; in addition, several endemic inverte- brates occur in that small portion of the St. Johns drainage inhabited by the above fishes, including the crayfish, *Procambarus pictus*. The historical basis of this natural distributional hiatus was discussed by Burgess and Franz (1978) and Gilbert (1987).

BASIS OF STATUS CLASSIFICATION: *Etheostoma olmstedi* has been re- corded from only three closely adjacent localities in the state, and in only one of these (Orange Creek) can it currently be found with any regular- ity. It cannot be definitely proven, but the construction of Rodman Res- ervoir almost certainly eliminated other populations of this species from the Oklawaha River, as suggested by the fact that the Orange Creek lo- cality (at the state Highway 315 bridge) is in very close proximity to im- pounded waters of the reservoir. At the present time, the Orange Creek locality continues to support a good population of fish; however, in re- cent years, increasingly dense growths of the water weed *Hydrilla* have been seen at this site and conceivably could begin to have an adverse ef- fect on *E. olmstedi*, as well as on other fish species. The potential reduc- tion in habitat quality in Orange Creek, together with the geographic limitation of the tessellated darter in Florida to this locality, places the species in a vulnerable position. For this reason, we continue to accord this species "threatened" status.

RECOMMENDATIONS: Additional ichthyological surveys in the St. Johns River drainage (particularly the Oklawaha River system) would be desir- able to find other localities of the tessellated darter. Continued protec- tion of the Oklawaha against further habitat modification is necessary to ensure its survival.

Literature Cited

Published Information

Burgess, G. H., and R. Franz. 1978. Zoogeography of the aquatic fauna of the St. Johns River system with comments on adjacent peninsular faunas. Am. Midl. Nat. 100 (1):160–170.

Burgess, G. H., C. R. Gilbert, V. Guillory, and D. C. Taphorn. 1977. Distribu- tional notes on some north Florida freshwater fishes. Fla. Sci. 40(1):33–41.

Cole, C. F. 1965. Additional evidence for separation of *Etheostoma olmstedi* Storer and *Etheostoma nigrum* Rafinesque. Copeia 1965(1):8–13.

_____. 1967. A study of the Eastern johnny darter, *Etheostoma olmstedi* Storer (Teleostei, Percidae). Chesapeake Sci. 8(1):28–51.

Gilbert, C. R. 1987. Zoogeography of the freshwater fish fauna of southern Georgia and peninsular Florida. Brimleyana 13:25–54.

Hildebrand, S. F., and W. C. Schroeder 1928. Fishes of Chesapeake Bay. Bull. U.S. Bur. Fish. (1927), 43(1):1–366.

Lee, D. S., and D. E. McAllister. 1980. *Etheostoma olmstedi* Storer, tessellated darter. Page 677 *in* D. S. Lee et al., eds., Atlas of North American freshwater fishes. North Carolina State Museum of Natural History, Raleigh. i–x+854 pp.

Page, L. M. 1983. Handbook of darters. T. F. H. Publications, Inc., Neptune City, N.J. 271 pp.

Unpublished information

McLane, W. M. 1955. The fishes of the St. Johns River system. Ph.D. diss., University of Florida, Gainesville.

Prepared by: Carter R. Gilbert, *Florida Museum of Natural History, University of Florida, Gainesville, Florida 32611.*

Saddleback Darter

Percina vigil

FAMILY PERCIDAE

Order Perciformes

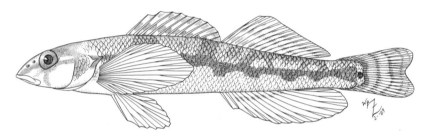

Saddleback darter, *Percina vigil* (Hay, 1882). UF 73348. Adult female, 41.2 mm SL. Escambia River, Santa Rosa County, Florida. 28 November 1974.

OTHER NAMES: Yellow darter; stargazing darter (latter name applied to *Percina uranidea*, which before 1974 was considered to be a single species that included both *P. uranidea* and *Percina vigil*).

DESCRIPTION: *Percina vigil* is a moderately small darter (maximum SL about 65 mm) with an emarginate caudal fin; four forwardly directed and usually distinct oblique dorsal saddles (the first saddle beneath anterior part of spinous dorsal fin), with a fifth saddle (usually indistinct) just in front of caudal fin; saddles not quite touching series of 8–10 rectangular blotches along midside of body; a distinct suborbital bar and preorbital stripe; a small and usually discrete black basicaudal spot; black (or dusky) basal and marginal stripes in spinous dorsal fin, the fin otherwise clear; opercle and nape scaled, cheek either scaled or naked, and breast usually naked; lateral line straight and complete, usually with 47–56 scales (range 46–62); dorsal-fin rays usually X–XI, 13–14; anal-fin rays usually II, 10–11; pectoral-fin rays usually 14–15.

TAXONOMIC COMMENTS: The scientific name of this species has been characterized by change over the past 15 years. It was known as *P. urani-*

93

dea before 1974, when Douglas (1974), based on information supplied by Bruce Thompson and Robert Cashner, showed it to be a complex of two species: the true *P. uranidea*, a comparatively rare species confined almost entirely to west of the Mississippi River; and the more common and widespread *Percina ouachitae*, which occurs both west and east of the Mississippi River and along the central Gulf slope. Suttkus (1985) later showed that the species name *vigil* also applies to the saddleback darter; since it antedates *ouachitae* by five years, the species should henceforth be called *P. vigil*.

RANGE: Spot-distribution maps appear in Thompson and Cashner (1980) and in Page (1983). *Percina vigil* ranges from southeastern Missouri and

Distribution map of *Percina vigil*.

the Wabash River system of extreme southwestern Indiana south through western Kentucky, western Tennessee, and the lower Mississippi Valley to southern Arkansas and Louisiana. From there it occurs eastward along the Gulf slope below the Fall Line to the Mobile Bay basin of Alabama and Mississippi and the Escambia River drainage of extreme western Florida. The following ten lots (comprising 34 specimens) from this drainage are present in the Florida Museum of Natural History collection, of which six are from Florida and four are from closely adjacent areas in Alabama: UF 53434 (4), UF 53536 (1), UF 54365 (1), UF 55913 (6), UF 75328 (1), UF 76426 (1) (Florida), UF 44652 (5), UF 44664 (4), UF 44682 (10), and UF 74147 (1) (Alabama). All but two of the above series are from the Escambia River proper; the other two are from the lowermost sections of large tributaries, of which the one from Canoe Creek at the U.S. Highway 29 bridge (UF 76426) is most distant from the main river.

HABITAT: The saddleback darter typically occupies shallow riffles with moderate current in large creeks and rivers, usually over a substrate of sand and gravel. According to Kuehne and Barbour (1983, p. 51), "These conditions usually prevail toward the foot of a chute or riffle but also where snags and log jams create enough current to sweep away silt and finely divided organic material. Although usually associated with clean, relatively clear waters, it may also be found in murky waters characteristic of much of the Mississippi lowlands."

LIFE HISTORY AND ECOLOGY: Heins and Baker (1986, 1989) found that reproductive activities during 1984–1985 in the Homochitto River in southwestern Mississippi began in late February or early March and had ended by mid-May. Mettee et al. (1987) reported on collections of ripe males and females from the Escambia River drainage of southeastern Alabama and surmised that spawning in this area occurs from January into March. Heins and Baker (1986, 1989) found reproductively mature females to contain two distinct groups of yolk-bearing oocytes, indicating that *P. vigil* produces multiple clutches of eggs. Based on analysis of 23 individuals, they found from 60 to 317 ova per clutch with the eggs averaging 0.78 mm in diameter. Thompson (1974) found that *P. vigil* and the closely related *P. uranidea* (with which *P. vigil* was once synonymized) occur syntopically in certain tributaries of the Mississippi River in Arkansas and Missouri. In these areas the two species are ecologically segregated, *P. vigil* occupying the slower riffles and eddies and *P. uranidea* the deeper, swifter, gravel-rubble bottom riffles. He found *P. vigil* to have a typical darter diet of insect larvae and small crustaceans, in contrast to *P. uranidea*, which feeds almost exclusively on snails and limpets. *Percina vigil* sometimes achieves population densities that are high compared with most other species of darters.

BASIS OF STATUS CLASSIFICATION: *Percina vigil* is one of six species native to Florida whose range in the state is limited to the Escambia River drainage. All are in a vulnerable position and accordingly are regarded as "threatened" by the FCREPA subcommittee on fishes. It should be noted, however, that of the six species (which also include *Moxostoma carinatum, Hybognathus hayi, Fundulus dispar blairae, Crystallaria asprella,* and *Etheostoma histrio*), the saddleback darter probably is the most generally common throughout its range. Thus, although classified here as "threatened," as in the previous FCREPA account (Yerger 1978), the ability of this fish to sometimes achieve high populations may place it in a less vulnerable position than the other five species.

RECOMMENDATIONS: Continue to monitor known populations of this species, search for new localities, and protect the general environment of the Escambia River and its tributaries.

Literature Cited

Douglas, N. H. 1974. Freshwater fishes of Louisiana. Claitor's, Baton Rouge, La. 443 pp.

Heins, D. C., and J. A. Baker, 1986. Natural history of *Percina vigil* Hay in the Homochitto River, Mississippi. ASB Bull. 33(2):82.

———. 1989. Natural history of *Percina vigil* Hay in the Homochitto River, Mississippi. Copeia 1989(3):727–736.

Kuehne, R. A., and R. W. Barbour. 1983. The American darters. University Press of Kentucky, Lexington. 177 pp.

Mettee, M. F., P. E. O'Neil, R. D. Suttkus, and J. M. Pierson. 1987. Fishes of the lower Tombigbee River system in Alabama and Mississippi. Bull. Geol. Surv. Ala. 107:1–186.

Page, L. M. 1983. Handbook of darters. T.F.H. Publications, Inc., Neptune City, N.J. 271 pp.

Suttkus, R. D. 1985. Identification of the percid, *Ioa vigil* Hay. Copeia 1985(1): 225–227.

Thompson, B. A. 1974. An analysis of sympatric populations of two closely related species of *Percina*, with notes on food habits of the subgenus *Imostoma*. ASB Bull. 21(2):87.

Thompson, B. A., and R. C. Cashner. 1980. *Percina ouachitae* (Jordan and Gilbert), Yellow darter. Page 732 *in* D. S. Lee et al., eds., Atlas of North American freshwater fishes. North Carolina State Museum of Natural History, Raleigh. i–x+854 pp.

Yerger, R. W. 1978. Saddleback darter, *Percina ouachitae* (Jordan and Gilbert). Pages 26–27 *in* Carter R. Gilbert, ed., Rare and endangered biota of Florida. Vol. 4. Fishes. University Presses of Florida, Gainesville. 58 pp.

Prepared by: Carter R. Gilbert, *Florida Museum of Natural History, University of Florida, Gainesville, Florida 32611*; and Ralph W. Yerger (retired), *Department of Biological Science, Florida State University, Tallahassee, Florida 32306.*

Shoal Bass

Micropterus n. sp. cf *coosae*

FAMILY CENTRARCHIDAE

Order Perciformes

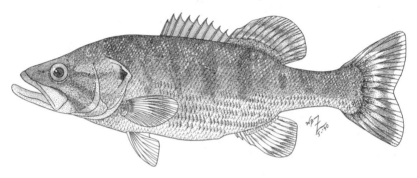

Shoal bass, *Micropterus* n. sp. cf *coosae*. UF 79980. Adult, 378 mm SL. Chipola River, Jackson County, Florida. 8 May 1989.

OTHER NAMES: Chipola bass, Flint River bass, Flint River smallmouth, Redeye bass, Apalachicola redeye bass.

DESCRIPTION: The shoal bass is a medium-sized species of black bass, reaching a maximum SL of 420 mm (about 16.5 in) (20-in TL) and a maximum confirmed weight of 5.33 lbs (greatest unconfirmed weight 7 lbs). It belongs to the *Micropterus punctulatus* (spotted bass) species complex and is most closely related to the redeye bass (*Micropterus coosae*), with which it occurs syntopically at several localities in the upper Chattahoochee River system in Georgia. It differs from *M. coosae* primarily in the absence of white on the upper- and lower-posterior margins of the caudal fin, in having a higher average caudal-peduncle circumferential scale count (range 28–34 vs. 25–31), and in reaching a larger maximum body size. Both species have parallel, longitudinally situated rows of spots along the lower part of the body, as is true for all members of the spotted bass complex, and prominent transverse bars along the side of the body (these are comparatively narrower and more evenly spaced in the young). *Micropterus* new species and *M. coosae* are primarily distinguished from *Micropterus punctulatus* and *Micropterus notius* (the Suwannee bass) in having smaller (and thus more) lateral-line scales and more scales in the caudal-peduncle circumferential series. A color illustration appears in McClane (1972).

TAXONOMIC REMARKS: The shoal bass was first discussed by Hubbs and Bailey (1940), who had available a single adult specimen collected in the Chipola River in January 1933. Bailey and Hubbs (1949) later provided additional information on this specimen, as well as a comparison

Distribution map of *Micropterus* n. sp. cf *coosae*.

with *M. coosae*. They listed as possible differences (1) the more emarginate shape of the dorsal fin (i.e., depth of break between spinous and soft portions of fin) in the shoal bass; (2) the absence of glossohyal teeth (usually present in *M. coosae*); (3) the unusually large size of the Chipola River specimen (388-mm TL vs. 261-mm TL maximum for specimens of *M. coosae* available at that time); and (4) the high caudal-peduncle circumferential scale count (31), which is at the upper meristic limit for *M. coosae* (range 25–31 [mean 28.3] in 73 specimens examined). They concluded that the Chipola River specimen probably represented an undescribed species. However, subsequent examination (by Bailey) of additional specimens taken from the Chipola River in 1957 led him to conclude that the shoal and redeye basses are conspecific (Parsons and Crittenden 1959).

McClane (1972), in a popular article that included excellent color illustrations and means for separating the various species of *Micropterus*, discussed both forms. He referred to the shoal bass as the "Apalachicola River form" of the redeye bass and listed several supposed differences for separating it from the "Alabama River form." In addition to the dorsal-fin shape and absence of glossohyal teeth that had been mentioned by Bailey and Hubbs (1949), McClane indicated that the Apalachicola River form possessed both a more prominent basicaudal and opercular spot and had higher scale counts in both the lateral-line series and series of scale rows below the lateral line (72–77 vs. 67–72 and 18–19 vs. 16–17, respectively); however, he made no reference either to differences in caudal-peduncle circumferential scale count or to maximum body size. The Apalachicola specimen illustrated by McClane (1972) also had narrower and more prominent barring on the side than the Alabama specimen, but there was no indication that this constituted a possible diagnostic difference.

Ramsey and Smitherman (1972) compared juveniles of the two forms, and although they indicated that the pigmentation pattern was essentially the same, they suggested that the lateral bars along the side of the body were somewhat broader and more widely spaced in the Apalachicola form. Ramsey (1973), who concluded that the two forms were valid species, was the first to point out the critical difference in caudal-fin pigmentation. He also reaffirmed the specific difference in maximum body size, which had first been suggested by Bailey and Hubbs (1949), but he was apparently unable to verify the other supposed differences indicated by McClane (1972).

Gilbert (1978) provided the first comprehensive account of the shoal bass, based largely on information provided by John Ramsey (then at Auburn University). In addition to the specific differences mentioned above, Gilbert (1978) indicated that the shoal and redeye basses differ in caudal-peduncle circumferential scale count, as suggested earlier by Bailey and Hubbs (1949).

RANGE: The shoal bass is endemic to the Apalachicola River basin of Florida, Alabama, and Georgia, with most of its range concentrated in the last state. In Florida, it is fairly common in a 30-mile segment of the Chipola River between Marianna and Clarksville, but elsewhere has been taken only in very small numbers in the main Apalachicola River below Jim Woodruff Dam. It also occurs in widely scattered populations in suitable habitats of the Flint and Chattahoochee river drainages in Georgia. Populations have been greatly reduced in the lower half of the main Chattahoochee River in Georgia and Alabama because of loss of favorable habitat resulting from dam construction.

HABITAT: The shoal bass is restricted to large riverine shoals of Piedmont and Coastal Plain rivers and large creeks in the Apalachicola River basin, where it has been taken at temperatures as high as 27.3° C (81° F) during the summer (Carlander 1977). Parsons and Crittenden (1959), who provided a thorough habitat summary for that segment of the Chipola River inhabited by the species, indicated that the stream varies from 75 to 100 feet in width, with normal summer flow about 300 cubic feet per second, and with the bottom consisting principally of sand, rubble, and limestone outcroppings. Much of the stream flow here comes from large springs, and thus the water is usually clear with turbidity less than 5 ppm. Annual water temperatures usually range from about 10°–23° C (50°–75° F). On 19 July 1957, the water temperature was 70° F, pH 8.7, and total alkalinity 95 ppm.

The type of habitat described above is not particularly common in areas below the Fall Line, and results in a more-or-less discontinuous distribution of the shoal bass throughout its range.

LIFE HISTORY AND ECOLOGY: Parsons and Crittenden (1959) provided information on growth of the shoal bass in Florida. Smitherman and Ramsey (1972) discussed spawning and early growth in ponds based on stock taken from the Chattahoochee River drainage in eastern Alabama. Carlander (1977) summarized information included in these and other papers. Gilbert's (1978) summary was taken from the above reference sources, as well as from data supplied by Ramsey (1973).

Small shoal bass (40–80 mm TL) usually feed on aquatic insects, particularly mayfly nymphs, but at larger sizes they feed predominantly on crayfish and fish (Carlander 1977; Gilbert 1978). Smitherman and Ramsey (1972) said that spawning was first observed in ponds at Auburn University on 5 May, when the water temperature was 79° F (26.1° C), and effective spawning occurred on 19 May at a temperature of 77° F (25° C). Fry were noted on 29 May, but they soon disappeared from surface and inshore areas and were presumed to have moved to deeper water. Eggs were 2.0 mm in diameter, and the fry measured 4.5 mm at hatching. By comparison, redeye bass (*M. coosae*) maintained under the same conditions had begun to spawn by 14 April, when the water temperature was 73° F (22.8° C). Spawning of both species was enhanced by the addition of gravel or limestone chips, but it often occurred over a hard-clay substrate, independent of other materials. Gilbert (1978) indicated that spawning occurs from April through June, with nests located in eddies adjacent to shoals in water eight inches to a foot deep. Although the species spawns when held in experimental ponds, its absence from reservoirs suggests a strong preference for flowing water and possibly an inability to compete with lacustrine species such as the largemouth bass.

Parsons and Crittenden (1959) examined 32 shoal bass from the Chipola River, ranging from 7.5 to 16.9 in (191–429 mm) TL and from 3.1 to 40 oz (87–1134 g) in weight. They found shoal bass from the Chipola River to have a faster growth rate than redeye bass from Tennessee, and attributed this to a combination of longer growing season, larger stream habitat, clearer water, and more productive shoal areas. They compiled age/length data from 21 fish, with the following results (TL expressed in inches, with millimeters in parentheses): I = 3.8 (97); II = 8.1 (206); III = 11.4 (290); IV = 13.9 (353); V = 15.3 (388). By comparison, comparable lengths of redeye bass from Sheeds and Spring creeks in Tennessee were found to be 1.9, 3.4, 4.7, 5.9, and 7.0 in, respectively (Parsons 1954). The largest and oldest redeye bass from Sheeds Creek was 10.2 in and was determined to be ten years old. Dendy (1954) calculated the age of a 19 in (TL), 3-lb 10-oz shoal bass from Alabama as ten years.

SPECIALIZED OR UNIQUE CHARACTERISTICS: *Micropterus* new species is of scientific interest because of its restriction to the Apalachicola River basin. It is a favored game species in those areas where it occurs and is the only large game fish found in the rapids of the lower Apalachicola basin.

BASIS OF STATUS CLASSIFICATION: Although the shoal bass, because of its preferred habitat, probably has always had a more-or-less scattered distribution throughout its range, there can be no question that the species has become greatly depleted within the past 50 years. This has resulted partly from siltation of its habitat especially in the lower half of the Chattahoochee River proper and particularly from the construction of dams, inasmuch as the most favorable construction sites are those areas having the highest stream gradient, which are thus favored by this species. Probably the largest population of shoal bass still existing occurs in the upper Flint River drainage in Georgia, an area for which a major dam was once proposed. The shoal bass probably has never been widespread in Florida, inasmuch as that section of the Chipola River near Marianna seems to be the only really favorable habitat for this species within its range in the state.

The Chipola River appears not to have undergone any noticeable environmental changes since appearance of the 1978 FCREPA report, at which time the shoal bass was accorded "threatened" status. Furthermore, the fact that the segment of stream inhabited by this species is largely spring fed means that a large pollution spill on the river would be partially diluted by spring water. Nevertheless, we feel that any species whose distribution in the state is essentially limited to one 30-mile stretch of a large river remains at risk, and thus we recommend retention of "threatened" status.

RECOMMENDATIONS: Preserve present habitat in the Chipola River by keeping close controls on pollution or other types of environmental disturbance. Outside Florida, preserve suitable habitat by stopping pollution, channelization, and particularly dam construction in those areas where the species occurs.

Literature Cited

Bailey, R. M., and C. L. Hubbs. 1949. The black basses (*Micropterus*) of Florida, with description of a new species. Occ. Pap. Mus. Zool. Univ. Mich. 516:1–40.

Carlander, K. D. 1977. Handbook of freshwater fishery biology. Vol. 2. Iowa State University Press, Ames. 431 pp.

Dendy, J. S. 1954. How large do redeye bass grow? Ala. Conserv. 26(3):1.

Gilbert, C. R. 1978. Shoal bass, *Micropterus* new species. Pages 27–28 *in* Carter R. Gilbert, ed., Rare and endangered biota of Florida. Vol. 4. Fishes. University Presses of Florida, Gainesville. 58 pp.

Hubbs, C. L., and R. M. Bailey. 1940. A revision of the black basses (*Micropterus* and *Huro*) with descriptions of four new forms. Misc. Publ. Mus. Zool. Univ. Mich. 48:1–51.

McClane, A. J. 1972. I.D. guide to all the American bass. Field and Stream 76(10):52–57.

Parsons, J. W. 1954. Growth and habits of the redeye bass. Trans. Amer. Fish. Soc. (1953) 83(1):202–211.

Parsons, J. W., and E. Crittenden. 1959. Growth of the redeye bass in Chipola River, Florida. Trans. Amer. Fish. Soc. (1958) 88(3):191–192.

Ramsey, J. S. 1973. The *Micropterus coosae* complex in southeastern U.S. (Osteich-thyes, Centrarchidae). ASB Bull. 20(2):76.

Ramsey, J. S., and R. O. Smitherman. 1972. Development of color pattern in pond-reared young of five *Micropterus* species of southeastern U.S. Proc. 25th Ann. Conf. Southeast. Assoc. Game Fish Comm. (1971):348–356.

Smitherman, R. O., and J. S. Ramsey. 1972. Observations on spawning and growth of four species of basses (*Micropterus*) in ponds. Proc. 25th Ann. Conf. Southeast. Assoc. Game Fish Comm. (1971):357–365

Prepared by: Carter R. Gilbert, *Florida Museum of Natural History, University of Florida, Gainesville, Florida 32611.*

Bigmouth Sleeper

Gobiomorus dormitor

FAMILY ELEOTRIDIDAE

Order Perciformes

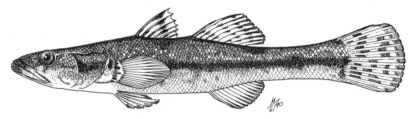

Bigmouth sleeper, *Gobiomorus dormitor* Lacepède, 1798. UF 40065. Adult, 212 mm SL. North Relief Canal, Brevard County, Florida. 23 December 1983.

OTHER NAMES: *Guavina.*

DESCRIPTION: *Gobiomorus dormitor* is the largest species of eleotridid in the Western Hemisphere, reaching a length of 317-mm SL (12.5 in) in Florida waters and reputedly as much as 610 mm (24 in) in Central America (Jordan and Evermann 1898). Body is fusiform; head wide and flattened, averaging 36% of SL; mouth wide, the maxillary reaching to middle of pupil, with lower jaw projecting in front of upper; teeth very small, slender, and depressible; dorsal-fin rays VI–I,9; anal-fin rays I,9; pectoral-fin rays 16; lateral scales 55–65; ventral fins not fused; caudal fin rounded; color dark brown or olive, with a dark stripe of pigment along side of body extending from base of pectoral fin to caudal fin, the stripe very dark and continuous in juveniles but becoming progressively lighter and more broken in adults; body with dark spots and mottling; anal and ventral fins unpigmented or mottled, the remainder of the fins dusky and with series of dark lines and spots; dorsal fin with prominent dark bar extending from tip of first spine to base of sixth spine, the bar particularly prominent in juveniles.

RANGE: *Gobiomorus dormitor* ranges from eastern Florida south to Cuba,
Puerto Rico, Jamaica, Martinique, Nicaragua, Costa Rica, Panama, and
Surinam (Gilmore and Hastings 1983), with its center of abundance in
the Caribbean region. It also occurs in the Rio Grande and is common in
the Rio Tamesi drainage, Mexico, and in other tributaries to the southern Gulf of Mexico (Darnell 1955; Treviño-Robinson 1959; Pezold and
Edwards 1983). It has not been recorded from tributaries to the eastern
and northern Gulf of Mexico. *Gobiomorus dormitor* apparently also occurs
in the western Bahamas, Breder (1932) having listed two specimens from
Lake Forsyth on Andros Island. It is surprising that Böhlke and Chaplin
(1968) did not include this species in their book on Bahaman fishes and

Distribution map of *Gobiomorus dormitor*.

also made no indication that the Lake Forsyth record might have been based on a misidentification. Although the specimens on which Breder's record is based (presumably housed in the American Museum of Natural History) have not been examined, it seems unlikely that such a distinctive species as *G. dormitor* would have been misidentified. Assuming that this record was simply overlooked by Böhlke and Chaplin, the western Bahamas are included in the range of this species.

The bigmouth sleeper was first recorded from Florida by Briggs (1958), although no specific locality information was given. It has consistently been collected only in the Loxahatchee River drainage (Palm Beach County) (Christensen 1965), the St. Lucie River (Martin and St. Lucie counties), Sebastian Creek (Indian River and Brevard counties), and in relief canals associated with these streams. It also occurs in Lake Okeechobee (Lindquist 1980), in an artificial freshwater stream in Parrot Jungle (Miami) (Loftus et al. 1984), and in other freshwater tributaries to Biscayne Bay (Loftus and Kushlan 1987). Several specimens have been captured in canals inland from migratory barriers such as salinity dams and flood-control locks (W. F. Loftus and C. R. Robins, personal communication), which indicates ability of the species to move around these structures. A 330-mm-SL specimen, supposedly collected in the lower St. Johns River by William McLane, is present in the Florida Museum of Natural History collection (UF 31431). Since no specific locality data accompanies this specimen and since McLane (1955) made no mention of *G. dormitor* in his study on St. Johns River drainage fishes, this locality undoubtedly is in error.

Routine monthly and exploratory ichthyological collections from 1978 through 1982, using a variety of techniques, resulted in the capture of around 100 individuals (ranging from 16.0 to 317 mm SL) in freshwater tributaries to the southern Indian River. Christensen (1965) observed 15–20 individuals in one location below a floodgate in the Loxahatchee River. The species is considered to be a year-round freshwater resident, although it is rather infrequently encountered. This may result in part because the species appears to be less susceptible to conventional seining techniques than are most species and is more readily collected by gear types that are difficult to quantify, such as electroshockers, hook and line, cast nets, and gill nets.

HABITAT: Although a euryhaline fish, *G. dormitor* is typically found in flowing fresh water. In tributaries to the Indian River lagoon, *G. dormitor* occurs principally over an open-sand substrate along undercut banks, but it may also be found in heavy vegetation or around rock or wood structures (Nordlie 1979). Gilmore and Hastings (1983) found juveniles ranging from 16 to 23.5 mm SL in fresh to brackish water (0.0–13.0 ppt) on the downstream side of salinity barriers. Temperatures at which juveniles have been taken range from 10.5°–29.5° C.

LIFE HISTORY AND ECOLOGY: The bigmouth sleeper is a large predator that is primarily nocturnal or crepuscular in its feeding habits (Darnell 1955, 1962; Koenig et al. 1976). Analysis of a small number of adults from Tortuguero, Costa Rica, indicates that, in frequency of occurrence, shrimp and fish comprise approximately 80 percent of the species' diet (Nordlie 1981).

Darnell (1962) reported G. dormitor as spawning in brackish water, a situation that receives confirmation from Nordlie (1981), who reported both large, sexually mature adults and small juveniles (down to 21-mm SL) from the lower part of Tortuguero estuary. As indicated above, Gilmore and Hastings (1983) found juveniles of 16–23.5 mm in both fresh and brackish water on the downstream side of salinity barriers in tributaries to Indian River lagoon, in Florida. However, juveniles were not present in the sample taken from the tismiche moving into Tortuguero estuary in August 1964 (Gilbert and Kelso 1971), although juveniles of two other species of eleotridids were included. Observations of reproduction in Lago de Yojoa, Honduras (Darnell 1962), and Lago Jiloa, Nicaragua (Lim et al. 1976; McKaye et al. 1979), both of which are entirely freshwater lakes, indicate that estuarine migrations are not necessary for effective reproduction in this species. Insufficient numbers of specimens have been collected in Florida to allow isolation of specific spawning locations; however, the simultaneous capture of young-of-the-year individuals as well as of a ripe female of G. dormitor in Sebastian Creek indicates apparent spawning in this particular stream.

Occurrences above stream barriers and the observation of nocturnal semiterrestrial behavior in G. dormitor (Darnell 1955) indicate that this species is capable of migrating overland for short distances. This was verified when a large (300-mm SL) specimen was collected and left in a bucket in a stationary truck. It was found on the ground about four hours later and had moved approximately 10 feet. It was relatively dry and covered by loose soil but was still alive and, when placed in water, appeared to have suffered no ill effects (Gilmore, personal observation).

SPECIALIZED OR UNIQUE CHARACTERISTICS: Gobiomorus dormitor is one of a small number of euryhaline Florida freshwater fish species of basically Caribbean affinities, whose distribution in the state is limited to a small area around the lower Indian River lagoon. It most likely reached this area via transportation by the Gulf Stream.

BASIS OF STATUS CLASSIFICATION: The dependence of the bigmouth sleeper on accessible freshwater habitat along the lower east Florida coast, from the southern portion of the Indian River lagoon to Biscayne Bay, results in the species being almost entirely limited to coastal reaches of small tributary streams. These localized populations in turn are surrounded by the most rapidly growing human populations on the east-central coast of Florida (Miami–West Palm Beach, Port St. Lucie, Sebastian Highlands, and Palm Bay). As a consequence, all freshwater tributaries in which the bigmouth sleeper is found in southeastern Florida are under the control of regional water-management districts. These freshwater habitats have experienced major declines in water quality, natural vegetative cover, and natural freshwater hydrodynamics with the increase in regional human populations. Floodgates and salinity dams placed upstream 2–25 km from tributary mouths may inhibit but appear not to totally block inland migration of this species; however, these barriers may limit most of the usable habitat for this species to downstream areas.

A portion of the range of this species (the North Fork of the St. Lucie River) is a state wildlife preserve. The Loxahatchee River is a National Wild and Scenic River, and part of the North Fork of the Loxahatchee River is within Jonathan Dickinson State Park. The artificial stream in Parrot Jungle (Miami) presumably will continue to be maintained in its present condition. Although the species thus receives some degree of protection, much of its range is still in an area subject to heavy human population encroachment. This situation, together with the limited distribution of *G. dormitor* in Florida, justifies our according this species "threatened" status, as we have for several other fish species whose distribution is largely or entirely limited to this part of the state.

RECOMMENDATIONS: Human population encroachment on freshwater tributaries to both Indian River lagoon and Biscayne Bay should be limited and a buffer zone established. The artificial stream in Parrot Jungle should be maintained in its present condition. Water-management practices should result in duplication, insofar as possible, of natural hydrologic and vegetative conditions. The remaining "natural" portions of various creeks and streams (e.g., Sebastian Creek) should be preserved. Nonpoint and point-source pollutants should be eliminated. Herbicide-spraying programs should be eliminated along portions of tributaries (streams and canals) between water-control structures and coastal estuaries. Additional research is needed to determine spatial and temporal population dynamics, microhabitat requirements, and aspects of early life history, particularly for egg, larval, and juvenile stages.

Literature Cited

Published Information

Böhlke, J. E., and C. C. G. Chaplin. 1968. Fishes of the Bahamas and adjacent tropical waters. Livingston, Wynnewood, Pa. xxiii+771 pp.

Breder, C. M., Jr. 1932. An annotated list of fishes from Lake Forsyth, Andros Island, Bahamas, with the descriptions of three new forms. Amer. Mus. Novit. 551:1–8.

Briggs, J. C. 1958. A list of Florida fishes and their distribution. Bull. Fla. St. Mus. Biol. Sci. 2(8):223–318.

Darnell, R. M. 1955. Nocturnal terrestrial habits of the tropical gobioid fish *Gobiomorus dormitor*, with remarks on its ecology. Copeia 1955(3):237–238.

_____. 1962. Fishes of the Rio Tamesi and related coastal lagoons in east-central Mexico. Publ. Inst. Mar. Sci. 8:299–365.

Gilbert, C. R., and D. P. Kelso. 1971. Fishes of the Tortuguero area, Caribbean Costa Rica. Bull. Fla. St. Mus. Biol. Sci. 16(1):1–54.

Gilmore, R. G., and P. A. Hastings. 1983. Observations on the ecology and distribution of certain tropical peripheral fishes in Florida. Fla. Sci. 46(1):31–51.

Jordan, D. S., and B. W. Evermann. 1898. Fishes of North and Middle America. Bull. U.S. Nat. Mus. 47(3):2188–2236.

Koenig, K. W., R. J. Beatty, and S. Martinez. 1976. Species diversity and distribution of fish in Lake Nicaragua. Pages 321–325 *in* T. B. Thorson, ed., Investigations of the ichthyofauna of Nicaraguan lakes. School of Life Sciences, University of Nebraska, Lincoln. iv–x+663 pp.

Lim, T. M., K. R. McKaye, and D. J. Weiland. 1976. An investigation into the use of artificial habitats as a means of increasing the fishery productivity of the great lakes complex of Nicaragua. Pages 311–320 *in* T. B. Thorson, ed., Investigations of the ichthyofauna of Nicaraguan lakes. School of Life Sciences, University of Nebraska, Lincoln. iv–x+663 pp.

Lindquist, D. G. 1980. *Gobiomorus dormitor* Lacepède, Bigmouth sleeper. Page 784 *in* D. S. Lee et al., eds., Atlas of North American freshwater fishes. North Carolina State Museum of Natural History, Raleigh. i–x+854 pp.

Loftus, W. F., and J. A. Kushlan. 1987. Freshwater fishes of southern Florida. Bull. Fla. St. Mus. Biol. Sci. 31(4):147–344.

Loftus, W. F., J. A. Kushlan, and S. A. Voorhees. 1984. Status of the mountain mullet in southern Florida. Fla. Sci. 47(4):256–263.

McKaye, K. R., D. J. Weiland, and T. M. Lim. 1979. Comments on the breeding biology of *Gobiomorus dormitor* (Osteichthyes: Eleotridae) and the advantage of school behavior to its fry. Copeia 1979(3):542–544.

Nordlie, F. G. 1979. Niche specificities of eleotrid fishes in a tropical estuary. Rev. Biol. Trop. 27(1):35–50.

———. 1981. Feeding and reproductive biology of eleotrid fishes in a tropical estuary. J. Fish Biol. 18:97–110.

Pezold, F. L., and R. J. Edwards. 1983. Additions to the Texas marine ichthyofauna, with notes on the Rio Grande estuary. Southwest. Nat. 28(1):102–105.

Treviño-Robinson, D. 1959. The ichthyofauna of the lower Rio Grande, Texas and Mexico. Copeia 1959(3):253–256.

Unpublished Information

Christensen, R. F. 1965. An ichthyological survey of Jupiter Inlet and Loxahatchee River, Florida. M.Sc. thesis, Florida State University, Tallahassee.

McLane, W. M. 1955. The fishes of the St. Johns River system. Ph.D. diss., University of Florida, Gainesville.

Prepared by: R. Grant Gilmore, *Harbor Branch Oceanographic Institution, Ft. Pierce, Florida 33450.*

River Goby

Awaous tajasica

FAMILY GOBIIDAE

Order Perciformes

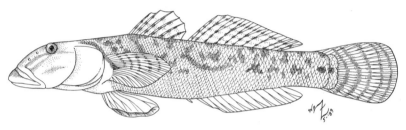

River goby, *Awaous tajasica* (Lichtenstein, 1822). UF 44708. Adult male, 109 mm SL. Sebastian Creek, Indian River County, Florida. 21 July 1955.

OTHER NAMES: Guavina hoyera; Aboma de rio.

DESCRIPTION: *Awaous tajasica* is a large goby, with Florida specimens reaching a SL of 280 mm (11 in). Distinguishing features include the pelvic fins fused to form a sucking disk and lateral line absent from body; caudal fin rounded; snout long (42%–46% of head length); head depressed in mature males; mouth large and lips thick, with upper lip extending well beyond the lower; inner edge of shoulder girdle with two or more conspicuous dermal flaps; dorsal-fin rays usually VI–I,10 (occasionally VI–I,9); anal-fin rays usually I,10 (occasionally I,9); scales ctenoid over most of body but cycloid on head, belly, predorsal midline of back, and in region beyond hypural base; 61–69 scales in lateral series, the scales more crowded anteriorly. Body olivaceous or yellowish tan; head, back, and sides spotted and mottled with dark brown markings; dorsal, caudal, and pectoral fins with parallel rows of spots, forming crossbars.

TAXONOMIC REMARKS: An apparently unique character of the genus *Awaous* involves the respiratory surfaces of the gills, which are much re-

duced in area and have the outer surface covered by a complex array of
sensory papillae.

Although treated here under the specific name *tajasica*, Ronald Watson indicates that the proper name for this species should be *Awaous banana* (Valenciennes, 1837). Watson, who is currently involved in a taxonomic revision of the genus *Awaous*, states that there are three species in the western Atlantic region: *A. tajasica* and *Awaous badius*, which have restricted ranges along the coast of South America; and the more widely ranging *A. banana*, which is the species found throughout the West Indies and adjacent areas (including Florida) to the north (R. Watson, per-

Distribution map of *Awaous tajasica*.

sonal communication). The name *tajasica* will continue to be used in this account until such time as Watson's study is formally published.

RANGE: The following range statement takes into account the new information concerning the taxonomy of *Awaous* in the western Atlantic region, as discussed in the preceding paragraph.

Awaous tajasica ranges from South Carolina south to northern South America. Within this area it has been recorded from the Savannah River (South Carolina), eastern and western Florida, and from larger islands and continental land areas around the Caribbean: Cuba, Puerto Rico, Jamaica, Belize, Guatemala, Honduras (Bonacca Island), Nicaragua, Costa Rica, Panama, mainland and insular Colombia (Providencia Island), Venezuela, Tobago, St. Vincent, Dominica, Martinique, and Barbados (R. Watson, personal communication). It has not been recorded from the Bahama Islands or from areas bordering the western Gulf of Mexico.

One might suspect that the more northerly records do not represent permanent populations. This would appear to be substantiated by a recent record from the Santa Fe River (a tributary of the Suwannee River), at the U.S. Highway 27 bridge, which is based on an underwater photograph (on file in the Florida Museum of Natural History) of a large adult individual, taken by William Streever on 7 October 1990. Fish sampling using various gears and methods has been carried out on both the Santa Fe and Suwannee rivers throughout the years, and were the species regularly present it should have been seen or collected before now. Conversely, collections of *A. tajasica* from Garnier's Creek (a tributary to Choctawhatchee Bay near Ft. Walton Beach), in the Florida panhandle, suggest either temporary or permanent establishment, since specimens were taken over an eight-year period (1959–1966, UF 55161, UF 56052, UF 63772, UF 64786), and there are unpublished reports of its having been taken there still later during the 1960s (James D. Williams, personal communication). It would be instructive to see if the species is still present there today.

In addition to the Gulf drainage localities, the species has occasionally (1949–1950 and an unspecified year recently) been collected in the St. Johns River (three records, of which one is based on material in our collection [UF 31432]) (McLane 1955). In Florida, the species has consistently been collected only from the St. Lucie River in Martin and St. Lucie counties; various freshwater relief canals constructed to drain fresh water into the adjacent estuary for flood control in Martin, Indian River, and Brevard counties; and Sebastian Creek in Indian River and Brevard counties (Gilmore and Hastings 1983).

HABITAT: *Awaous tajasica* characteristically inhabits lotic waters of streams and rivers of the Greater and Lesser Antilles, Central America, and northern South America. It is closely restricted to fast-flowing, well-oxygenated waters and apparently does not adapt well to lentic conditions, even though the water may be well oxygenated (R. Watson, personal communication). Watson believes the close dependence of the species on flowing water is a direct result of the peculiar modification of the gills (in which the outer surfaces are covered with sensory papillae), which apparently results in attendant loss of respiratory function. In view of this, the absence of the species from the Bahamas and from other low islands with streams of base-level gradient is understandable. Although present in Florida, the preponderance of low-gradient streams is obviously a factor limiting the distribution of the species throughout much of the state. Along the southeast coast, its upstream distribution is restricted by water-control structures. Gilmore and Hastings (1983), during their work in Indian River lagoon, never found any individuals at tributary mouths or in the lagoon itself. They collected specimens in tributary streams, with most being found over a sand substrate at salinities of 0.0–4.0 ppt and at temperatures of 20°–28° C. Most were found below bridges, which Gilmore and Hastings (1983) theorized was an indication of preference for shaded areas of the stream and/or sediment deposited around bridge pilings. It has been suggested that adult and subadult *A. tajasica* are probably intolerant of salinities higher than those indicated above (R. Watson, personal communication), as indicated both by experimental observations and analysis of ecological data accompanying collections of the species.

LIFE HISTORY AND ECOLOGY: Little has been published on the life history of this species, as was also true at the time of the 1978 FCREPA report (Yerger 1978). Much of the following has again been communicated to us by Watson.

Young and adult *A. tajasica* inhabit freshwater streams, and there is no evidence that they ever leave there and move into estuaries or the ocean to spawn. Spawning occurs in fresh water with the small eggs (numbering from 2,400 to 3,000 in large females) presumably drifting downstream, where they either hatch in brackish or salt water or do so before reaching there. Larval development takes place in brackish or salt waters at the mouths of tributaries, as has been documented for *Awaous stamineus* in Hawaiian waters (Ford and Kinzie 1982). Most larvae probably reenter the parental stream, but some may be dispersed via ocean currents before returning to fresh water. Evidence for this is seen from the distribution of *A. tajasica* on many West Indian islands, as well as from the collection of small juveniles (all about 12.5 mm long) in an aggregation of juvenile fish that were entering Tortuguero lagoon, Costa Rica, on 7 August 1964 (Gilbert and Kelso 1971). The life history of this species probably parallels that of the mountain mullet (*Agonostomus monticola*), another euryhaline species whose distribution is similar to that of *A. tajasica* and the individuals of which, once transformed from the larval stage, apparently spend their entire lives in fresh water (Loftus and Gilbert, this volume).

SPECIALIZED OR UNIQUE CHARACTERISTICS: As may also be true for *A. monticola*, the river goby may be one of the few euryhaline fishes in North America in which only the larval stages occur in salt water.

BASIS OF STATUS CLASSIFICATION: With the possible exception of the St. Johns and Santa Fe rivers and Garnier's Creek in the Florida panhandle (the latter of which has not been surveyed for over 20 yr), the tributaries of Indian River lagoon are the only places in Florida where *A. tajasica* is presently known to occur. Within this area, deterioration in quality and quantity of habitat has increased in recent years and represents a serious threat to Florida river goby populations. Water-flow manipulation, degradation of water quality, and sedimentation may influence life-history patterns of this species to the point that successful reproduction and egg and larval survival are threatened. Floodgates and salinity dams commonly placed upstream, from 2 to 25 km above the tributary mouths in the Indian River lagoon, apparently block the inland migration of this species, as no specimens have been captured upstream from these barriers. This results in the habitat of the species being limited to that portion of stream situated between the barriers and the lagoon. Since this also is the area where most human habitation is concentrated, it makes the habitat highly vulnerable to human disturbance. The situation outlined above has caused us to recommend this species for "threatened" status, as we have done for several other species whose distribution in Florida is limited, or nearly limited, to the Indian River lagoon area. This also represents one of only two situations in which a fish has been listed in a "higher" category than in the 1978 FCREPA publication, in which it was only listed as "rare."

RECOMMENDATIONS: Human population encroachment on freshwater tributaries to the Indian River lagoon should be limited and buffer zones established. Water managers should consider modifying their policies in order to "mimic" natural stream hydrologic and vegetative conditions. The remaining natural portions of various creeks and streams (e.g., Sebastian Creek) should be preserved. Nonpoint and point-source pollutants should be eliminated. Additional research should be done on the life history of this species, which is essentially unknown, to determine spatial and temporal population dynamics, microhabitat requirements and early life history, particulary with regard to egg, larval, and juvenile stages.

Literature Cited

Published Information

Ford, J. I., and R. A. Kinzie III. 1982. Life crawls upstream. Nat. Hist. 91:61–66.

Gilbert, C. R., and D. P. Kelso. 1971. Fishes of the Tortuguero area, Caribbean Costa Rica. Bull. Fla. St. Mus. Biol. Sci. 16(1):1–54.

Gilmore, R. G., and P. A. Hastings. 1983. Observations on the ecology and distribution of certain tropical peripheral fishes in Florida. Fla. Sci. 46(1): 31–51.

Yerger, R. W. 1978. River goby, *Awaous tajasica* (Lichtenstein). Pages 46–47 *in* Carter R. Gilbert, ed., Rare and endangered biota of Florida. Vol. 4. Fishes. University Presses of Florida, Gainesville. 58 pp.

Unpublished information

McLane, W. M. 1955. The fishes of the St. Johns River system. Ph.D. diss., University of Florida, Gainesville.

Prepared by: R. Grant Gilmore, *Harbor Branch Oceanographic Institution, Ft. Pierce, Florida 33450*; and Ralph W. Yerger (retired), *Department of Biological Sciences, Florida State University, Tallahassee, Florida 32306.*

Slashcheek Goby

Gobionellus pseudofasciatus

FAMILY GOBIIDAE

Order Perciformes

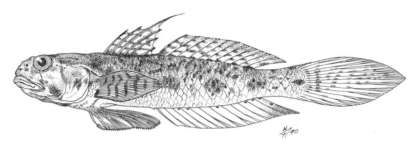

Slashcheek goby, *Gobionellus pseudofasciatus* Gilbert and Randall, 1971. UF 84981. Adult male, 43.0 mm SL. North Fork of Sebastian Creek, Brevard County, Florida. 5 June 1990.

OTHER NAMES: None.

DESCRIPTION: *Gobionellus pseudofasciatus* is a small goby that reaches a maximum SL of 44 mm (1.7 in). Its most prominent diagnostic feature is a bar of dark pigment that crosses the cheek diagonally from the lower angle of the preopercle to just above the corner of the jaw; pelvic fins completely fused to form a disc; caudal fin elongate; dorsal-fin rays VI–I,11; anal-fin rays I,12; pectoral-fin rays 16–18, usually 17; lateral scales 29–34, usually 30–31, these relatively more numerous on anterior third of body; body light brownish to straw colored, with five dark lateral blotches on midline; orange pigment on distal edge of spinous dorsal membrane; males often with elongated third spine in first (spinous) dorsal fin and a large recurved canine tooth midlaterally in lower jaw.

RANGE: *Gobionellus pseudofasciatus* is known from Costa Rica, Panama, Surinam, and Trinidad, with a widely disjunct population in eastern Florida. Within the Caribbean region, to which the species is largely confined, all records are from streams and rivers of continental coastal areas,

118

and it has not yet been recorded from islands of the Greater or Lesser Antilles. In Florida, the slashcheek goby is limited to the Loxahatchee River (Palm Beach County), St. Lucie River (Martin and St. Lucie counties), Sebastian Creek (Indian River and Brevard counties), and freshwater relief canals associated with these streams. It was only recently discovered in the state, Hastings (1978) first reporting collections from the South Relief Canal and Sebastian Creek in Indian River and Brevard counties.

Gilmore and Hastings (1983) theorized that the presence of the slashcheek goby in Florida could either be relictual or could have resulted from Holocene population expansions from the Caribbean region, with

Distribution map of *Gobionellus pseudofasciatus.*

larval individuals having been transported there via the Gulf Stream. The latter explanation is the more plausible one.

HABITAT: In tributaries to Indian River lagoon, *G. pseudofasciatus* occurs principally in flowing fresh water over an open-sand bottom on the downstream side of sandbars, banks, or coves at salinities of 0.0–13.0 ppt and temperatures of 17°–32° C (Gilmore and Hastings 1983). It may be patchily distributed within this microhabitat, however. All specimens have been taken in areas downstream of water-control structures and above the tributary mouths in Indian River lagoon.

LIFE HISTORY AND ECOLOGY: No comprehensive life-history study has yet been conducted on the slashcheek goby. However, intensive survey efforts between 1978 and 1982 (involving the capture of more than 400 specimens) have permitted the distribution of the species in Florida to be clearly defined. Populations become concentrated at upstream locations below water-control structures from March to May (Gilmore and Hastings 1983). Seasonal movements upstream and downstream have prevented accurate total population estimates at long-term, nearshore sampling stations. Additional research is needed to determine spatial and temporal population dynamics, microhabitat requirements, and details of the early life history of the species, particularly as regards egg, larval, and juvenile stages.

SPECIALIZED OR UNIQUE CHARACTERISTICS: The slashcheek goby is one of a small group of essentially estuarine/freshwater fish species in Florida whose distribution is mainly centered in the Caribbean area. The small area to which it is confined on the central east coast of Florida is the only place on the North American continent where it is known to occur.

BASIS OF STATUS CLASSIFICATION: The slashcheek goby requires a specific type of freshwater habitat that is only available along the southern portion of the Indian River lagoon. This area in turn is surrounded by the most rapidly growing human populations on the east-central coast of Florida (Port St. Lucie, Sebastian Highlands, and Palm Bay). As a result, the freshwater habitat of this species has experienced a major decline in water quality, natural vegetative cover, and natural freshwater hydrodynamics. All freshwater tributaries to the Indian River lagoon are regulated by regional water-management districts, which determine artificial flow rates according to anthropogenic needs, principally storm runoff control to prevent urban flooding or for agricultural purposes (drainage or irrigation). Associated with these streams are major canals capable of releasing exceptionally large quantities of low-quality water into the remaining natural portions of the streams.

The North Fork of the St. Lucie River is a state wildlife preserve, the North Fork of the Loxahatchee River is a National Wild and Scenic River, and a portion of the North Fork of the Loxahatchee River is within the Jonathan Dickinson State Park. The slashcheek goby thus receives some protection in the state. Despite this, the Florida habitat of the slashcheek goby remains highly vulnerable to human impact, and the species therefore is accorded "threatened" status on the present FCREPA list. It was not known to occur in Florida at the time of publication of the 1978 FCREPA report, and thus it represents a new addition to the list.

RECOMMENDATIONS: Human population encroachment in the area inhabited by *G. pseudofasciatus* should be limited and buffer zones established. Water-management authorities should consider mimicking natural stream hydrologic and vegetative conditions. The remaining "natural" portions of various creeks and streams (e.g., Sebastian Creek) should be preserved. Nonpoint and point-source pollutants, as well as herbicide-spraying programs, should be eliminated for those portions of the tributary streams and canals between the water-control structures and Indian River lagoon. Additional research should be undertaken to determine spatial and temporal population dynamics, microhabitat requirements, and early life history, particularly for egg, larval, and juvenile stages.

Literature Cited

Gilmore, R. G., and P. H. Hastings. 1983. Observations on the ecology and distribution of certain tropical peripheral fishes in Florida. Fla. Sci. 46(1):31–51.

Hastings, P. H. 1978. First North American continental records of *Gobionellus pseudofasciatus* (Pisces: Gobiidae). Northeast Gulf Sci. 2:140–144.

Prepared by: R. Grant Gilmore, *Harbor Branch Oceanographic Institution, Fort Pierce, Florida 33450.*

Sea Lamprey

Petromyzon marinus

FAMILY PETROMYZONTIDAE

Order Petromyzontiformes

Sea lamprey, *Petromyzon marinus* Linnaeus, 1758. UF 26441. Adult, 212 mm TL. St. Johns River, Putnam County, Florida. February 1978.

OTHER NAMES: Lamprey eel

DESCRIPTION: The sea lamprey has an elongated eel-like body and is further distinguished by the absence of movable jaws (the mouth instead comprising a funnel-like disc lined with conical epidermal teeth), absence of paired (i.e., pectoral and pelvic) fins, absence of scales, seven circular gill openings on each side of the body just behind the head, a single nostril located in the middle of top of head just in front of and between the eyes, and an entirely cartilagenous internal skeleton. It is reputed to attain a length of 1,200 mm (nearly 4 ft) (Rohde 1980), although Bigelow and Schroeder (1948) listed a maximum length of about 3 ft (900 mm), with most adults no longer than 2–2.5 ft (600–750 mm). Male length averages slightly less than for females. The only other freshwater fishes in Florida with which the sea lamprey might be confused are the southern brook lamprey (*Ichthyomyzon gagei*), which attains a much smaller maximum size and is confined to freshwater streams along the northern Gulf Coast; and the freshwater eel (*Anguilla rostrata*), which possesses jaws, paired pectoral fins, a single gill opening on each side of the body, paired nostrils, and a bony internal skeleton.

RANGE: *Petromyzon marinus* occurs in the northern Atlantic Ocean, where it is found off both North America and Europe. In the eastern Atlantic region it ranges from Norway south to the Mediterranean Sea (Morocco), and in the western Atlantic it is found as far south as Florida, where it occasionally enters the St. Johns River (Mclane 1955). The species was first recorded from Florida in 1900, where it was reported as "not uncommon" in the vicinity of Lake George (Evermann and Kendall 1900). There are four unquestioned Florida records (each based on a single specimen) in the Florida Museum of Natural History collection, as follows: UF 6001 (Lake Jessup, Seminole County; January 1955); UF

Distribution map of *Petromyzon marinus*. Inset does not show northern limits of range in North America, distribution in eastern Atlantic region, or relict population in northern Gulf of Mexico.

7796 (Big Lake George, Putnam County; February 1953); UF 7797 (near Welaka, Putnam County; February 1949); and UF 26441 (Palatka; February 1978). A natural disjunct population probably existed also in the northern Gulf of Mexico, based on an apparently valid record of a newly-metamorphosed 136-mm specimen (USNM 174990) taken from a tidal pond near the tip of Cape San Blas in Gulf County, Florida, on 20 June 1932 (Vladykov and Kott 1980); and on two specimens with imprecise locality data (UF 9905 [possibly from Choctawhatchee Bay] and UF 23217 [probably Gulf of Mexico, ca 26°N, 90°W]) collected in August 1954 and May 1959, respectively. The construction during the 1950s of a series of dams on the Chattahoochee River (the most likely spawning area for the species) would have eliminated the sea lamprey from the region.

There is little question that the sea lamprey has never bred in Florida, inasmuch as suitable spawning habitat and sufficiently cold water do not exist in the state. All eastern Florida specimens were collected during January and February, which strongly suggests that they were brought here by host fish that had migrated south during the winter.

HABITAT: Adult sea lampreys are parasitic and may occur in both fresh water and salt water. Individuals found in the Great Lakes region of North America spend their entire lives in fresh water, as do certain land-locked populations elsewhere in eastern North America (Wigley 1959), whereas those found in Atlantic coastal areas probably spend most of the time in the ocean where they occur primarily in coastal waters. Because of the species' parasitic habits, its distribution is probably controlled more by the distribution of its hosts rather than by physical factors, as evidenced by the fact that individuals have been collected over a wide range of salinities, temperatures, and depths. Adults spawn in fresh water, and larval development also occurs there. As indicated previously, some populations of this species are landlocked and spend their adult lives in large, deep lakes.

LIFE HISTORY AND ECOLOGY: Sea lampreys are anadromous, ascending freshwater streams from the sea (or lakes) in the spring to spawn. They migrate upstream until they reach the cool, clear, gravel-to-rocky-bottomed flowing streams that are their preferred spawning sites. Spawning occurs at temperatures of 10° C or more and may continue up to temperatures of 20° or 21° C (Bigelow and Schroeder 1948). The eggs are small and spherical, with Bigelow and Schroeder (1948) giving a count of 236,000 for an individual of undetermined length. Pairs or small groups of individuals participate in building crude nests in riffle areas, at which time stones are moved about by means of the oral sucking disc, creating a shallow depression two to three feet in diameter and about six inches deep. On completion of the nest, the female attaches herself to a stone by means of her oral disc. The smaller male attaches himself to the body of the female so that their vents are approximately opposite one another. Their bodies intertwine, and they wriggle vigorously as eggs and sperm are deposited. The eggs are sticky, and sand particles, stirred up by the spawning activity, adhere to the eggs causing them to sink into the nest. Both parents die after spawning.

The newly hatched larvae, or ammocoetes, differ notably in appearance from the adults, especially in the structure of the mouth. The ammocoetes live burrowed in the substrate of the parent stream, usually in quiet sidewater areas, where they secure food by filtering minute organisms and organic detritus from the water. They remain in fresh water from four to seven years, attaining a length of about six inches. Transformation to the adult form apparently takes place in the fall, after which the young adults migrate downstream to the sea (or lakes).

As adults, sea lampreys are parasitic on other fish, to which they attach themselves to the outside of the body by applying suction through the oral disc. They then rasp a hole through the body wall by means of their muscular, scraping tongue. Modified salivary glands secrete an anticoagulant, and the lamprey feeds on the blood and body fluids of its host.

Host selection varies greatly, and it appears that virtually any species inhabiting near-coastal areas is open to attack if it is of suitable size. Little is known regarding the details of feeding, such as the duration of a feeding bout or the frequency of feeding. In some cases, several lampreys may be attached to one host. Such multiple attacks are usually fatal to the host. In some cases, however, host fish do not succumb from a lamprey attack, as evidenced by otherwise healthy fish bearing scars from encounters with lampreys.

Hardesty and Potter (1971) are mentioned here as an excellent source of information on all aspects of the biology, taxonomy, and distribution of lampreys in general.

SPECIALIZED OR UNIQUE CHARACTERISTICS: It is perhaps ironic that *P. marinus* is treated as a rare species whose possible disappearance from Florida is a matter of concern. In other parts of its range, the species is considered a pest and a nuisance. This is especially true in the upper Great Lakes, where the invasion of sea lampreys from Lake Ontario (through the Welland Canal, connecting Lakes Ontario and Erie) has contributed to the collapse of many important commercial and sport fish populations. A massive eradication program, described as the most extensive effort ever mounted to control populations of a vertebrate pest, has effected a reduction in lamprey populations in Lakes Superior and Michigan (Lawrie 1970).

BASIS OF STATUS CLASSIFICATION: The sea lamprey is regarded as a "rare" species in Florida. A general decrease in spawning sea lamprey populations has been noted along the Atlantic coast of the United States in recent years. Dams and locks block the upstream migration of adults, and polluted sections of streams possibly constitute an additional barrier.

As indicated, sea lampreys have never been reported to reproduce in Florida streams, and because of the lack of suitable habitat and sufficiently cool water temperatures spawning in state waters seems unlikely. Most confirmed Florida records are based on adults taken in the St. Johns River, where they apparently enter attached to anadromous host fish. Most likely the host is one of the species of shad (genus *Alosa*), especially the American shad (*Alosa sapidissima*), which ascends the river to spawn in winter and spring. The striped bass (*Morone saxatilis*) is another possibility; however, that species no longer spawns in the St. Johns River since construction of Rodman Dam, and only occasional adult individuals are now found there.

Literature Cited

Published Information

Bigelow, H. B., and W. C. Schroeder. 1948. Cyclostomes. *In* Fishes of the western North Atlantic. Mem. Sears Found. Mar. Res. 1(1):29–58.

Evermann, B. W., and W. C. Kendall. 1900. Check-list of the fishes of Florida. Rept. U.S. Comm. Fish Fish. 25:37–103.

Hardesty, M. W., and I. C. Potter, eds. 1971. The biology of lampreys. Vol. 1. Academic Press, New York. 423 pp.

Lawrie, A. H. 1970. The sea lamprey in the Great Lakes. Trans. Am. Fish. Soc. 99(4):766–775.

Rohde, F. C. 1980. *Petromyzon marinus* Linnaeus, Sea lamprey. Page 35 *in* D. S. Lee et al., eds., Atlas of North American freshwater fishes. North Carolina Museum of Natural History, Raleigh. i–x+854 pp.

Vladykov, V. D., and E. Kott. 1980. First record of the sea lamprey, *Petromyzon marinus* L., in the Gulf of Mexico. Northeast Gulf Sci. 4(1):49–50.

Wigley, R. L. 1959. Life history of the sea lamprey of Cayuga Lake, New York. Fish. Bull. 154, U.S. Fish Wildl. Serv. 59:561–617.

Unpublished Information

McLane, W. M. 1955. The fishes of the St. Johns River system. Ph.D. diss., University of Florida, Gainesville.

Prepared by: Carter R. Gilbert, *Florida Museum of Natural History, University of Florida, Gainesville, Florida 32611*; and Franklin F. Snelson, Jr., *Department of Biological Sciences, University of Central Florida, Orlando, Florida 32816.*

Alligator Gar

Atractosteus spatula

FAMILY LEPISOSTEIDAE

Order Lepisosteiformes

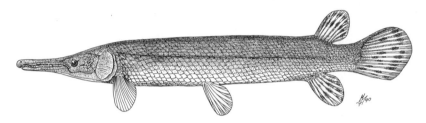

Alligator gar, *Atractosteus spatula* (Lacepède, 1803). Composite drawing. (1) UF 18446. Juvenile, 116 mm SL. Rancho Viejo floodway to Rio Grande, Cameron County, Texas. 17 July 1964. (2) An adult, 488.8 mm TL, from Lake Pontchartrain, Tangipahoa Parish, Louisiana (from *Fishes of the Western North Atlantic*).

OTHER NAMES: None.

DESCRIPTION: The alligator gar is a large heavy-bodied gar, which (as is true of all gars) has hard ganoid scales, an abbreviated heterocercal tail, and the dorsal and anal fins situated far back on body; snout short and broad compared to most other gar species, the width at nostrils going less than 4.6 times into its length and the snout length less than length of rest of head; teeth in upper jaw in two rows on each side; scales in a diagonal row from front of anal fin to midline of back 23–32; lateral-line scales, 58–62; gill rakers, 59–66. The young can be distinguished from young of other gars by a light-colored middorsal stripe that extends from tip of snout to dorsal fin origin (vs. a dark middorsal stripe in this area). An individual taken in Mississippi in 1951 measured 3,048 mm in total length (just over 10 ft long) and weighed 104.3 kg (Carlander 1969). Gudger (1942) reported a slightly shorter individual as weighing 137 kg (almost 300 lbs). Robison and Buchanan (1988) reported a weight of 350 lbs for an 8 ft 3 in individual from Arkansas.

TAXONOMIC COMMENTS: Wiley (1976) showed that living gars comprise two distinct phyletic lines, which date back at least to the Cretaceous period (75 million yr ago). On this basis, he concluded that the genus *Atractosteus* (with three living species) should be removed from the synonymy of *Lepisosteus* (with four living species) in which it had previously been placed. Although some (e.g., Robins et al. 1991) have continued to maintain the more conservative (i.e., earlier) arrangement, we maintain (as does Fink [1978]) that antiquity of these two distinct phyletic lines is in itself sufficient reason for their recognition as genera.

A morphologically distinctive gar from eastern Texas was, until re-

Distribution map of *Atractosteus spatula*.

cently, believed to represent an undescribed species of *Atractosteus*. However, Gibbons (1990) has conclusively demonstrated that this instead represents an intergeneric hybrid between *Atractosteus spatula* and the longnose gar, *Lepisosteus osseus*.

RANGE: A spot-distribution map of *A. spatula* appears in Lee and Wiley (1980). The alligator gar ranges from Veracruz, Mexico, northward along the Gulf slope to the Florida panhandle, northward in the Mississippi Valley to the lower reaches of the Ohio and Missouri rivers. It also occurs disjunctly in Nicaragua (Rio Sapoa [Rivas Province] and Lake Nicaragua) and northwestern Costa Rica (Guanacaste Province) (Wiley 1976). In Florida, the alligator gar has been recorded from brackish waters of Pensacola and Choctawhatchee bays, from the Escambia and Choctawhatchee rivers (Hellman 1953), and from Econfina Creek (between the Choctawhatchee and Apalachicola rivers). In the Escambia River it has been taken upstream almost to the Alabama state line. Only one Florida specimen (UF 8747), from the Escambia River, is present in the Florida Museum of Natural History collection, although a specimen from the Choctawhatchee River was supposedly donated to the collection (Hellman 1953). The species has either disappeared or become increasingly scarce in many peripheral parts of its range, as for example Ohio (Trautman 1981) and Arkansas (Robison and Buchanan 1988). This probably is attributable in large degree to the channelization of large rivers and elimination of preferred backwater habitats.

Abundant fossil remains of this species have been taken from various late Pliocene and Pleistocene sites along the west coast of peninsular Florida, as far south as the Naples area (Hay 1919; Webb et al. 1989). There is no logical explanation why the alligator gar should have disappeared from this area since environmental conditions appear suitable today; however, it should be noted that this situation is paralleled by peninsular extirpations of certain other vertebrate and invertebrate animals, for example the alligator snapping turtle, which today does not occur south of the Suwannee River. In contrast to most other species, however, the alligator gar is highly salt tolerant and thus should have been able to repopulate river drainages from which it may earlier have been extirpated.

HABITAT: The species is found in sluggish pools and backwaters of large rivers, frequently entering brackish or salt water along the Gulf coast (Suttkus 1963; Robison and Buchanan 1988). It is capable of living for indefinite periods of time in full-strength sea water, as evidenced by an individual that lived for many years in the marine exhibition tank at Marineland, Florida.

LIFE HISTORY AND ECOLOGY: The alligator gar is said to eat large numbers of game fish in fresh water, but little has been published about its diet in brackish or salt water. Raney (1942) reported it feeding on ducks and other birds in Texas, and Gunter (1945) found mullet in the gut tract. Suttkus (1963) reported it eating blue crabs in estuarine waters of Lake Pontchartrain and said that *A. spatula* is in large degree a scavenger. Spawning occurs from April to June in Louisiana (Suttkus 1963) and in May in Oklahoma (May and Echelle 1968). Its reproductive habits have not been described, but they probably do not differ much from those of other gars (Robison and Buchanan 1988); spawning in the spotted gar (*Lepisosteus oculatus*) has been reported to occur in shallow backwater areas, over dead vegetation and algal mats, with the adhesive eggs being scattered over the substrate.

SPECIALIZED OR UNIQUE CHARACTERISTICS: The alligator gar is a member of an ancient family of fishes once found in South America, Europe, Africa, and southern Asia (India), but now confined to North and Central America, as well as Cuba (Wiley 1976). Specimens clearly referable to the genus *Atractosteus* are known from upper Cretaceous deposits (approximately 75 million yr old) in Africa and North America.

BASIS OF STATUS CLASSIFICATION: Although the alligator gar occurs throughout much of panhandle Florida, actual records of the species are scarce. The species therefore is regarded as "rare" in the state.

RECOMMENDATIONS: Surveys should be conducted to determine more precisely the range and abundance of this species in Florida. The species is not readily collected with small seines (especially adult specimens), and specialized gear (gill nets, electroshockers, or large commercial seines in the lower parts of large rivers or bays) are required for effective sampling. The absence of specimens in collections is in part a reflection of the large size of most specimens encountered.

Literature Cited

Published Information

Carlander, K. D. 1969. Handbook of freshwater fishery biology. Vol. 1. Iowa State University Press, Ames. 752 pp.

Fink, W. L. 1978. *Review of:* The phylogeny and biogeography of fossil and recent gars (Actinopterygii: Lepisosteidae), by E. O. Wiley. Copeia 1978(2):374–377.

Gudger, E. W. 1942. Giant fishes of North America. Nat. Hist. 49:115–121.

Gunter, G. 1945. Studies on marine fishes of Texas. Publ. Inst. Mar. Sci. Univ. Tex. 1(1):1–190.

Hay, O. P. 1919. Descriptions of some mammalian and fish remains from Florida of probably Pleistocene age. Proc. U.S. Nat. Mus. 56(2291):103–112.

Hellman, R. E. 1953. The alligator gar in Florida. Q. J. Fla. Acad. Sci. 16(3): 198–199.

Lee, D. S., and E. O. Wiley. 1980. *Atractosteus spatula* (Lacepède), Alligator gar. Page 47 *in* D. S. Lee et al., eds., Atlas of North American freshwater fishes. North Carolina State Museum of Natural History, Raleigh. i–x+854 pp.

May, E. B., and A. A. Echelle. 1968. Young-of-year alligator gar in Lake Texoma, Oklahoma. Copeia 1968(3):629–630.

Raney, E. C. 1942. Alligator gar feeds upon birds in Texas. Copeia 1942(1):50.

Robins, C. R., R. M. Bailey, C. E. Bond, J. R. Brooker, E. A. Lachner, R. N. Lea, and W. B. Scott. 1991. Common and scientific names of fishes from the United States and Canada. 5th ed., Am. Fish. Soc. Spec. Publ. 20. 183 pp.

Robison, H. W., and T. M. Buchanan. 1988. Fishes of Arkansas. University of Arkansas Press, Fayetteville. 536 pp.

Suttkus, R. D. 1963. Order Lepisostei. Pages 61–88 *in* Fishes of the western North Atlantic. Mem. Sears Foun. Mar. Res. 1(3):vi–xxi, 1–630.

Trautman, M. B. 1981. The fishes of Ohio. Ohio State University Press, Columbus. vii–xxv+782 pp.

Webb, S. D., G. S. Morgan, R. C. Hulbert, Jr., D. S. Jones, B. J. MacFadden, and P. A. Mueller. 1989. Geochronology of a rich early Pleistocene vertebrate fauna, Leisey Shell Pit, Tampa Bay, Florida. Quat. Res. 32:96–110.

Wiley, E. O. 1976. The phylogeny and biogeography of fossil and recent gars (Actinopterygii: Lepisosteidae). Misc. Publ. Univ. Kans. Mus. Nat. Hist. 64:1–111.

Unpublished information

Gibbons, J. K. 1990. Identification and characterization of a putative intergeneric hybrid in the gars (Family Lepisosteidae). Abstract. 70th Annual ASIH meeting, Charleston, S.C.

Prepared by: Carter R. Gilbert, *Florida Museum of Natural History, University of Florida, Gainesville, Florida 32611.*

Florida Chub

Extrarius n. sp. cf *aestivalis*

FAMILY CYPRINIDAE

Order Cypriniformes

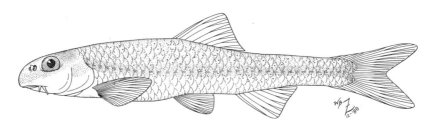

Florida chub, *Extrarius* n. sp. cf *aestivalis*. UF 57640. Adult, 48.2 mm SL. Mouth of Shoal River, Okaloosa County, Florida. 6 June 1961. Pigmentation pattern augmented from 37 mm SL specimen (UF 73336) from Little Choctawhatchee River, Dale County, Alabama. 23 Feburary 1975.

OTHER NAMES: Speckled chub (name used in 1978 FCREPA account). The vernacular name "Florida chub" is here used for the first time.

DESCRIPTION: A relatively small minnow (the largest specimen measuring 50 mm SL), the Florida chub is distinguished by having two pairs of prominent barbels (fleshy appendages) at the corners of the mouth; a ventrally situated mouth overhung by a fleshy snout; seven anal rays; a cylindrical body; body pallid or translucent and sides with a silvery longitudinal stripe; body marked with scattered pigment spots; breeding males with rows of tubercles on pectoral-fin rays. The combination of two pairs of barbels and seven anal rays are the main characters distinguishing this species from populations of the widespread *Extrarius aestivalis* (nearly all of which have one pair of barbels and eight anal rays), the species complex to which this fish belongs. In addition, individuals apparently reach a smaller maximum size (ca. 50-mm SL) than is true for most other populations of *E. aestivalis*. It was referred to by the species name *aestivalis* in the 1978 FCREPA account (Yerger 1978), and the photograph appearing in that publication (labeled there as fig. 7) actually is of another un-described member of the same species complex from central Alabama.

A formal description of this new species is being prepared by Carter R. Gilbert.

TAXONOMIC COMMENTS: Elevation of *Extrarius* from subgeneric to generic status follows the recommendation of Mayden (1989).

RANGE: A spot-distribution map of *Extrarius* new species, which actually shows the distribution of the entire *E. aestivalis* species complex, appears in Wallace (1980). The range statement given by Yerger (1978) in the

Distribution map of *Extrarius* n. sp. cf *aestivalis*.

first FCREPA volume refers to the distribution of this complex. The Florida chub occurs in western Florida and southeastern Alabama, where it is restricted to the Escambia and Choctawhatchee river drainages, as well as to the intervening Blackwater Bay drainage. This species was first reported (as *Hybopsis aestivalis*) by Suttkus (1961) and by Yerger and Suttkus (1962) from the Escambia and Choctawhatchee drainages and was later indicated by Yerger (1978) to be restricted to these two areas. Its presence in the Blackwater Bay drainage, which includes the Yellow and Shoal river systems, is here recorded for the first time. Although *Extrarius* new species has a fairly wide distribution in these three drainages, it has been collected at only five major localities in Florida, as can be seen from the accompanying distribution map, and thus can be considered as a rare fish overall. At several of these places, however, the fish is locally common and has been collected repeatedly throughout the years, most notably in the Escambia River at the state Route 4 bridge near Century. A total of 16 lots (totaling 176 specimens) are present in the Florida Museum of Natural History collection (11 from Florida and 5 from Alabama). Members of the *E. aestivalis* complex range widely in the Mississippi River and its larger tributaries from Minnesota and Pennsylvania south to the Gulf coast and from New Mexico and the Rio Grande eastward to western Florida.

HABITAT: This species is found in the main channels of wide, shallow, low-gradient streams with a moderate to strong current, over a sand or fine gravel bottom and clear to moderately turbid water.

LIFE HISTORY AND ECOLOGY: No life-history studies have been done on the Florida chub. The only specific information is Yerger's (1978) statement that individuals in spawning condition have been collected in Florida during July. Based on information on other Florida freshwater fishes, this is unusually late in the year, and it is suspected that the beginning of the spawning season may be much earlier. Yerger (1978) reported that the reproductive period of other members of this species complex (in Iowa) extends from late May through August, with spawning observed in late July and August. He also reported that few fish live more than 1.5 years.

Members of the *E. aestivalis* complex are bottom dwellers. Small eye size is correlated with the development of barbels and in an increase in the number of cutaneous taste buds. Dipteran larvae comprise the chief food, which is located primarily by taste.

SPECIALIZED OR UNIQUE CHARACTERISTICS: The *E. aestivalis* complex is extremely variable morphologically, probably more so than any other freshwater species or species complex in eastern North America. Standard practice has been to recognize a single species (*E. aestivalis*) and six subspecies, but this arrangement is now known to be incorrect. The Florida–southeastern Alabama population, which is unusual among members of the complex in having a combination of two pairs of maxillary barbels and seven anal rays (otherwise found only in the population from the upper Red River drainage in Texas and Oklahoma), apparently is also distinguished by a smaller average SL (maximum size 50-mm SL, and usually much less). It is here considered to be a distinct and as yet undescribed species, based on unpublished data by C. R. Gilbert.

BASIS OF STATUS CLASSIFICATION: The Florida chub was classified as "threatened" in the 1978 FCREPA report (Yerger 1978). Although recorded from only a relatively few localities in Florida, these are widely scattered and at some places the fish has been consistently present through the years. In addition, there are a number of records from closely adjacent areas in Alabama (Wallace 1980). This situation differs from those of several other fishes in extreme western Florida, as for example those whose distributions are limited to the main channel of the Escambia River that are consequently classified as threatened. Based on the perceived reduced vulnerability of this species, as compared to certain other fishes, we submit that a "rare" classification is more realistic and appropriate in this particular case.

RECOMMENDATIONS: Continued preservation of those sections of rivers or large streams having sand or gravel bottoms should ensure the survival of this species in the state.

Literature Cited

Mayden, R. L. 1989. Phylogenetic studies of North American minnows, with emphasis on the genus *Cyprinella* (Teleostei: Cypriniformes). Misc. Publ. Mus. Nat. Hist. Univ. Kans. 80:1–189.

Suttkus, R. D. 1961. *Review of:* Freshwater fishes in Mississippi, by Fannye A. Cook. Trans. Amer. Fish. Soc. 90(2):233–234.

Wallace, R. K. 1980. *Hybopsis aestivalis* (Girard), Speckled chub. Page 180 *in* D. S. Lee et al., eds., Atlas of North American freshwater fishes. North Carolina State Museum of Natural History, Raleigh. i–x+854 pp.

Yerger, R. W. 1978. *Hybopsis aestivalis* (Girard), speckled chub. Pages 12–13 *in* Carter R. Gilbert, ed., Rare and endangered biota of Florida. Vol. 4. Fishes. University Presses of Florida, Gainesville. 58 pp.

Yerger, R. W., and R. D. Suttkus. 1962. Records of freshwater fishes in Florida. Tulane Stud. Zool. 9(5):323–330.

Prepared by: Carter R. Gilbert, *Florida Museum of Natural History, University of Florida, Gainesville, Florida 32611*; and Ralph W. Yerger (retired), *Department of Biological Science, Florida State University, Tallahassee, Florida 32306*.

Southern Striped Shiner

Luxilus chrysocephalus isolepis

FAMILY CYPRINIDAE

Order Cypriniformes

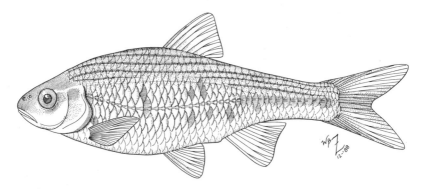

Southern striped shiner, *Luxilus chrysocephalus isolepis* (Hubbs and Brown, 1929). UF 15835. Adult, 83.1 mm SL. Tallapoosa River, Haralson County, Georgia. 23 April 1968.

OTHER NAMES: Common shiner. *Luxilus chrysocephalus* has, in the past, been regarded as a subspecies of the common shiner, *Luxilus cornutus*.

DESCRIPTION: The southern striped shiner is a moderately large, deep-bodied species of Cyprinidae with 2,4–4,2 pharyngeal teeth and nine anal rays; the dorsal-fin origin directly over the pelvic insertion; mouth terminal and slightly oblique; anterior dorsolateral scale rows and anterior dorsolateral stripes (usually three in number) very straight and even (Gilbert 1964, fig. 15), the number of scales in a series (counted from head posteriorly to below dorsal-fin origin) usually numbering 13 or 14; total body circumferential scales usually 24–28; lateral stripe usually not well developed (sometimes moderately well developed in juveniles) and caudal spot absent; scales in and above anterior part of lateral line distinctly elevated; lateral line complete; various degrees of yellow, rose, or red pigment present on body and fins of breeding males. It is distin-

138

guished from the subspecies *chrysocephalus* in having lower average dorso-lateral and body circumferential scale counts and especially in having the dorsolateral stripes distinctly straighter. Maximum recorded size 178-mm SL (Robison and Buchanan 1988), but in general adults range from 65–100-mm SL (Gilbert 1980).

TAXONOMIC COMMENTS: Elevation of *Luxilus* from subgeneric to generic status follows the recommendation of Mayden (1989).

Distribution map of *Luxilus chrysocephalus isolepis*. Open area on inset indicates distribution of *L. chrysocephalus chrysocephalus*; blacked-in area indicates distribution of *L. chrysocephalus isolepis*.

RANGE: A spot-distribution map of both subspecies of *L. chrysocephalus* appears in Gilbert (1980). The species ranges from the central Gulf slope northward throughout the Mississippi River basin (including the Ohio River drainage) into the eastern Great Lakes basin (Lakes Michigan, Huron, and Erie) from southeastern Wisconsin to western New York. *Luxilus chrysocephalus isolepis* is confined to the lower Mississippi Valley and the central and eastern Gulf slope. It occurs in tributaries on the eastern side of the Mississippi embayment northward into western Tennessee and from the eastern half of the Red River drainage in extreme northeastern Texas and southeastern Oklahoma eastward to the Mobile Bay basin, where it ranges east to the Tallapoosa River system of western Georgia. In the Mobile Bay basin, it is limited to areas below the Fall Line, with the typical subspecies (*L. chrysocephalus chrysocephalus*) occurring in those areas above. Intergrades between the two subspecies occur in certain areas around the Fall Line in Alabama and in a very small portion of the Tennessee River drainage in western Tennessee and northwestern Alabama (Gilbert 1980). In Florida, the southern striped shiner was, until recently, apparently limited to the Canoe Creek watershed of the Escambia River drainage in Escambia County (UF 47669, UF 79475), where it was first reported only within the past few years; however, as reported in the account of *Notropis baileyi*, the striped shiner was taken by James D. Williams in Big Escambia Creek, another tributary of the Escambia River in Alabama, as long ago as 1966. Its presence is believed to have resulted from human introduction, as it was absent from all early collections from Canoe Creek, the earliest of which date back to 1959. Specimens collected in October 1988 from Moore Creek, an eastern tributary of the Escambia River in Santa Rosa County (UF 81082), confirm its recent dispersal outside of Canoe Creek proper.

HABITAT: The species typically occurs in medium-sized streams having clear weedless waters, a moderate to swift current, and alternating pools and riffles over a gravel or rubble bottom, often with some silt. Some flow is usually present, but in general the species avoids the strongest currents and is frequently found either at the head or foot of riffles. Canoe Creek at the state Route 4 bridge is a narrow (probably about 5–7 ft wide), clear, sand-bottomed stream with numerous snags and undercut banks. Farther downstream at the U.S. Highway 29 bridge, it broadens out into a shallow stream with a sand-gravel bottom, as is typical of many of those in western Florida.

LIFE HISTORY AND ECOLOGY: Various aspects of the ecology of *L. chry-socephalus* have been reported on or summarized by different authors (Gilbert 1964, 1980; Smith 1979; Robison and Buchanan 1988). Habits and ecology are essentially identical to those of the very closely related common shiner (*Luxilus cornutus*), with which the striped shiner occurs sympatrically over a broad area in the upper Ohio River drainage and lower Great Lakes region and which has been studied even more intensively. Both species usually spawn at or near the bases of riffles, in water three to eight inches deep. Spawning occurs over a bottom of fine to coarse rubble, with the nests of other species often being utilized, particularly those constructed by species of the chub genus *Nocomis*. Spawning of *L. cornutus* takes place at temperatures of at least 18° C and has been reported to occur in waters as high as 29° C; in New York this was found to occur from mid-May to mid-July (Raney 1940). Based on its more southerly distribution, it may be assumed that spawning in *L. chry-socephalus* occurs at somewhat higher temperatures and also begins earlier in the year. Both common and striped shiners are carnivorous sight feeders and apparently prefer aquatic insects and their larvae, although other invertebrates and even plant material are commonly taken. They usually feed at the surface or in the upper water levels, but they may also take food on the bottom. This versatility in feeding habits probably is an important factor in explaining their broad distributions and abundance. Lewis (1957) found that occasional individuals live into their fourth or occasionally even their fifth year in southern Illinois, but most do not live beyond their third year.

BASIS OF STATUS CLASSIFICATION: The striped shiner is believed to have been introduced into Florida, where it occupies a limited area in the Escambia River drainage. Unlike *Notropis baileyi* and *Nocomis leptocephalus bellicus*, which are also confined to this area and which were known to have been established in the state by 1975, the first definite records of *L. chrysocephalus isolepis* have been very recent. Inasmuch as the striped shiner appears to be far less common than the rough shiner and probably less common also than the Alabama chub, it is possible that it was introduced at the same time but has simply been overlooked until recently (see account of *N. baileyi* for further discussion). Because of the geographic position and physical setting of Canoe and Moore creeks, these streams and their contained faunas appear much less vulnerable to pollution or other adverse modifications than the Escambia River proper, to which certain other Florida species are confined. The striped shiner therefore is accorded "rare" status on the FCREPA list.

RECOMMENDATIONS: Continue to monitor the striped shiner population in Canoe Creek and adjacent streams in order to determine population stability and possible spread to other areas.

Literature Cited

Dowling, T. E., and W. S. Moore. 1984. Level of reproductive isolation between two cyprinid fishes, *Notropis cornutus and N. chrysocephalus.* Copeia 1984(3): 617–628.

Gilbert, C. R. 1961. Hybridization versus intergradation: an inquiry into the relationship of two cyprinid fishes. Copeia 1961(2):181–192.

———. 1964. The American cyprinid fishes of the subgenus *Luxilus* (genus *Notropis*). Bull. Fla. St. Mus. Biol. Sci. 8(2):95–194.

———. 1980. *Notropis chrysocephalus* (Rafinesque), Striped shiner. Page 256 *in* D. S. Lee et al., eds., Atlas of North American freshwater fishes. North Carolina State Museum of Natural History, Raleigh. i–x+854 pp.

Lewis, W. M. 1957. The fish population of a spring-fed stream system in southern Illinois. Trans. Ill. Acad. Sci. 50:23–29.

Mayden, R. L. 1989. Phylogenetic studies of North American minnows, with emphasis on the genus *Cyprinella* (Teleostei: Cypriniformes). Misc. Publ. Mus. Nat. Hist. Univ. Kans. 80:1–189.

Menzel, B. W. 1976. Biochemical systematics and evolutionary genetics of the common shiner species group. Biochem. Syst. Ecol. 4:281–293.

Miller, R. J. 1968. Speciation in the common shiner: an alternate view. Copeia 1968(3):642–647.

Raney, E. C. 1940. The breeding behavior of the common shiner, *Notropis cornutus* (Mitchill). Zoologica 25(1):1–14.

Robison, H. W., and T. M. Buchanan. 1988. Fishes of Arkansas. University of Arkansas Press, Fayetteville. 536 pp.

Smith, P. W. 1979. The fishes of Illinois. University of Illinois Press, Urbana. 314 pp.

Prepared by: Carter R. Gilbert, *Florida Museum of Natural History, University of Florida, Gainesville, Florida 32611.*

Bandfin Shiner

Luxilus zonistius

FAMILY CYPRINIDAE

Order Cypriniformes

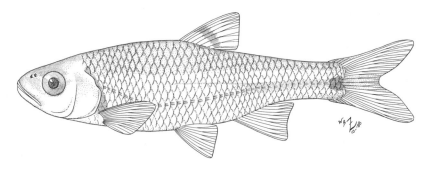

Bandfin shiner, *Luxilus zonistius* Jordan, 1880. UF 54035. Adult, 62.6 mm SL. Tributary to Flint River, Gadsden County, Florida. 26 January 1959.

OTHER NAMES: None.

DESCRIPTION: *Luxilus zonistius* is a moderately large cyprinid species (maximum SL 85 mm), characterized by a relatively deep, compressed body; 2,4–4,2 pharyngeal teeth; anal rays nine or ten (latter count prevalent in Florida specimens); dorsal fin with a strongly oblique dark band (orange-red in young individuals), beginning on lower third of anterior margin and terminating at middle of posterior margin; caudal spot present, moderately large and distinct, about equal to diameter of eye; a faint red bar along cheek in life; a distinct black scapular bar in adults; eye relatively large, about equal in length to snout; mouth large and moderately oblique; origin of dorsal fin directly above (or very slightly behind) insertion of pelvic fins; nuptial tubercles in two or three rows on lower jaw, extending to tip of chin; peritoneum speckled with dark pigment but not appearing uniformly black. The only Florida cyprinid with which *Luxilus zonistius* might possibly be confused is *Luxilus chrysocephalus isolepis*, which

143

is the only other member of this genus occurring in Florida but which is confined to the Escambia River drainage in the extreme western panhandle.

TAXONOMIC COMMENTS: Elevation of the subgenus *Luxilus* to generic status follows the recommendation of Mayden (1989). Among other members of the genus, *L. zonistius* clearly has its closest relationships with *Luxilus coccogenis* (the warpaint shiner), a species whose range is centered in the upper half of the Tennessee River drainage of Tennessee, North Carolina, and Virginia. Although no subspecies of *L. zonistius* are recognized, Gilbert (1964) found a north to south clinal gradation (from

Distribution map of *Luxilus zonistius*.

nine to ten) in anal-ray count, which he attributed to higher developmental temperatures at more southerly latitudes.

RANGE: The range of *L. zonistius* is largely restricted to the Chattahoochee River system of the Apalachicola River drainage. It also occurs in the upper Savannah River drainage, which it probably reached by natural stream capture, and in a limited part of the Oconee River system of the Altamaha River drainage where it may also be native (Satterfield 1961; Ramsey 1965). It is also established in parts of the Coosa and Tallapoosa river drainages (Dahlberg and Scott 1971; Williams 1967), where it has presumably been introduced. In Florida, the bandfin shiner occurs only in a few small tributaries of the Flint and Apalachicola rivers in Gadsden and Jackson counties, where it is reasonably common.

HABITAT: *Luxilus zonistius* typically occurs in small- to medium-sized, clear headwater streams of 20 feet or less in width, with a rubble-gravel or sand-gravel substrate and no aquatic vegetation. The current is moderately swift in such areas, although the fish seems to prefer flowing pools to the riffles themselves.

LIFE HISTORY AND ECOLOGY: Except for a report on spawning behavior (Johnston and Birkhead 1988), nothing specific is known regarding the life history of *L. zonistius*. Because of its close phylogenetic relationship to *L. coccogenis*, however, it may logically be assumed that certain life-history details of the two species are similar.

Johnston and Birkhead (1988) observed aggregations of the bandfin shiner spawning over nests of the cyprinid fishes *Campostoma pauciradii* and *Nocomis leptocephalus*, in April 1985 and April 1987, in two clear headwater tributaries of the Chattahoochee River in eastern Alabama and northwestern Georgia. This type of spawning site has also been reported for other species of *Luxilus* (as well as for at least two other cyprinid genera), although Johnston and Birkhead (1988) were not certain whether this association was obligatory or facultative in *L. zonistius*. Both streams had a sand and gravel substrate and well-defined pools and riffles. The nest studied in 1985, in Halawakee Creek, Alabama, involved an aggregation of 20–30 bandfin shiners, was situated below a riffle and above a deep pool that was 0.5–1 meter deep, and had a cover of overhanging vegetation. Water temperature was 15° C. Male *L. zonistius* held loose, moving territories, and these individuals chased intruding males (usually with less intense coloration) that had gathered around the periphery of the nest and occasionally tried to enter the nest area. An individual female would periodically enter this area, and if she was not chased away, the pair would press their bodies together and swim down close to the substrate where spawning was consummated. Other males rapidly joined the pair at these times, pressing their bodies together as close as possible and perhaps also releasing sperm in an apparent spawning attempt.

Outten (1957) found *L. coccogenis* to exhibit spawning behavior basically similar to *L. zonistius*. He also made other observations (see below), which, considering the two species' close taxonomic relationship, may ultimately be shown to be similar in *L. zonistius*. Sex ratios in the warpaint shiner were approximately the same during the first year of life but gradually changed so that by the third year over three-fourths of the living individuals were females. Individuals occasionally live as long as four years. *Luxilus coccogenis* feeds on terrestrial and aquatic animals, principally insects, with occasional small amounts of vegetable matter, which are usually taken at the surface or in the upper water levels.

SPECIALIZED OR UNIQUE CHARACTERISTICS: Although *L. zonistius* is not completely restricted geographically to the Apalachicola River basin, it can to all intents and purposes be considered to comprise an endemic element. Six other fish species are similarly restricted, but of these only two (the bluestripe shiner, *Cyprinella callitaenia*, and the shoal bass, *Micropterus* new species) also occur in Florida.

BASIS OF STATUS CLASSIFICATION: The bandfin shiner is regarded as a "rare" species in Florida, a judgment that might appear inconsistent when compared to the "threatened" status accorded the other two Apalachicola endemics found in the state (see above). Another apparent inconsistency concerns the fact that the total geographic area in Florida inhabited by *L. zonistius* actually is smaller than that occupied by the other species. The decision to accord this species only "rare" status is based primarily on the fact that *L. zonistius* occurs in small streams that are less subject to widespread pollution or other types of habitat disturbance than are the large rivers occupied by the other two species. Although not directly related to this decision, it is also worth noting that the bandfin shiner, in contrast to both the bluestripe shiner and the shoal bass, is a widespread and common species in other parts of its range.

RECOMMENDATIONS: None.

Literature Cited

Published Information

Dahlberg, M. D., and D. C. Scott. 1971. The freshwater fishes of Georgia. Bull. Ga. Acad. Sci. 29:1–64.

Gilbert, C. R. 1964. The American cyprinid fishes of the subgenus *Luxilus*, genus *Notropis*. Bull. Fla. St. Mus. Biol. Sci. 8(2):95–194.

Johnston, C. E., and W. S. Birkhead. 1988. Spawning in the bandfin shiner, *Notropis zonistius* (Pisces: Cyprinidae). J. Ala. Acad. Sci. 59(2):30–33.

Mayden, R. L. 1989. Phylogenetic studies of North American minnows, with emphasis on the genus *Cyprinella* (Teleostei: Cypriniformes). Misc. Publ. Univ. Kans. Mus. Nat. Hist. 80:1–189.

Outten, L. M. 1957. A study of the life history of the cyprinid fish *Notropis coccogenis*. J. Elisha Mitchell Sci. Soc. 73(1):68–84.

Williams, J. D. 1967. Records of three cyprinid fishes from the Tallapoosa River system. J. Ala. Acad. Sci. 38:307–310 .

Unpublished Information

Ramsey, J. S. 1965. Zoogeographic studies on the freshwater fish fauna of rivers draining the southern Appalachian region. Ph.D. diss., Tulane University, New Orleans.

Satterfield, J. D. 1961. A study of the distribution of fishes in the headwaters of streams in northern Georgia. M.Sc. thesis, University of Georgia, Athens.

Prepared by: Carter R. Gilbert, *Florida Museum of Natural History, University of Florida, Gainesville, Florida 32611.*

Blacktip Shiner

Lythrurus atrapiculus

FAMILY CYPRINIDAE

Order Cypriniformes

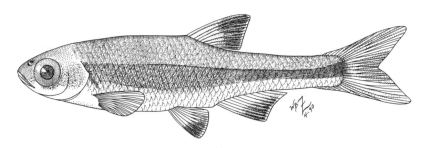

Blacktip shiner, *Lythrurus atrapiculus* (Snelson, 1972). UF 73362. Adult male, 49.3 mm SL. West Branch of Choctawhatchee River, Dale County, Alabama. 23 Feburary 1975. Pigment in dorsal, pelvic, and anal fins augmented from illustration in Snelson (1972).

OTHER NAMES: None.

DESCRIPTION: The blacktip shiner is a species of *Lythrurus* characterized by usually having 2,4–4,2 pharyngeal teeth and 11 (occasionally 10) anal rays; a body shape that tends to be somewhat compressed laterally; the dorsal, anal, pectoral, and pelvic fins with dark pigment on the outer edges and/or limited to the tips in adult males; relatively small scales, the predorsal scales usually 21–25 (range 18–28), lateral-line scales usually 39–41 (range 36–45); body-circumferential scales usually 33–34 (range 31–36), caudal-peduncle circumferential scales 14; and a maximum SL of 53 mm.

TAXONOMIC REMARKS: Until recently, the blacktip shiner and its close relatives were included in the subgenus *Lythrurus* of the genus *Notropis*. Elevation of *Lythrurus* to full generic status results from Mayden's (1989) phylogenetic studies of this and other related cyprinid groups.

Lythrurus atrapiculus is most closely related to *Lythrurus bellus* and *Ly-*

148

thrurus roseipinnis (both of which are allopatric to *L. atrapiculus* and neither of which occur in Florida) and is intermediate to those species (in the case of *L. bellus* specifically the typical subspecies) in the following qualitative and quantitative characters: (1) dorsal-, anal-, pelvic-, and pectoral-fin pigmentation in adult males; (2) anal-fin ray count; (3) scale reduction index (i.e., variation from naked to fully scaled condition in predorsal and dorsolateral areas and on breast); (4) predorsal length; (5) body depth; (6) caudal-peduncle length; (7) caudal-peduncle depth; and (8) dorsal-fin length. Despite its intermediate appearance, *L. atrapiculus* was described by Snelson (1972) as a full species, largely because of its allopatric distribution. Stein et al. (1985), however, who studied the bio-

Distribution map of *Lythrurus atrapiculus*.

chemical systematics of this species complex, found *L. atrapiculus* and *L. bellus* to be very similar electrophoretically, whereas *L. roseipinnis* displayed a number of independent biochemical characters. Furthermore, they found that *L. atrapiculus* actually clustered more closely with *L. bellus alegnotus* than with the geographically closer typical subspecies. They stated that the electrophoretic similarities displayed by the latter three forms is in line with those usually reported for conspecific populations. Stein et al. (1985) suggested the possibility that *L. atrapiculus* and *L. roseipinnis* both arose independently from *L. bellus*.

RANGE: *Lythrurus atrapiculus* ranges from the Escambia River drainage eastward to the Chattahoochee and Flint river drainages (Apalachicola River basin) in Florida, Alabama, and Georgia. It is limited to the middle part of the Chattahoochee drainage (thus does not range south into Florida) and is found only in the uppermost sections of the Flint River drainage of Georgia. It is common in southeastern Alabama, but in Florida is essentially limited to a few tributaries of the Yellow and Choctawhatchee rivers, in Okaloosa, Walton, and Holmes counties; it is known from the Escambia drainage of Florida only from a single specimen (UF 75329) collected in May 1976. In all cases but one the Florida records are in close proximity to the Alabama state line, the one exception being a series of 24 specimens collected in Crooked Creek (tributary to the Choctawhatchee River) near Redbay, Walton County, in September 1959 (UF 55416). A spot-distribution map appears in Snelson (1980).

HABITAT: Snelson (1972) listed the typical habitat of the blacktip shiner as small- to moderate-sized (5–35 ft wide) streams with a moderate gradient and characterized by pools alternating with shorter stretches of riffles or runs. The species usually inhabits the deep pools, where there is little current, and may be rare or absent from intervening areas. Bottom substrate is comprised principally of sand, occasionally mixed with some silt, clay, or gravel. Water ranges from colorless to brown stained. The species probably is not tolerant of continuous turbidity but is often collected in streams temporarily roiled by recent rains. Vegetation may or may not be present.

LIFE HISTORY AND ECOLOGY: Little is known regarding the life history of the blacktip shiner. Snelson (1980), on the basis of tubercle development, indicated that it probably spawns in early summer.

The life history of *L. atrapiculus* is probably similar in most respects to that of the closely related *L. roseipinnis*, a study of which was conducted in the Jourdan River system in Mississippi (Heins and Bresnick 1975). *Lythrurus roseipinnis* was found to have an extended spawning season, which lasts from late March into August or early September. Based on analysis of mature ova, two reproductive peaks were noted, one at the beginning of the reproductive season and one in the latter half. Sex ratio was 1:1, and mean sizes of the two sexes were very similar. Most fish were mature by about 30 mm SL. The number of mature ova was correlated with the size of the female and ranged from 58 to 293 in individuals 29.6–46.6-mm SL, but individual ova size did not vary with size of the adult. *Lythrurus roseipinnis* appears to be short-lived, and probably few individuals live beyond one year.

SPECIALIZED OR UNIQUE CHARACTERISTICS: *Lythrurus atrapiculus* is one of several species endemic to streams entering the Gulf of Mexico east of the Mobile Bay basin. It has the widest range of any of these species, however, ranging from the Escambia drainage eastward to the Apalachicola River basin.

BASIS OF STATUS CLASSIFICATION: *Lythrurus atrapiculus* is classified as "rare" in Florida, based on its limited occurrence from the Escambia drainage eastward to the Choctawhatchee drainage. It is a common species in adjacent areas of Alabama. It also prefers medium-sized creeks, which makes the species less vulnerable than it would be if it were confined to large rivers. It was not included in the 1978 FCREPA report.

Literature Cited

Heins, D. C., and G. I. Bresnick. 1975. The ecological life history of the cherryfin shiner, *Notropis roseipinnis*. Trans. Amer. Fish. Soc. 104(3):516–523.

Mayden, R. L. 1989. Phylogenetic studies of the North American minnows, with emphasis on the genus *Cyprinella* (Teleostei: Cypriniformes). Misc. Publ. Mus. Nat. Hist. Univ. Kans. 80:1–189.

Snelson, F. F., Jr. 1972. Systematics of the subgenus *Lythrurus*, genus *Notropis* (Pisces: Cyprinidae). Bull. Fla. St. Mus. Biol. Sci. 17(1):1–92.

———. 1980. *Notropis atrapiculus* Snelson, Blacktip shiner. Page 233 *in* D. S. Lee et al., eds., Atlas of North American freshwater fishes. North Carolina State Museum of Natural History, Raleigh. i–x+854 pp.

Stein, D.W., J.S. Rogers, and R.C. Cashner. 1985. Biochemical systematics of the *Notropis roseipinnis* complex (Cyprinidae: subgenus *Lythrurus*). Copeia 1985(1):154–163.

Prepared by: Carter R. Gilbert, *Florida Museum of Natural History, University of Florida, Gainesville, Florida 32611.*

Southern Bluehead Chub

Nocomis leptocephalus bellicus

FAMILY CYPRINIDAE

Order Cypriniformes

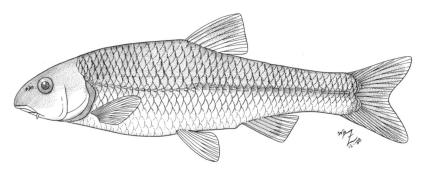

Southern bluehead chub, *Nocomis leptocephalus bellicus* Girard, 1856. UF 23396. Adult, 112.5 mm SL. Canoe Creek, Escambia County, Florida. 21 April 1976.

OTHER NAMES: Alabama chub (name dates from time *bellicus* was regarded as a distinct species); Bluehead chub (name applied to *Nocomis leptocephalus leptocephalus.*

DESCRIPTION: *Nocomis leptocephalus bellicus* is a relatively large cyprinid fish with 4–4 pharyngeal teeth; seven anal rays; a small maxillary barbel at each corner of the mouth; a small nasal crest and up to seven large cephalic tubercles (all situated anterior to the eyes) in adult males; body moderately deep and only slightly compressed in lateral view in adults; origin of dorsal fin directly above or very slightly behind insertion of pelvic fins; head relatively deep and eye small, going about six times in head length in adults; scales on upper part of back somewhat elevated and outlined with dark pigment; total body-circumferential scales usually 28–29 (range 26–31); lateral-line scales usually 39–40 (range 38–42); overall body tone greenish olive on upper two-thirds of body, grading to a lighter shade below; intestine long and convoluted, more so than in any other

153

species of *Nocomis*. The maximum SL of males is approximately 180 mm and of females approximately 140 mm (Lachner and Wiley 1971).

TAXONOMIC REMARKS: The form *bellicus* was regarded as a full species until 1971, at which time Lachner and Wiley (1971) downgraded it to a subspecies of *N. leptocephalus*.

RANGE: Spot-distribution maps appear in Lachner and Wiley (1971) and Jenkins and Lachner (1980). The latter map does not differentiate between the ranges of the three subspecies of *N. leptocephalus*. *Nocomis lep-*

Distribution map of *Nocomis leptocephalus bellicus*. Blacked-in area of inset indicates overall distribution of *N. leptocephalus bellicus*; open area indicates combined range of other two subspecies of *N. leptocephalus*.

tocephalus bellicus occurs throughout the Mobile Bay basin west to the Pearl River drainage and a few eastern tributaries of the lower Mississippi River in Louisiana and southwestern Mississippi. It also is present in part of the Bear Creek system of the Tennessee River drainage in northwestern Alabama and extreme northeastern Mississippi.

Nocomis leptocephalus bellicus was not reported from Florida by Lachner and Wiley (1971), although in 1966 the species had been taken (along with the rough shiner, *Notropis baileyi*) by James D. Williams in Big Escambia Creek, a tributary of the Escambia River in Alabama. Stephen A. Bortone (personal communication) apparently was the first to record the species from Florida, having taken specimens in Canoe Creek (a western tributary of the Escambia River in Escambia County) in 1975. Until recently, all records of the Alabama chub and the two other species with nearly identical distributions and presumed distributional histories in the state (rough shiner and southern striped shiner) were from Canoe Creek. Evidence for dispersal from this area was not obtained until 20 October 1988, when the three species were taken together in Moore Creek, a nearby eastern tributary of the Escambia River in Santa Rosa County. A more complete discussion of the pros and cons of introduction versus natural occurrence of these western panhandle species appears in the account of *N. baileyi*.

HABITAT: *Nocomis leptocephalus bellicus* prefers small- to medium-sized, generally weedless streams of about 10 to 50 feet in width but avoids the larger streams and rivers preferred by certain other species of *Nocomis*, as well as extreme headwaters. It inhabits clear streams composed of gravel and rubble, particularly those having shallow areas swept by current, although below the Fall Line the substrate also contains a considerable amount of sand. Slack waters are generally avoided, but in those places where lower gradients predominate and the waters tend to be turbid, some gravel-rubble areas occur.

LIFE HISTORY AND ECOLOGY: Flemer and Woolcott (1966), who studied the food and feeding habits of *N. leptocephalus*, found that this species like other *Nocomis* species is a sight feeder and feeds largely on adult aquatic insects and their larvae, with lesser percentages of other aquatic invertebrates. Fish are rarely eaten. *Nocomis leptocephalus* also consumes large quantities of plant materials (both algae and vascular plants) to a much greater degree than do other members of the genus. This is reflected by the morphology of the intestinal tract, which is longer and more convoluted than in other members of the genus. All species of *Nocomis* are nest builders and carry small stones or gravel, which are piled together to form dome-shaped nests for use as spawning sites (Lachner and Jenkins 1971). These nests vary in size (depending on the species) and are often used for the same purpose by other cyprinid species. *Nocomis leptocephalus*, which has a smaller body size and a consequently smaller mouth than most other species of *Nocomis*, builds smaller nests comprised mostly of gravel. Lachner (1952), reporting on the typical subspecies (*N. leptocephalus leptocephalus*), indicated that tuberculate males approaching spawning condition were taken from the Neuse River drainage of North Carolina on 2 April 1940. It matures, and probably spawns, at three years of age, but the fish overall is relatively short-lived, only about 1.5 percent of the 819 specimens examined (from Virginia and North Carolina) being in their fourth summer's growth. Lachner (1952) also reported egg complements of from 710–800 eggs in females of 84–92 mm SL and that, in age groups 0 and 1 at least, females outnumbered males by a ratio of about 2.5 to 1.

BASIS OF STATUS CLASSIFICATION: *Nocomis leptocephalus bellicus* is known only from Canoe Creek in Escambia County and from Moore Creek in Santa Rosa County, where it is believed to have been introduced presumably from some area in the closely adjacent lower Mobile Bay basin. It is classified as "rare" for reasons discussed in greater detail in the account of *Notropis baileyi*. This species was not included in the previous FCREPA volume (1978).

RECOMMENDATIONS: Continue to monitor for other populations of the Southern bluehead chub and also to assess change in population size of known populations.

Literature Cited

Flemer, D. A., and W. S. Woolcott. 1966. Food habits and distribution of the fishes of Tuckahoe Creek, Virginia, with special emphasis on the bluegill, *Lepomis m. macrochirus* Rafinesque. Chesapeake Sci. 7(2):75–89.

Jenkins, R. E., and E. A. Lachner. 1980. *Nocomis leptocephalus* (Girard), Bluehead chub. Page 213 *in* D. S. Lee et al., eds., Atlas of North American freshwater fishes. North Carolina State Museum of Natural History, Raleigh. i–x+854 pp.

Lachner, E. A. 1952. Studies of the biology of the cyprinid fishes of the chub genus *Nocomis* of northeastern United States. Am. Midl. Nat. 48(2):433–466.

Lachner, E. A., and R. E. Jenkins. 1971. Systematics, distribution, and evolution of the chub genus *Nocomis* Girard (Pisces, Cyprinidae) of eastern United States, with descriptions of new species. Smithsonian Contr. Zool. 85:1–97.

Lachner, E. A., and M. L. Wiley. 1971. Populations of the polytypic species *Nocomis leptocephalus* (Girard) with a description of a new subspecies. Smithsonian Contr. Zool. 92:1–35.

Prepared by: Carter R. Gilbert, *Florida Museum of Natural History, University of Florida, Gainesville, Florida 32611.*

Rough Shiner

Notropis baileyi

FAMILY CYPRINIDAE

Family Cypriniformes

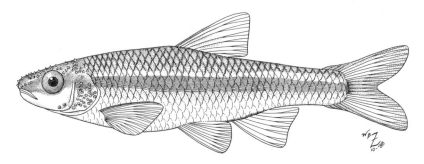

Rough shiner, *Notropis baileyi* Suttkus and Raney, 1955. UF 47668. Adult breeding male, 49.6 mm SL. Canoe Creek, Escambia County, Florida. 13 April 1988.

OTHER NAMES: None.

DESCRIPTION: *Notropis baileyi* is a small deep-bodied species of Cyprinidae with 2,4–4,2 pharyngeal teeth and seven anal rays; the dorsal-fin origin over or slightly behind pelvic-fin insertion; mouth terminal and slightly oblique; black lateral stripe well developed from tip of lower jaw and snout to caudal base; caudal spot square or rounded and slightly separated from it; lateral-line scales not elevated, usually numbering 35–37; breeding tubercles in males of moderate size, restricted to top of head, top of snout, surface of opercle, anterodorsal edge of lacrymals, and (in high-breeding males) on virtually all body scales; considerable amounts of chromatic pigments (yellow to red) present on body and fins of adults, particularly in breeding males. The maximum SL is 75 mm.

Swift (1970), in an unpublished work, studied systematics and variation in this species.

RANGE: A spot-distribution map appears in Swift and Gilbert (1980). *Notropis baileyi* occurs in coastal plain and piedmont areas (mostly below the Fall Line) from the Leaf and Chickasawhay rivers (Pascagoula River drainage), Mississippi, east through the Mobile Bay basin of Alabama to the lower Tallapoosa River system. The species has been introduced into the middle Chattahoochee River drainage of Georgia.

Its presence in the Escambia River drainage of Florida is also suspected to be the result of introduction, as indicated by Swift and Gilbert (1980). Bailey et al. (1954) did not report *N. baileyi* from the Escambia drainage, but this is not considered conclusive proof of its absence at that time, inasmuch as none of their collections were from Canoe Creek or

Distribution map of *Notropis baileyi*.

from other areas of the Escambia drainage in Alabama (especially Big and Little Escambia creeks) where the species has subsequently been collected. More definitive proof comes from two collections made in Canoe Creek at the state Route 4 bridge, Escambia County, in March 1959 (UF 54812–54821 and UF 54829–54836); neither of these produced specimens of *N. baileyi*, but they did turn up three other cyprinid species (*Pteronotropis hypselopterus, Pteronotropis signipinnis,* and *Notropis texanus*). No other collections apparently were taken in the Florida portion of this creek until April and June of 1975, at which time specimens of *N. baileyi* (as well as *Nocomis leptocephalus bellicus,* another presumed introduction) were taken at the U.S. Highway 29 bridge, which is downstream from Route 4. *Notropis baileyi* has been consistently common (although not dominant) in subsequent samples from the Highway 29 locality, but a collection made at the Route 4 locality (UF 47668) in April 1988 showed the species to be by far the dominant fish numerically, greatly outnumbering the other cyprinid species found there (*Pteronotropis hypselopterus, Luxilus chrysocephalus isolepis,* and *Notropis buccatus*). The total absence of a species from the 1959 collections at a locality where it is now dominant provides strong proof that an introduction has occurred. Similarly, the presence of *L. chrysocephalus isolepis* and *N. leptocephalus bellicus* in Canoe Creek are also believed to have resulted from introductions. James D. Williams reports (personal communication) having collected *N. baileyi, L. chrysocephalus isolepis,* and *N. leptocephalus bellicus* (together with *Campostoma oligolepis*), none of which had previously been reported from the Escambia River drainage, in Big Escambia Creek (shown on some maps as a continuation of the Escambia River proper) at the I-65 crossing in Alabama in 1966; however, he did not find any of these species farther downstream at the state Highway 31 crossing when he sampled there in the early 1970s. At the Highway 31 crossing, however, this stream assumes a big-river character and does not provide the ecological setting normally associated with the species in question. Other recent records of *N. baileyi* and *L. chrysocephalus isolepis* have been reported from farther up in the drainage (Mettee 1983). Until recently, all Florida records of *N. baileyi,* as well as *N. leptocephalus bellicus* and *L. chrysocephalus isolepis,* have been from Canoe Creek. On 20 October 1988, all three species were taken together in Moore Creek, a nearby eastern tributary of the Escambia River in Santa Rosa County, thus indicating that dispersal has occurred out from Canoe Creek.

HABITAT: *Notropis baileyi* occurs in small- to medium-sized (usually five to fifteen feet wide), wooded, moderate- to high-gradient streams with clear water. The bottom substrate consists of sand and gravel, and sub-mergent vegetation is normally absent. Conditions at the Route 4 locality on Canoe Creek, where the species is especially abundant, are very close to those described above. The creek at this particular locality is probably no more than five to seven feet wide.

LIFE HISTORY AND ECOLOGY: Mathur and Ramsey (1974a, 1974b) published on the food habits and reproduction of *N. baileyi*. The species has an extended spawning period (May to early October) with a peak in early or mid-June. It feeds on aquatic insect larvae and terrestrial insects. The life span is usually two years.

BASIS OF STATUS CLASSIFICATION: The rough shiner apparently has been introduced into Florida. As such, the question arises as to whether it should be included on the present FCREPA list, as it does also for the southern striped shiner (*L. chrysocephalus isolepis*) and the southern blue-head chub (*N. leptocephalus bellicus*), two other species that in Florida are confined to the Escambia River drainage and that are suspected to be in-troductions. In response to this, it is not absolutely certain that these species are not native to the state, even though circumstantial evidence seems to suggest otherwise. Whatever the situation, all are now perman-ent members of the Florida freshwater fish fauna and occupy very limited ranges within the state. The areas to which the three species are confined are medium-sized creeks that do not flow through areas that are heavily developed or farmed, and thus these fish are not vulnerable to anywhere near the same degree as those species whose ranges in Florida are limited to the Escambia River proper. Both Canoe and Moore creeks seem to be in stable condition, and it appears highly likely that populations of the above three species are permanently established. Under the circumstances a "rare" classification seems entirely appropriate. *Notropis baileyi* was not included in the 1978 FCREPA volume.

RECOMMENDATIONS: Very few recommendations are called for in this particular case. Canoe Creek appears to be a pristine creek, particularly in the upper reaches where *N. baileyi* is especially common.

Literature Cited

Published Information

Bailey, R. M., H. E. Winn, and C. L. Smith. 1954. Fishes from the Escambia

River, Alabama and Florida, with ecologic and taxonomic notes. Proc. Acad. Nat. Sci. Phila. 106:109–164.

Mathur, D., and J. S. Ramsey. 1974a. Reproductive biology of the rough shiner, *Notropis baileyi*, in Halawakee Creek, Alabama. Trans. Amer. Fish. Soc. 103(1): 88–93.

———. 1974b. Food habits of the rough shiner, *Notropis baileyi* Suttkus and Raney, in Halawakee Creek, Alabama. Am. Midl. Nat. 92(1):84–93.

Mettee, M. F. 1983. A biological inventory of streams draining the Citronelle, Pollard and Gilbertown oil fields in Alabama. Geol. Survey Ala. Circ. 108. 101 pp.

Swift, C. C., and C. R. Gilbert. 1980. *Notropis baileyi* Suttkus and Raney, Rough shiner. Page 235 *in* D. S. Lee et al., eds., Atlas of North American freshwater fishes. North Carolina State Museum of Natural History, Raleigh. i–x+854 pp.

Unpublished information

Swift, C. C. 1970. A review of the eastern North American cyprinid fishes of the *Notropis texanus* species group (subgenus *Alburnops*), with a definition of the subgenus *Hydrophlox*, and materials for a revision of the subgenus *Alburnops*. Ph.D. diss., Florida State University, Tallahassee.

Prepared by: Carter R. Gilbert, *Florida Museum of Natural History, University of Florida, Gainesville, Florida 32611.*

Mountain Mullet

Agonostomus monticola

FAMILY MUGILIDAE

Order Perciformes

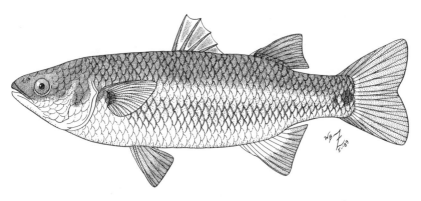

Mountain mullet, *Agonostomus monticola* (Bancroft, 1846). UF 40906. Adult, 218 mm SL. Parrot Jungle Pond, South Miami, Dade County, Florida. 26 April 1983.

OTHER NAMES: Tepemechin, Dajao.

DESCRIPTION: The mountain mullet is a relatively small species of mullet, reaching a maximum size of 250–300 mm total length (no Florida specimens in museum collections approach that size, however) and characterized by the following meristic counts: dorsal rays IV–I, 8; anal rays II, 9–10; and lateral scales 38–42. The overall body pigmentation is darker than in species of *Mugil* and the pattern shows distinct countershading. The entire dorsum is dark, with each scale outlined in black, shading to gray on the sides, and the ventral third of the body is white. A line of pigment, equal in width to the pupil, runs from the snout to the posterior edge of the operculum. One black spot is situated at the base of the pectoral fins and another on the caudal peduncle; both spots are slightly smaller than the eye diameter. The unpaired fins are often yellowish, and the soft dorsal fin is darkened along the base of the first few rays.

163

The genus *Agonostomus* is distinguished from the genus *Mugil* in having the teeth not ciliiform; the stomach not gizzardlike; the lower jaw
not angular in front; and in having brownish rather than silvery coloration.

RANGE: *Agonostomus monticola* ranges from southern United States (from
North Carolina to Texas), Mexico, Central America, and the West Indies
south to northern South America (Colombia and Venezuela) (Suttkus
1956; Rohde 1980; Pezold and Edwards 1983). Its distribution in the
United States is very patchy and is probably dependent on the occurrence
of suitable habitat near a source of recruitment. The species may also inhabit streams on the Pacific coast of Central America, but the taxonomic

Distribution map of *Agonostomus monticola*.

status of Pacific drainage *Agonostomus* is uncertain. Juveniles (>30 mm SL), subadults, and adults inhabit fresh waters, whereas larvae are found in marine waters often well out to sea (Anderson 1957; Erdman 1972).

In Florida, *A. monticola* has been found on a more-or-less regular basis in various isolated parts of the state throughout the years. The first specimens from Florida of which we are aware were collected in 1948 from several localities on the upper Atlantic coast (McLane 1955), and a total of seven series (all in the Florida Museum of Natural History collection) were taken from this general area from 1948–1952. Specimens were found in the Apalachicola River below Jim Woodruff Dam in 1959–1960 (UF 55971, UF 57835). The record from the Florida Bay area, which is not represented by material in our collection, is based on the Tabb et al. (1974) report and was later discussed by Loftus and Kushlan (1987). Occurrence on the middle Atlantic coast of Florida is based on information appearing in Gilmore (1977) and Gilmore et al. (1981, 1983). Rohde (1980), in his North American distribution map of the species, showed records from the lower St. Johns River and from the middle west coast of the peninsula (Sarasota County); these also are based on material not in our collection. Loftus et al. (1984) and Loftus and Kushlan (1987) reported what appears to be a permanent population from the Parrot Jungle area of Miami and from closely adjacent areas. There are three recent records available from the Waccasassa and Suwannee river drainages, each of which has been verified by photographs or specimens. William J. B. Miller observed and photographed adults in Wekiva Spring (tributary to the Waccasassa River) in 1985. A 104-mm SL specimen (UF 79993) was collected by Florida Game and Fresh Water Fish Commission personnel in the Withlacoochee River (upper Suwannee River drainage) at the state Highway 6 bridge on 8 August 1989; and James D. Williams observed three individuals in Ichetucknee River at the U.S. Highway 27 bridge on 5 and 8 November 1990.

HABITAT: The larvae of the mountain mullet undergo a period of development in salt water, where they have been collected both in coastal waters (Erdman 1972) and far offshore in the Florida current (Anderson 1957). Larger individuals typically inhabit high-gradient streams (Erdman 1972; Cruz 1987), although they have also been collected in slowly flowing waters and in pools (McLane 1955; Loftus et al. 1984). In tropical regions, this is one of the few fishes able to ascend streams to their headwaters (hence the vernacular name "mountain mullet") (Gilbert and Kelso 1971).

LIFE HISTORY AND ECOLOGY: The pattern of reproduction of *A. monti-cola* remains something of a mystery. Gilbert and Kelso (1971) presumed that it is catadromous and that adults made spawning runs downstream into the ocean. However, they presented the alternative hypothesis that it may spawn in fresh water with the eggs or larvae subsequently being carried out to sea. The actual pattern has not been definitely described, although several recent studies have presented circumstantial evidence in support of the latter theory. Corujo-Flores (1980) believed that mountain mullet make downstream migrations to spawn in or around the estuaries of Puerto Rican rivers, a view shared by D.S. Erdman (personal communication). Cruz (1987) was unable to verify in-stream spawning movements by *A. monticola* in Honduras, although he did document in-migration of postlarvae. Loftus et al. (1984) surveyed the literature dealing with life history and concluded that amphidromy was the most likely pattern for *A. monticola*. Their conclusions were based on the fact that ripe adults have been taken only in fresh waters, out-migrations of adults into the ocean have never been reported, and only larvae and juveniles have been found at sea. This particular reproductive strategy extends across phylogenetic lines in many fish species inhabiting tropical streams and presumably has evolved in response to the dearth of larval foods available in such habitats. Adults are reproductively active during the wettest times of the year, which are during spring and summer in Florida and Puerto Rico (Erdman 1972; Corujo-Flores 1980; Loftus et al. 1984) and late fall in Honduras (Cruz 1987). Erdman (1972) proposed that increased river flows wash the eggs and larvae out to sea. Based on the size of specimens and the period of time required to attain those lengths, Anderson (1957) believed that Cuba was the most likely source of recruits for Florida waters. It is unknown if the larvae are obligatory marine inhabitants. Observations on mountain mullet in the Rio Grande suggest that, in Texas at least, *A. monticola* may pass its entire life cycle in fresh water (R.J. Edwards, personal communication). Loftus et al. (1984) reported the first population of adult *A. monticola* from Florida and thought that the population might be self-sustaining. Adults were subsequently observed and photographed by W.J.B. Miller (then at the Florida Museum of Natural History) in Wekiva Spring (Levy County), which flows into the Waccasassa River and thence to the Gulf of Mexico.

The diet of mountain mullet in Florida fresh waters includes seeds, algae, aquatic insects, detritus, and crustaceans (Loftus et al. 1984). In Honduras, Cruz (1987) found that the species feeds mainly on aquatic insects and crustaceans, with small amounts of filamentous algae also included. Anderson (1957) described changes in body proportions of juveniles as they switch from a marine to freshwater existence. Erdman (1972) indicated that growth rates of mountain mullet are slow.

SPECIALIZED OR UNIQUE CHARACTERISTICS: *Agonostomus monticola* may be one of the few catadromous fishes in North America, although this has never actually been demonstrated. Conversely, Loftus et al. (1984) and Cruz (1987) presented arguments that the species is amphidromous, a life-history strategy employed by other tropical, peripheral fish species in Florida (Gilmore and Hastings 1983).

BASIS OF STATUS CLASSIFICATION: Because *A. monticola* is infrequently and sporadically observed in Florida fresh waters, it qualifies as a "rare" species. It cannot be considered "threatened" because of its independence from any stream system, as well as the lack of clearcut evidence for any established, breeding populations in the state. However, the Miami population reported by Loftus et al. (1984), which includes ripe adults, may be permanently established, and if so it would be the first verified sustaining population in Florida. Human impacts that could be detrimental to this particular population include channelization of natural streams, which would change their hydrology and impede access of fish from downstream.

RECOMMENDATIONS: Because the habitat requirements for the mountain mullet seem restrictive, steps should be taken to preserve habitats in which persistent populations are known to occur. The recent discovery of adults in Wekiva Spring and Ichetucknee River should spur searches for mountain mullet populations in other stenothermic springs and spring runs in the state. Life-history studies, especially those investigating mode of reproduction and migrations by juveniles into salt water, should be supported.

Literature Cited

Published Information

Anderson, W. W. 1957. Larval forms of the fresh-water mullet (*Agonostomus monticola*) from the open ocean off the Bahamas and south Atlantic coast of the United States. Fish. Bull. 120, U.S. Fish Wildl. Serv. 57:415–425.

Cruz, G. A. 1987. Reproductive biology and feed habits of cuyamel, *Joturus pichardi*, and tepemechin, *Agonostomus monticola* (Pisces; Mugilidae) from Rio Platano, Mosquitia, Honduras. Bull. Mar. Sci. 40:63–72.

Erdman, D. S. 1972. Inland game fishes of Puerto Rico. Department of Agriculture, Commonwealth of Puerto Rico, P.R. Fed. Aid Proj. F-1-20. Job. No. 7. Vol. 4(2):1–96.

Gilbert, C. R., and D. P. Kelso. 1971. Fishes of the Tortuguero area, Caribbean Costa Rica. Bull. Fla. St. Mus. Biol. Sci. 16(1):1–54.

Gilmore, R. G. 1977. Fishes of the Indian River lagoon and adjacent waters. Bull. Fla. Mus. Nat. Hist. Biol. Sci. 22(3):101–147.

Gilmore, R. G., C. J. Donohoe, D. W. Cooke, and D. J. Herema. 1981. Fishes of the Indian River lagoon and adjacent waters, Florida. Harbor Branch Found., Tech. Rept. 41:1–64.

Gilmore, R. G., and P. A. Hastings. 1983. Observations on the ecology and distribution of certain tropical peripheral fishes in Florida. Fla. Sci. 46(1):31–51.

Gilmore, R. G., P. A. Hastings, and D. J. Herrema. 1983. Ichthyofaunal additions to the Indian River lagoon and adjacent waters, east-central Florida. Fla. Sci. 46(1):22–30.

Loftus, W. F., and J. A. Kushlan. 1987. Freshwater fishes of southern Florida. Bull. Fla. St. Mus. Biol. Sci. 31(4):147–344.

Loftus, W. F., J. A. Kushlan, and S. A. Voorhees. 1984. Status of the mountain mullet in southern Florida. Fla. Sci. 47(4):256–263.

Pezold, F. L., and R. J. Edwards. 1983. Additions to the Texas marine ichthyofauna, with notes on the Rio Grande estuary. Southwest. Nat. 28:102–105.

Rohde, F. C. 1980. *Agonostomus monticola* (Bancroft), Mountain mullet. Page 778 *in* D. S. Lee et al., eds., Atlas of North American freshwater fishes. North Carolina State Museum of Natural History, Raleigh. i–x+854 pp.

Suttkus, R. D. 1956. First record of the mountain mullet, *Agonostomus monticola* (Bancroft), in Louisiana. Proc. La. Acad. Sci. 19:43–46.

Tabb, D. C., B. Brummond, and N. Kenny. 1974. Coastal marshes of southern Florida as habitat for fishes and effects of changes in water supply of these habitats. Final Rpt. to Bur. Sport Fish Wildl. (Contract No. 14-16-004-56). Rosensteil School Mar. Atmospheric Sci., University of Miami, Miami, Florida.

Unpublished information

Corujo-Flores, I. N. 1980. A study of fish populations in the Espiritu Santo river estuary. M.Sc. thesis, University of Puerto Rico, Rio Piedras.

McLane, W. M. 1955. The fishes of the St. Johns River system. Ph.D. diss., University of Florida, Gainesville.

Prepared by: William F. Loftus, *South Florida Research Center, Everglades National Park, Homestead, Florida 33030*; and Carter R. Gilbert, *Florida Museum of Natural History, University of Florida, Gainesville, Florida 32611.*

Goldstripe Darter

Etheostoma parvipinne

FAMILY PERCIDAE

Order Perciformes

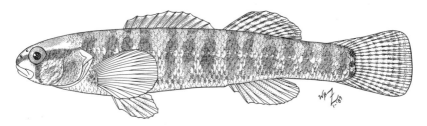

Goldstripe darter, *Etheostoma parvipinne* Gilbert and Swain, 1887. UF 54678. Adult female, 52.6 mm SL. Tributary to Holmes Creek, Washington County, Florida. 12 January 1978.

OTHER NAMES: None.

DESCRIPTION: *Etheostoma parvipinne* is a small- to medium-sized, rather robust darter (maximum SL 56 mm), the most noticeable morphological characteristics of which are (1) the lateral-line scales typically without dark pigment adjacent to the pores, thus producing a narrow pale stripe along the side of the body; (2) a thick vertical bar extending ventrally from the eye; and (3) a pair of small spots located on the middle third of the base of the tail. In addition, it is characterized by gill membranes that are broadly connected across the isthmus; the cheek, opercle, nape, and breast usually scaled; a complete, or nearly complete, lateral line; a complete infraorbital canal; color dusky olive, with about 10 short, black cross-bars that are interrupted by the light lateral-line stripe; dorsal rays usually IX–XI,10 (range VIII–XII, 9–11); anal rays II, 7–8; and total lateral-line scales 48–57, of which all but 0–7 are pored.

RANGE: Spot-distribution maps of *E. parvipinne* appear in Rohde (1980) and Page (1983, map 57). The geographic range of the species is centered in the lower Mississippi Valley and in the Mobile Bay basin of Alabama. To the west it occurs from the Mississippi River drainage in northeastern Arkansas south to the middle Red River drainage of southwestern Arkansas, southeastern Oklahoma, northwestern Louisiana, and northeastern Texas. To the east it ranges from extreme western Kentucky and Tennessee south throughout much of Mississippi and Alabama (west and south of the Tennessee River drainage) and eastward to western Florida (Choctawhatchee and Apalachicola drainages) and east-central Georgia (Altamaha River drainage). Yerger and Suttkus (1962) first reported the species from Florida, where it is still known from a total of only eleven specimens in six collections, three from the Apalachicola drainage (UF 69008 [2], UF 75606 [4], UF 81075 [1]), and three from the Choc-

Distribution map of *Etheostoma parvipinne*.

tawhatchee drainage (UF 54678 [2], UF 55128 [1], UF 55326 [1]). Although *E. parvipinne* has not yet been found in either the Perdido or Escambia river drainages in Florida, there are several records from Alabama portions of these drainages which are in close proximity to the Florida state line (Rohde 1980; Page 1983).

HABITAT: The goldstripe darter characteristically occurs in very small- to medium-sized creeks and in seepage outlets from springs, often where there is an abundance of aquatic vegetation. The bottom usually consists of sand or fine gravel.

LIFE HISTORY AND ECOLOGY: Very little is known regarding the life history and ecology of this species, other than descriptions of the habitat indicated above.

BASIS OF STATUS CLASSIFICATION: *Etheostoma parvipinne* was listed as "threatened" in Florida in the 1978 FCREPA account (Gilbert 1978). Although apparently rare in the state, this may be partly a sampling artifact. The species is often found in extremely small bodies of water (tiny brooks and spring seeps), which contain heavy vegetation and detritus and are frequently overlooked during routine sampling operations. In these situations it is not readily collected with a seine, and it may be more easily taken with dipnets or handnets. Because the habitat preferred by the goldstripe darter is not uncommon in western Florida, the rarity of the species may be more apparent than real, and further collecting efforts likely will reveal additional populations in the state. The often remote and scattered nature of this type of habitat may well afford the goldstripe darter a higher level of protection than would be true for many other species. For this reason, we feel that a "rare" classification is more appropriate for this species than the "threatened" classification accorded it earlier.

RECOMMENDATIONS: Continue to survey suitable-looking habitats in western Florida to find additional localities for this species.

Literature Cited

Gilbert, C. R. 1978. Goldstripe darter, *Etheostoma parvipinne* Gilbert and Swain. Pages 23–25 *in* Carter R. Gilbert, ed., Rare and endangered biota of Florida. Vol. 4. Fishes. University Presses of Florida, Gainesville. 58 pp.

Page, L. M. 1983. Handbook of darters. T. F. H. Publications, Inc., Neptune City, N.J. 271 pp.

Rohde, F. C. 1980. *Etheostoma parvipinne* Gilbert and Swain. Goldstripe darter. Page 680 *in* D. S. Lee et al., eds., Atlas of North American freshwater fishes. North Carolina State Museum of Natural History, Raleigh. i–x+854 pp.

Yerger, R. W., and R. D. Suttkus. 1962. Records of freshwater fishes in Florida. Tulane Stud. Zool. 9(5):323–330.

Prepared by: Carter R. Gilbert, *Florida Museum of Natural History, University of Florida, Gainesville, Florida 32611.*

Cypress Darter

Etheostoma proeliare

FAMILY PERCIDAE

Order Perciformes

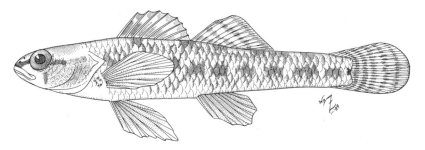

Cypress darter, *Etheostoma proeliare* (Hay, 1881). UF 73046. Adult male, 25.3 mm SL. Big Escambia Creek, Escambia County, Florida. 27 November 1974.

OTHER NAMES: None.

DESCRIPTION: One of the smallest darters, the cypress darter has a maximum SL of 39.6 mm (rarely over 30 mm); lateral line slightly arched and very short (9 or fewer [usually fewer than 6] pored scales); dorsal-fin spines usually 7–8, occasionally 9; pectoral-fin rays usually 10, occasionally 9 or 11; body olive yellow-brown with numerous brown flecks, with a row of 9–10 irregular dark brown blotches on sides; dorsal and caudal fins with rows of brown spots; bar below eyes well developed.

RANGE: Spot-distribution maps of *Etheostoma proelaire* appear in Burr (1980) and Page (1983, map 88). The cypress darter ranges from Illinois south to Texas and east to western Florida. In Florida, it is known only from the Escambia and Choctawhatchee river drainages. Burr (1978), in his revision of the subgenus *Microperca* (to which *E. proeliare* belongs), listed only two records from the Choctawhatchee drainage, based on a total of only two specimens (UF 50351, TU [Tulane University] 46278), collected in 1951 and 1967, respectively; that paper, and Yerger's account in the first FCREPA volume (1978) are the first published records for the species from the drainage. Based on the number of available museum collection records, the species appears to be much more common in the Escambia drainage. Bailey et al. (1954) listed four collections (totaling 37 specimens), all collected during the fall and spring of 1952–1953 from closely adjacent stations in the lower reaches of the river in Florida; they also listed three lots (totaling 10 specimens), all taken during the fall of 1929 in the headwaters of the Escambia drainage in Butler County, Alabama. There are presently five series from this drainage in the Florida Museum of Natural History collection, one of which (UF 44648 [2]) was taken in 1986 from a nearby locality in Ala-

Distribution map of *Etheostoma proeliare*.

bama. The remaining four series, collected between 1959 and 1976, are from sidewater areas of the Escambia River as follows: UF 55011 (2), UF 64251 (8), UF 73046 (2), and UF 75377 (1).

HABITAT: *Etheostoma proeliare* inhabits pools and sloughs of sluggish streams and quiet sidewaters of flowing creeks and rivers. The species usually occurs over a mud-silt bottom, often in association with a protective cover of woody debris or aquatic vegetation.

LIFE HISTORY AND ECOLOGY: Burr and Page (1978) published a life-history study of *E. proeliare* from Max Creek in southern Illinois, which is near the northernmost limit of its range. Maximum life span was found to be only about 18 months, with fewer than 10 percent of the population apparently living longer than 12 months. Both sexes reproduce at one year of age. Breeding occurs in April and May in Illinois but may occur as early as January in Louisiana and (presumably) Florida. Spawning occurs during the day, and one to three eggs are laid at a time on the undersides of leaves, twigs, and rocks or in algae, and subsequent parental care apparently does not occur. Individuals feed primarily on small crustaceans but less heavily on insects other than chironomids.

SPECIALIZED OR UNIQUE CHARACTERISTICS: The cyprus darter is one of the smallest species of darters and consequently may be easily overlooked in the field and may sometimes be confused with the southern swamp darter (*Etheostoma fusiforme barratti*), which also lacks bright colors, has a similarly incomplete lateral line, and lives in a similar habitat.

BASIS OF STATUS CLASSIFICATION: The cypress darter was listed as "threatened" in the 1978 FCREPA volume (Yerger 1978), based on its restricted occurrence in the state and in particular its rarity in the Choctawhatchee drainage. The habitat of this species (sidewaters and sloughs), however, places it in a much less vulnerable position than those species of restricted distribution living largely or entirely in the main Escambia River. In addition, *E. proeliare*, unlike most other species of restricted distribution in western Florida, is widely distributed throughout the Escambia drainage and has been collected regularly over the years. It apparently is extremely rare in the Choctawhatchee drainage. Based on these considerations, it is here downgraded to "rare" status in Florida.

RECOMMENDATIONS: Continue to monitor existing populations of this species and search for additional populations in the Choctawhatchee drainage. Protection of habitat where the species is presently found is important for maintaining existing populations of the species.

Literature Cited

Bailey, R. M., H. E. Winn, and C. L. Smith. 1954. Fishes from the Escambia River, Alabama and Florida, with ecologic and taxonomic notes. Proc. Acad. Nat. Sci. Phila. 106:109–164.

Burr, B. M. 1978. Systematics of the percid fishes of the subgenus *Microperca*, genus *Etheostoma*. Bull. Ala. Mus. Nat. Hist. 4:1–53.

_____. 1980. *Etheostoma proeliare* (Hay), Cypress darter. Page 680 *in* D. S. Lee et al., eds., Atlas of North American freshwater fishes. North Carolina State Museum of Natural History, Raleigh. i–x+854 pp.

Burr, B. M., and L. M. Page. 1978. The life history of the cypress darter, *Etheostoma proeliare*, in Max Creek, Illinois. Ill. Nat. Hist. Surv. Biol. Notes 112:1–15.

Page, L. M. 1983. Handbook of darters. T.F.H. Publications, Inc., Neptune City, N.J. 271 pp.

Yerger, R. W. 1978. Cypress darter, *Etheostoma proeliare* (Hay). Pages 25–26 *in* Carter R. Gilbert, ed., Rare and endangered biota of Florida. Vol. 4. Fishes. University Presses of Florida, Gainesville. 58 pp.

Prepared by: Carter R. Gilbert, *Florida Museum of Natural History, University of Florida, Gainesville, Florida 32611*; and Ralph W. Yerger (retired), *Department of Biological Science, Florida State University, Tallahassee, Florida 32306.*

Florida Logperch

Percina n. sp. cf *caprodes*

FAMILY PERCIDAE

Order Perciformes

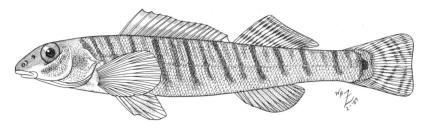

Florida logperch, *Percina* n. sp. cf *caprodes*. UF 55461. Adult female, 85.3 mm SL. Chocta-whatchee River, Holmes County, Florida. 11 September 1959.

OTHER NAMES: Logperch; listed as *Percina caprodes carbonaria* by Bailey et al. (1954). The vernacular name "Florida logperch" is here employed for the first time.

DESCRIPTION: This species is a member of the *P. caprodes* species complex, which is characterized by having a projecting snout and numerous (up to 20) vertical dark bars along the side of the body that extend over the dorsum and join those from the opposite side. Each individual bar is of uniform width throughout and not expanded on midside of body (as in certain other logperch species), but collectively the bars differ in width, length, and pigmentary intensity and are in turn distributed in a definite sequence in relation to one another. A small, intense caudal spot is present at middle of caudal base, and a red or orange stripe is present on outer edge of dorsal fin (faint in juveniles), but chromatic pigments are absent elsewhere on body and fins. Nape fully scaled; breast and top of head scaleless; cheek and opercle scaled. Dorsal-fin rays usually XV–XVI,17; anal-fin rays usually II,10–11; lateral-line scales usually 88 or more (average about 91); scales in diagonal series from dorsal midline to ventral midline 59–72 (average about 64); pectoral-fin rays usually 15–15. The species is most closely related to another undescribed species of logperch that occurs below the Fall Line in the Mobile Bay basin and adjacent river drainages to the west, from which it differs in usually having 15 (vs. 14) pectoral-fin rays, usually 88 or more scales in lateral-line series (vs. fewer than 88), and a higher diagonal-scale count on side of body (more than 59 vs. fewer than 57). Part of the preceding information appears in a taxonomic key to the species and subspecies of the *P. caprodes* complex (Thompson 1985). The remaining data were supplied by Bruce A. Thompson (Louisiana State University), who is preparing a formal description of the Florida logperch.

Distribution map of *Percina* n. sp. cf *caprodes*.

RANGE: Spot-distribution maps of *Percina* new species, which actually show the distribution of the entire *P. caprodes* species complex, appear in Thompson (1980) and Page (1983). The Florida logperch was first reported from Florida by Bailey et al. (1954), and all subsequent collections have been from either the Escambia or Choctawhatchee river drainages, with none from the intervening Blackwater Bay drainage.

HABITAT: All recorded specimens of the Florida logperch have come from rivers and large creeks having a substrate of clean sand and gravel. Other logperch species typically occur in fast-flowing riffles of rubble, gravel, or sand, but unlike the Florida logperch they have successfully invaded a wide variety of environments, such as small- to medium-size creeks, mud-bottomed oxbows, and gravel-bottomed or sand lakes (Page 1983). Although the close restriction of the Florida logperch to large open streams with sand and gravel substrates may reflect absence of some of the other habitats described above, it may also indicate a basic genetic difference between this and other logperch species.

LIFE HISTORY AND ECOLOGY: No specific life-history study has been conducted on the Florida logperch, although considerable published information exists for certain other members of the *P. caprodes* complex, as summarized by Page (1983) and Kuehne and Barbour (1983). Spawning in other closely related species occurs in areas of swift current (often in riffles) over a sand and gravel bottom, with no territoriality being observed. Eggs are buried in the substrate, as is true for all other species of *Percina* but not for all *Etheostoma* species (Page 1985). The earliest spawning date recorded (in Oklahoma) was late March (Miller and Robison 1973), and presumably earlier spawning dates are true for the Florida logperch. About 10–20 eggs are fertilized at any one time, and females may spawn successively with several males. Winn (1958) recorded egg counts of up to 3,000 in females from Michigan (average of about 2,000 in two-year-old individuals), but Nance (1978) listed much lower egg counts (average of only about 300) for individuals from West Virginia. The oldest individuals reported for any members of the *P. caprodes* complex are over three years. Logperch species feed mainly on small crustaceans, and adults feed primarily on the larvae of midges, mayflies, and caddisflies. Logperches as a group possess the unique habit (among darters) of using their protruding snout to turn stones and other bottom objects in search of food (Keast and Webb 1967).

SPECIALIZED OR UNIQUE CHARACTERISTICS: The Florida logperch is one of six species (three cyprinids and three percids [only three of which have been formally described]) that are endemic to one or more of the independent eastern Gulf slope drainages situated between the Mobile Bay and Apalachicola river basins. Although its restricted distribution in the Escambia and Choctawhatchee drainages parallels those of several other species in the western Florida–southeastern Alabama area, none of the other five species endemic to the panhandle area exhibits this particular distribution pattern.

BASIS OF STATUS CLASSIFICATION: Most records of the Florida logperch are from the main channels of the Escambia and Choctawhatchee rivers, in western Florida. Those species confined to this habitat and that occur only in the Escambia are regarded as threatened by the FCREPA subcommittee on fishes, on the theory that one disastrous event could cause them to be eliminated from the state. *Percina* new species is more widely distributed and accordingly is only classified as "rare." Actually, however, it occupies an intermediate position in terms of its conservation status (it perhaps could be called "semithreatened") compared with other west Florida species that are classified as "rare" but which are less closely restricted to a big-river habitat. Although collections of Florida logperch have been made regularly down through the years, the species never appears to be particularly common, as indicated by the fact that the species is represented by only 20 lots (total of 67 specimens) in the Florida Museum of Natural History collection. It is encouraging to note that the species has continued to survive in the Choctawhatchee River, despite the heavy loads of pesticides that have periodically entered the river as a result of cotton-field spraying upstream, mostly in Alabama. In general, there does not appear to have been any change in distribution and numbers of this species in recent years. The Florida logperch was not included in the 1978 FCREPA list, but in retrospect it probably should have been.

RECOMMENDATIONS: Continue to survey areas of potentially suitable habitat in western Florida to locate additional populations. Protect the Escambia and Choctawhatchee rivers from additional pesticides or other forms of pollution.

Literature Cited

Bailey, R. M., H. E. Winn, and C. L. Smith. 1954. Fishes from the Escambia River, Alabama and Florida, with ecologic and taxonomic notes. Proc. Acad. Nat. Sci. Phila. 106:109–164.

Keast, A., and D. Webb. 1967. Mouth and body form relative to feeding ecology in the fish fauna of a small lake, Lake Opinicon, Ontario. J. Fish. Res. Bd. Can. (1966) 23:1845–1874.

Kuehne, R. E., and R. W. Barbour. 1983. The American darters. University of Kentucky Press, Lexington. 177 pp.

Miller, R. J., and H. W. Robison. 1973. The fishes of Oklahoma. Oklahoma State University Press, Stillwater. 246 pp.

Nance, S. 1978. Some aspects of the reproductive biology of the logperch, *Percina caprodes* (Rafinesque), from East Lynn Lake, Wayne County, West Virginia. Proc. W. Va. Acad. Sci. 50:25.

Page, L. M. 1983. Handbook of darters. T.F.H. Publications, Inc., Neptune City, N.J. 271 pp.

———. 1985. Evolution of reproductive behaviors in percid fishes. Ill. Nat. Hist. Surv. Bull. 33(3):275–295.

Thompson, B. A. 1980. *Percina caprodes* (Rafinesque), Logperch. Pages 719–720 *in* D. S. Lee et al., eds., Atlas of North American freshwater fishes. North Carolina State Museum of Natural History, Raleigh. i–x+854 pp.

———. 1985. *Percina jenkinsi*, a new species of logperch (Pisces, Percidae) from the Conasauga River, Tennessee and Georgia. Occ. Pap. Mus. Zool. La. St. Univ. 61:1–23.

Winn, H. E. 1958. Comparative reproductive behavior and ecology of fourteen species of darters (Pisces-Percidae). Ecol. Monogr. 28:155–191.

Prepared by: Carter R. Gilbert, *Florida Museum of Natural History, University of Florida, Gainesville, Florida 32611.*

Blackbanded Sunfish

Enneacanthus chaetodon

FAMILY CENTRARCHIDAE

Order Perciformes

Blackbanded sunfish, *Enneacanthus chaetodon* (Baird, 1855). UF 77070. Adult, 50.8 mm SL. Aucilla River, Jefferson County, Florida. 8 September 1977.

OTHER NAMES: Southern blackbanded sunfish (based on *Enneacanthus chaetodon elizabethae* [Bailey] 1941).

DESCRIPTION: The blackbanded sunfish has a deep and compressed body, as is true of all centrarchids except the black basses (genus *Micropterus*). It is characterized by a small maximum body size (66-mm SL), which is slightly less than for the other two species of *Enneacanthus* or for any other centrarchid. As is true for the other species of *Enneacan-*

thus, it has the caudal fin rounded or truncate (vs. emarginate in all other centrarchid genera except *Acantharchus*); anal spines three (vs. five to eight in the genera *Pomoxis, Acantharchus, Centrarchus,* and *Ambloplites*); lateral-line scales 26–35 (vs. 31–54 in species of *Lepomis*); and the opercle emarginate in area of opercular flap (vs. rounded in species of *Lepomis*). Distinguished from the other two species of *Enneacanthus* by a color pattern consisting of a light background overlain by six bold black vertical bars on side of head and body; anteriormost three dorsal spines sharply set apart from more posterior parts of fin by dark pigment; dorsal spines usually ten in northern populations, grading to nine in southern populations (vs. usually nine; see remarks below); anal soft rays usually

Distribution map of *Enneacanthus chaetodon.*

12 (vs. usually 10); and dorsal fin distinctly emarginate (vs. slightly or not at all emarginate). The largest specimen (out of 322) examined by Schwartz (1961) from Maryland measured 69 mm total length, which is slightly more than the 66-mm-SL maximum given by Lee (1980).

TAXONOMIC COMMENTS: Bailey (1941) described the Florida population as a new subspecies, *elizabethae*, based on the presence of nine (vs. ten) dorsal spines and 18–19 (vs. 20–21) rows of caudal-peduncle circumferential scales. His description was based on only six specimens, four from the Ocala National Forest area and two from Okefenokee Swamp, Georgia, with the closest records of *E. chaetodon chaetodon* being from South Carolina. Sweeney (1972) determined the difference in dorsal-spine count to be clinal in nature. Counts made on specimens in our collection confirm the reduced average dorsal-spine and caudal-peduncle circumferential scale counts in south Georgia and Florida specimens.

RANGE: A spot-distribution map appears in Lee (1980). The blackbanded sunfish occurs sporadically in sluggish streams and ponds of the Atlantic coastal plain, from central New Jersey south to the northern half of peninsular Florida and from a few widely disjunct and geographically limited areas of the Gulf coastal plain in Florida and southern Georgia. It is known from the upper Suwannee River drainage in Georgia (Turner and Atkinson counties; UF 18959 and UF 25175, respectively), but has yet to be taken in the Suwannee drainage in Florida. It occurs in the Okefenokee Swamp in Georgia (Wright 1926) and in a closely adjacent area in Baker County, Florida (UF 65438). Five collections are known from Gulf coastal drainages, including three from the Aucilla River drainage (UF 66688 [from Georgia]); UF 73635 and UF 77108 [from Florida]), one from the Econfina River drainage in Taylor County, Florida (specimen in University of Tennessee collection), and one widely disjunct location in Pasco County, on the middle western coast north of Clearwater (UF 20608) (Burgess et al. 1977; Lee 1980). In Florida, there are two old (i.e., 1947) records from Orange Lake in Marion County (UF 31 and UF 2515) (Reid 1950), but the species has not been taken there since. The greatest concentration of records are from in and around the Ocala National Forest, and there are a total of 11 series in the Florida Museum of Natural History collection taken from this area at various times between 1946 and 1973.

HABITAT: Although populations of the blackbanded sunfish are scattered throughout its range, there appear to be four areas of concentration. Three of these, the pine barrens of New Jersey, the sandhills in southeastern North Carolina, and the central highlands of Florida, are characterized by high, well-drained sandy soils with vegetation consisting primarily of pine and scrubby oak species. The fourth area of concentration is the Okefenokee Swamp in Georgia.

Preferred habitat of *E. chaetodon* is the shallow marginal areas of sluggish streams, ponds, or lakes. Rooted aquatic vegetation is usually dense, and the bottom material is typically comprised of sand overlain with varying amounts of organic detritus. The character of the water in most areas is acidic, and water color varies from clear to dark brown.

Underlying reasons for the unusually spotty and disjunct distribution of *E. chaetodon* are unclear. Smith (1953, 1957), Hastings (1979, 1984), and Graham and Hastings (1984) showed that both the blackbanded sunfish and banded sunfish (*Enneacanthus obesus*) occur in more acid waters (pH often <5), on the average, than the bluespotted sunfish (*Enneacanthus gloriosus*) (see also Collette's [1962] summary of Smith's studies), and Graham and Hastings (1984) reported collecting *Enneacanthus obesus* in waters as acidic as pH 3.7. This is evidenced by the relative distributions of these species in New Jersey, where both the banded and blackbanded sunfishes are mostly confined to acidic streams in the southern pine barrens, whereas the bluespotted sunfish is widely distributed throughout the state. However, both *E. chaetodon* and *E. obesus* are sometimes found in waters over pH. 7.0 (Graham and Hastings 1984), and Hoedeman (1974) stated that *E. chaetodon* can reproduce in neutral water. Although this helps explain differences in occurrence and distribution of *Enneacanthus gloriosus*, in comparison to the other two species, it does not explain why *E. obesus* on the whole should have a much more even and predictable distribution overall than *E. chaetodon*. Fox (1969) investigated this in conjunction with his study of the life history of *E. gloriosus*, but his results were inconclusive.

LIFE HISTORY AND ECOLOGY: Schwartz's (1961) study of *E. chaetodon* from Maryland is the only detailed information on the life history of this species, and his results were summarized by Fox (1969) and Carlander (1977). Aquatic insects, gammarids, filamentous algae, and plant leaves were present in the stomachs of 90 individuals collected in July and November, with chironomid larvae dominating in the July collections and trichopterans dominating in the November collections. Schwartz (1961) also suggested that the species is a nocturnal feeder, based on a comparison of time of collections and proportions of empty stomachs. Reid

(1950) and McLane (1955) reported copepods, cladocerans, and insect larvae from a limited number of Florida individuals. Schwartz (1961) determined that *E. chaetodon* may live as long as four years. Smith (1907) reported that the species spawns in March in North Carolina.

BASIS OF STATUS CLASSIFICATION: Although fairly widespread in northern Florida, the blackbanded sunfish is seldom common, with the greatest concentration of records in the sandhill lakes of Marion and northern Lake counties. Even in this area of greatest concentration, it was found in only one of 45 collections made during a survey of the Ocala National Forest during the early 1970s (Snelson 1978). The spotty distribution of *E. chaetodon* in Florida also characterizes the species elsewhere throughout its geographic range. As much of the Florida range is within the Ocala Forest boundaries and also because the type of habitat where the fish occurs is not likely to be subjected to widespread destruction, the species is classified as "rare."

RECOMMENDATIONS: As indicated above, most Florida records of this species are from Ocala National Forest. Assuming this area continues to be maintained in its present state, there is no reason to recommend any change in the status quo. Localities outside this area should also be maintained in their present ecological state.

Literature Cited

Published Information

Bailey, R. M. 1941. Geographic variation in *Mesognistius chaetodon* (Baird), with description of a new subspecies from Georgia and Florida. Occ. Pap. Mus. Zool. Univ. Mich. 454:1–7.

Burgess, G. H., C. R. Gilbert, V. Guillory, and D. C. Taphorn. 1977. Distributional notes on some north Florida freshwater fishes. Fla. Sci. 40(1):33–41.

Carlander, K. D. 1977. Handbook of freshwater fishery biology. Vol. 2. Iowa State University Press, Ames. 431 pp.

Collette, B. B. 1962. The swamp darters of the subgenus *Hololepis* (Pisces: Percidae). Tulane Stud. Zool. 9(4):115–211.

Graham, J. H., and R. W. Hastings. 1984. Distributional patterns of sunfishes on the New Jersey coastal plain. Environ. Biol. Fishes 10(3):137–148.

Hastings, R. W. 1979. Fish of the Pine Barrens. Pages 489–504 *in* R. T. Forman, ed., Pine Barrens: ecosystem and landscape. Academic Press, New York. 624 pp.

———. 1984. The fishes of Mullica River, a naturally acid water system of the New Jersey Pine Barrens. Bull. N.J. Acad. Sci. 29(1):9–23.

Hoedeman, J. J. 1974. Naturalist's guide to freshwater aquarium fish. Sterling, New York. Pp. 932–934.

Lee, D. S. 1980. *Enneacanthus chaetodon* (Baird), Blackbanded sunfish. Page 587 *in* D. S. Lee et al., eds., Atlas of North American freshwater fishes. North Carolina State Museum of Natural History, Raleigh. i–x+854 pp.

Reid, G. K., Jr. 1950. Notes on the centrarchid fish *Mesognistius chaetodon elizabethae* in peninsular Florida. Copeia 1950(3):239–240.

Schwartz, F. J. 1961. Food, age, growth and morphology of the black-banded sunfish, *Enneacanthus c. chaetodon*, in Smithville Pond, Maryland. Chesapeake Sci. 2:82–88.

Smith, H. M. 1907. The fishes of North Carolina. North Carolina Geol. Econ. Survey. Vol. 2. Raleigh, E. N. Uzzell & Co. 453 pp.

Smith, R. F. 1953. Some observations on the distribution of fishes in New Jersey. N.J. Fish. Surv. Div. Fish Game Rept. 2:165–174.

––––––. 1957. Lakes and ponds. N.J. Fish. Surv. Div. Fish Game Rept. 3:1–198.

Snelson, F. F, Jr. 1978. Blackbanded sunfish, *Enneacanthus chaetodon* (Baird). Pages 41–43 *in* Carter R. Gilbert, ed., Rare and endangered biota of Florida. Vol. 4. Fishes. University Presses of Florida, Gainesville. 58 pp.

Wright, A. H. 1926. The vertebrate life of Okefenokee Swamp in relation to the Atlantic Coastal Plain. Ecology 7(1):77–95.

Unpublished information

Fox, R. S., III. 1969. A study of the life history of the centrarchid *Enneacanthus gloriosus* (Holbrook) near the southern limit of its range. M.Sc. thesis, University of Florida, Gainesville.

McLane, W. M. 1955. The fishes of the St. Johns River system. Ph.D. diss., University of Florida, Gainesville.

Sweeney, E. F. 1972. The systematics and distribution of the centrarchid fish tribe Enneacanthini. Ph.D. diss., Boston University, Boston.

Prepared by: Carter R. Gilbert, *Florida Museum of Natural History, University of Florida, Gainesville, Florida 32611*; and Franklin F. Snelson, Jr., *Department of Biological Sciences, University of Central Florida, Orlando, Florida 32816.*

Bluenose Shiner

Pteronotropis welaka

FAMILY CYPRINIDAE

Order Cypriniformes

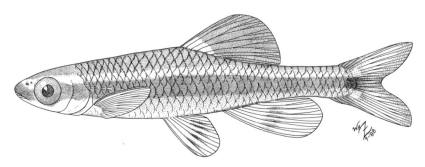

Bluenose shiner, *Pteronotropis welaka* (Evermann and Kendall, 1898). UF 43308. Adult male, 37.5 mm SL. Alexander Springs run, Lake County, Florida. 25 April 1985.

OTHER NAMES: None.

DESCRIPTION: A relatively small cyprinid species (maximum SL 53 mm), the bluenose shiner is characterized by a dark lateral stripe bordered above by a narrow light stripe that extends onto the snout; a dark caudal spot that is broadly joined to the lateral stripe and is bordered above and below by depigmented areas on the caudal fin (thus imparting a "halo" effect) and from which streaks of pigment extend posteriorly to the fork of the fin; 1,4–4,1 pharyngeal teeth; eight anal rays; no maxillary barbel at the corner of the mouth; a sharply pointed snout; the upper jaw longer than the lower (thus a slightly inferior mouth); and an incomplete lateral line. The two most prominent characters, however, which are well developed only in adults and are found only in one other species of North American Cyprinidae, are the caerulean blue nose (both sexes) and extensive development (males only) in both size and pigmentation of the dorsal, pelvic, and anal fins (usually these fins are darkly pigmented

188

throughout). Although adults are unmistakable, the young may be confused with several other species of black-striped Cyprinidae occurring in
southern lowland areas; this is particularly true with regard to *Notropis
chalybaeus*, which, like *Pteronotropis welaka*, normally has eight anal rays.
The most important characters to be looked for (in the bluenose shiner)
are the halo effect around the caudal spot, in company with the more
projecting and pointed snout and the slightly posterior position of the
dorsal fin in relation to the pelvics. In addition, *P. welaka* has 1,4–4,1
pharyngeal teeth, whereas these number 2,4–4,2 in *N. chalybaeus*.

TAXONOMIC COMMENTS: The bluenose shiner was previously placed in
the genus *Notropis* and was included in that genus in the earlier FCREPA

Distribution map of *Pteronotropis welaka*.

volume (Gilbert 1978). Placement in *Pteronotropis* follows Mayden (1989), who elevated to generic status this and several other groups previously considered subgenera of *Notropis*. Although superficially more similar to certain species still retained in *Notropis*, the bluenose shiner's closest relatives in Florida apparently are the sailfin and flagfin shiners, which are now also included in *Pteronotropis* (as *P. hypselopterus* and *P. signipinnis*, respectively).

Interestingly, the species to which *P. welaka* would appear to be most closely related is *Notropis hubbsi* (the bluehead shiner) of the lower Mississippi Valley. Despite remarkable similarities in overall appearance (caerulean blue on the head, together with markedly expanded and darkly pigmented dorsal, anal, and pelvic fins), as well as strong similarities in habitat preference, Dimmick (1987), on the basis of electrophoretic evidence, concluded that these species are not intimately related. However, Dimmick's conclusions differ from those of Amemiya and Gold (1990) who concluded, based on similarities of chromosomal NOR phenotypes, that *N. hubbsi* is closely related to *P. welaka* and thus is congeneric.

RANGE: *Pteronotropis welaka* occurs in lower sections of the Pearl River drainage in Mississippi and Louisiana, eastward to the lower Apalachicola River drainage in Florida, southeastern Alabama, and southwestern Georgia (Gilbert 1980). The species also occurs disjunctively in a limited area of the middle St. Johns River drainage in eastern peninsular Florida, having been recorded from the Oklawaha River upstream (i.e., south) to the Wekiva River in Seminole County. The species has never been found in the intervening 200 miles between the St. Johns and Apalachicola drainages and almost certainly does not occur there.

Generally speaking, the species can be found with reasonable consistency in the western parts of its range but is extremely difficult to find in the St. Johns drainage. Although originally described from the St. Johns River, near Welaka (Evermann and Kendall 1898), most subsequent collections from the drainage were taken by William McLane during his ichthyological survey during the late 1940s and early 1950s (McLane 1955). He collected the species on nine different occasions from 1948 through 1952 (data for four of these collections appear in Yerger and Suttkus [1962]) in the Oklawaha River, Alexander Springs run, Juniper Creek (at mouth), and the Wekiva River. Except for one series taken from the Wekiva River in 1956, only three other collections (a total of 13 specimens) have subsequently been taken from the drainage (in 1976, 1985, and 1988), all from Alexander Springs run at the state Highway 445 bridge in Lake County.

Discussions of the zoogeography of this and three other fish species displaying similarly isolated distributions in the middle St. Johns drainage appear in Burgess and Franz (1978) and in Gilbert (1987). Based on evidence presented, these species were believed to have reached this area during the Pliocene epoch (between 2 and 5 million years ago) or conceivably even earlier, with isolation from other populations likely having occurred during Pleistocene glacial maxima. At these times, lowered sea and groundwater levels would have resulted in increased percolation of water into the underlying limestone substrate, with a corresponding loss of surface water. Although this by itself would not have caused elimination of *P. welaka* and certain other fish species (many species obviously continued to survive in the Suwannee drainage), the related factors of a more restricted habitat and increased competition could well have resulted in the disappearance of some species, including the bluenose shiner.

HABITAT: The bluenose shiner inhabits quiet, often weedy waters, although aquatic vegetation is not an absolute requisite. Water may range from clear to turbid. More importantly, the species (particularly adults) typically occurs in deeper pools and holes of streams, where brush and other debris tend to accumulate, and the consequent difficulties of routine sampling in this type of habitat probably is a major contributing factor to the supposed rarity of this fish. It is not unusual to collect without success, as far as *P. welaka* is concerned, at localities where the species has been found in the past.

LIFE HISTORY AND ECOLOGY: The only available ecological information on the bluenose shiner apparently is McLane's (1955) unpublished observations on specimens from the St. Johns drainage. He found breeding males and females during June and September and suggested a prolonged breeding season extending from early spring into the fall. Examination of nine adult females indicated a herbivorous diet, the guts of all being filled exclusively with filamentous algae. Baker and Ross (1981) also included this species in their analysis of spatial and temporal resource partitioning among eight cyprinid species in southern Mississippi.

SPECIALIZED OR UNIQUE CHARACTERISTICS: As discussed previously, *P. welaka* is of geographical significance because it is one of four fish species having a disjunct population in the middle St. Johns River drainage. It is also one of the most attractive and colorful of all native North American cyprinid species, does well in aquaria, and is widely sought by native-fish hobbyists. Thus it is of potential commercial importance.

BASIS OF STATUS CLASSIFICATION: The bluenose shiner is here regarded as a species "of special concern," as was also true in the previous FCREPA report (Gilbert 1978). Although this designation results in part from the unusual disjunct range of the species, it should be noted that two of the other three species with similarly disjunct distributions have not been included in the present FCREPA list. A more important reason relates to the infrequency with which the species has been encountered in the St. Johns drainage during the past 30 or more years, specifically since 1956. Although hundreds of fish collections have been made in this drainage during that time, *P. welaka* has been taken on only three occasions, all from the Alexander Springs run locality indicated previously. Also, the Wekiva River locality has been visited on numerous occasions during this time, but the bluenose shiner has not been seen. The total population may have been reduced to some degree by Rodman Reservoir, although it should be noted that one of the two collection sites on the Oklawaha River is situated below the actual dam site. Although the bluenose shiner is, for some reason, undoubtedly very rare in the St. Johns drainage, we feel that the absence of the species from collections is partly a function of its habitat, which as a rule is very difficult to sample. Were a concerted effort made to collect this fish, using shocking gear and minnow traps, in appropriate places, particularly in the lowermost parts of streams tributary to the St. Johns River (including Lake George), it is likely that the species would be found.

RECOMMENDATIONS: None.

Literature Cited

Published Information

Amemiya, C., and J. R. Gold. 1990. Chromosomal NOR phenotypes of seven species of North American Cyprinidae, with comments on cytosystematic relationships of the *Notropis volucellus* species-group, *Opsopoeodus emiliae*, and the genus *Pteronotropis*. Copeia 1990(1):68–78.

Baker, J. A., and S. T. Ross. 1981. Spatial and temporal resource utilization by southeastern cyprinids. Copeia 1981(1):178–189.

Burgess, G. H., and R. Franz. 1978. Zoogeography of the aquatic fauna of the St. Johns River system with comments on adjacent peninsular faunas. Am. Midl. Nat. 100(1):160–170.

Dimmick, W. W. 1987. Phylogenetic relationships of *Notropis hubbsi, N. welaka,* and *N. emiliae* (Cypriniformes: Cyprinidae). Copeia 1987(2):316–325.

Evermann, B. W., and W. C. Kendall. 1898. Descriptions of new or little-known genera and species of fishes from the United States. Bull. U.S. Fish Comm. (1897) 17:125–133.

Gilbert, C. R. 1978. Bluenose shiner, *Notropis welaka* Evermann and Kendall. Pages 48–50 *in* Carter R. Gilbert, ed., Rare and endangered biota of Florida. Vol. 4. Fishes. University Presses of Florida, Gainesville, 58 pp.

———. 1980. *Notropis welaka* Evermann and Kendall, Bluenose shiner. Page 323 *in* D. S. Lee et al., eds., Atlas of North American freshwater fishes. North Carolina State Museum of Natural History, Raleigh. i–x+854 pp.

———. 1987. Zoogeography of the freshwater fish fauna of southern Georgia and peninsular Florida. Brimleyana 13:25–54.

Mayden, R. L. 1989. Phylogenetic studies of North American minnows, with emphasis on the genus *Cyprinella* (Teleostei: Cypriniformes). Misc. Publ. Univ. Kans. Mus. Nat. Hist. 80:1–189.

Yerger, R. W., and R. D. Suttkus. 1962. Records of freshwater fishes in Florida. Tulane Stud. Zool. 9(5):323–330.

Unpublished Information

McLane, W. M. 1955. The fishes of the St. Johns River system. Ph.D. diss., University of Florida, Gainesville.

Prepared by: Carter R. Gilbert, *Florida Museum of Natural History, University of Florida, Gainesville, Florida 32611.*

Lake Eustis Pupfish

Cyprinodon variegatus hubbsi

FAMILY CYPRINODONTIDAE

Order Cyprinodontiformes

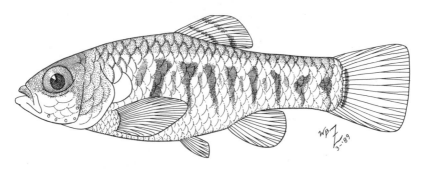

Lake Eustis pupfish, *Cyprinodon variegatus hubbsi* Carr, 1936. UF 68003. Adult female, 28.7 mm SL. Lake Weir, Lake County, Florida. 25 June 1967.

OTHER NAMES: None.

DESCRIPTION: *Cyprinodon variegatus hubbsi* is very similar to *Cyprinodon variegatus variegatus* (the typical subspecies) but can usually be distinguished by the following features: *C. variegatus hubbsi* is a smaller form, having a maximum standard length of 30–34 mm as opposed to 40–50 mm for *C. variegatus variegatus* (the Lake Dora population of *hubbsi* may be an exception, reaching a slightly larger maximum size). *Cyprinodon variegatus hubbsi* also has slightly lower average scale counts than the typical subspecies, as follows: dorsal-fin origin to midline of belly usually 15–16 in *hubbsi*, usually 17–21 in *variegatus*; dorsal-fin origin to pectoral-fin origin usually 11–12 in *hubbsi*, usually 12–15 in *variegatus*; body-circumference scales usually less than 30 in *hubbsi*, usually more than 30 in *variegatus*. *Cyprinodon variegatus hubbsi* also differs from the typical subspecies in several body proportions, with measurements for head depth, body depth, and interorbital width all averaging lower in *hubbsi* and the contour of the back at the dorsal-fin origin being much less elevated. Al-

194

though color pattern of the two subspecies is basically similar, in *hubbsi* it is much more pale overall.

TAXONOMIC REMARKS: Johnson (1974) studied the systematics of the Lake Eustis pupfish and concluded that this taxon, which previously had been recognized as a distinct species, was only subspecifically distinct from the widespread *C. variegatus.* Although the differences described above are distinctive, Johnson (1974) noted corresponding trends to-

Distribution map of *Cyprinodon variegatus hubbsi.* Open area on inset in central peninsular Florida indicates overall range of *C. variegatus hubbsi;* blackened areas elsewhere indicate range of *C. variegatus variegatus.* When taxonomy of *C. variegatus* is further clarified, range limits of species may be extended farther southward than indicated on inset.

ward reduction in both meristic values and morphometric depth measurements in other predominantly freshwater populations of *C. variegatus.*
These values and measurements, while extreme in *hubbsi,* are no more so
than would be expected in any population of *C. variegatus* that had been
isolated in fresh water for such an extended length of time. Johnson concluded that this may ultimately be correlated with decreased efficiency in
food conversion and physiological stress of this species in freshwater habitats. Nevertheless, he felt that recognition as a subspecies of *C. variegatus* was merited because of its degree of differentiation and unusual
habitat, together with its long period of isolation. Darling (1976), who
investigated electrophoretic characteristics of *C. variegatus hubbsi,* likewise concluded that species-level differentiation was not warranted. He
also found that genetically *C. variegatus hubbsi* bears a closer relationship
to the Gulf Coast population of *C. variegatus* rather than to the Atlantic
coast population.

Hildebrand and Schroeder (1928) noted that male *C. variegatus variegatus* reach a notably larger size than females, the average difference
being about 12 mm. This is in contrast to the situation among killifishes
in general and particularly in comparison to the closely related livebear-
ers, family Poeciliidae, in which females are invariably much larger.

RANGE: *Cyprinodon variegatus hubbsi* is endemic to central Florida, where
it is known only from Lakes Eustis, Harris, Dora, Griffin, and Yale in
Lake County; Lakes Beauclair and Carlton in Lake and Orange counties;
and Lake Weir in Marion County. These lakes are all interconnected and
form the headwaters of the Oklawaha River, which is the largest tributary
to the St. Johns River. Supposed populations from the Palm Beach area
(Christensen 1965) were identified as the typical subspecies by Johnson
(1974).

The distributions of the two subspecies of *C. variegatus* are sharply
limited by the Pleistocene Pamlico terrace, which is situated from 8–10 m
above present mean sea level. All records of the typical subspecies are
from below the terrace (Gilbert 1987, fig. 6). Stock from which the subspecies *hubbsi* evolved is believed to have reached the upper Oklawaha
area either during Pliocene or early Pleistocene times, when sea levels
were higher, and evolved to its present taxonomic level during the Pleistocene (Gilbert 1987). Guillory and Johnson (1986) discussed possible
migrational pathways into this area.

HABITAT: The Lake Eustis pupfish inhabits clean, white, sandy beaches
subject to heavy wave action and usually devoid of vegetation except for

sparse to moderate stands of *Panicum*. The species is most abundant in the wave-washed, shallow (less than 30 cm), narrow (30–90 cm wide) shoreline strip that may or may not be flanked by stands of emergent *Panicum*. The zone occupied is very narrow, but linearly may extend for long distances. *Cyprinodon variegatus hubbsi* is not common in deep water or in dense vegatation.

LIFE HISTORY AND ECOLOGY: No life-history studies have been conducted on the Lake Eustis pupfish, and the only specific information is that appearing in the earlier FCREPA report (Johnson and Snelson 1978). However, several studies have been published on various life-history aspects of *C. variegatus variegatus* (Hildebrand and Schroeder 1928; Raney et al. 1953). Kaill (1967) reviewed these and other related papers and provided original observations on behavior.

Spawning in the Lake Eustis pupfish probably occurs throughout much of the year. Mature ova are about one millimeter in diameter and an adult female carries between 7 and 29 (average 18) eggs at one time. It seems certain that a female spawns more than once during the year. The spawning act has not been described but probably is similar to that of *C. variegatus variegatus* (Raney et al. 1953). In that subspecies, the adult male assumes a distinctive coloration, consisting of a bright metallic-blue back and narrow black fin borders. Each male vigorously defends a small territory often around some fixed object. Near the center of the territory is a nest, a small saucer-shaped depression in the substrate. The male constructs the nest by vigorous sweeping motions of the body and occasionally by moving materials in the mouth. The nest and the entire territory are usually swept clean of silt by the incessant patrolling of the resident male. The male chases all invaders from his territory except receptive females, which are tersely courted. Spawning is consummated in a clasp, as eggs and milt are deposited. The site of deposition may be anywhere within the territory, not necessarily over the nest. The eggs are slightly heavier than seawater and are held together by minute adhesive strands.

Gunter (1945) and Springer and Woodburn (1960) found that, during colder months, individuals of *C. variegatus variegatus* move into deeper water, apparently in response to the warmer temperatures found there. Migration into deeper water by *C. variegatus hubbsi* during winter cold snaps has not yet been confirmed.

Johnson and Snelson (1978), citing McLane (1955), indicated that (on the basis of limited stomach analyses) *C. variegatus hubbsi* is carnivorous, feeding primarily on crustaceans and occasionally on aquatic insect larvae. No plant matter or sand was found among the stomach

contents. However, Hildebrand and Schroeder (1928) found the food of
C. variegatus variegatus from the Chesapeake Bay area to consist largely
of vegetable matter. They pointed out that the intestine of this fish is
long and convoluted, as is true for all species having a primarily herbivorous diet. However, they also noted that in the aquarium this fish feeds
readily on animal matter and has been observed to attack, kill, and feed
on other fish. The above observations indicate that *C. variegatus variegatus*, at least, has considerable dietary flexibility. Although it may be assumed that *C. variegatus hubbsi* is similar in this regard, this has yet to be
demonstrated.

SPECIALIZED OR UNIQUE CHARACTERISTICS: *Cyprinodon variegatus
hubbsi* is of interest because it represents a relictual population that
reached the upper Oklawaha River system at a time when sea levels were
higher than they are today. It also is of interest because it is the only endemic fish in the St. Johns River drainage.

BASIS OF STATUS CLASSIFICATION: The Lake Eustis pupfish was accorded "threatened" status in the 1978 FCREPA report. As a result, an
investigation was initiated by the Florida Game and Fresh Water Fish
Commission for the purpose of providing definitive information regarding this fish. These investigations indicated that *C. variegatus hubbsi*, despite heavy human population growth in the upper Oklawaha River system, continues to flourish within the limited microhabitat in which it
occurs. As a result, it was recommended that the species be considered a
species "of special concern," and this designation was adopted by the
commission in 1979 (Guillory and Johnson 1986). In concurrence with
this designation, the Lake Eustis pupfish is accordingly downgraded to
the same category here.

Literature Cited

Published Information

Gilbert, C. R. 1987. Zoogeography of the freshwater fish fauna of southern
    Georgia and peninsular Florida. Brimleyana 13:25–54.
Guillory, V., and W. E. Johnson. 1986. Habitat, conservation status, and zoogeo-
    graphy of the cyprinodont fish, *Cyprinodon variegatus hubbsi* (Carr). South-
    west. Nat. 31(1):95–100.
Gunter, G. 1945. Studies on marine fishes of Texas. Publ. Inst. Mar. Sci. Univ.
    Tex. 1(1):1–190.

Hildebrand, S. F., and W. C. Schroeder. 1928. Fishes of Chesapeake Bay. Bull. U.S. Bur. Fish. (1927) 43(1):1–366.

Johnson, W. E., and F. F. Snelson, Jr. 1978. Lake Eustis pupfish, *Cyprinodon variegatus hubbsi* Carr. Pages 15–17 *in* Carter R. Gilbert, ed., Rare and endangered biota of Florida. Vol. 4. Fishes. University Presses of Florida, Gainesville. 58 pp.

Raney, E. C., R. H. Backus, R. W. Crawford, and C. R. Robins. 1953. Reproductive behavior in *Cyprinodon variegatus* Lacepède, in Florida. Zoologica 38(2): 97–104.

Springer, V. G., and K. D. Woodburn. 1960. An ecological study of the fishes of the Tampa Bay area. Fla. St. Bd. Conserv. Mar. Lab. Prof. Pap. Ser. 1:1–104.

Unpublished Information

Christensen, R. F. 1965. An ichthyological survey of Jupiter Inlet and Loxahatchee River, Florida. M.Sc. thesis, Florida State University, Tallahassee.

Darling, J. 1976. Electrophoretic variation in *Cyprinodon variegatus* and systematics of some fishes of the subfamily *Cyprinodontidae*. Ph.D. diss., Yale University, New Haven.

Johnson, W. E. 1974. Morphological variation and local distribution of *Cyprinodon variegatus* in Florida. M.Sc. thesis, Florida Technological University, Orlando.

Kaill, W. M. 1967. Ecology and behavior of the cyprinodontid fishes *Jordanella floridae* (Goode and Bean), *Floridichthys carpio* (Günther), and *Cyprinodon variegatus* (Lacepède). Ph.D. diss. Cornell University, Ithaca.

McLane, W. M. 1955. The fishes of the St. Johns River system. Ph.D. diss., University of Florida, Gainesville.

Prepared by: Carter R. Gilbert, *Florida Museum of Natural History, University of Florida, Gainesville, Florida 32611*; William E. Johnson, *Florida Game and Fresh Water Fish Commission, Eustis, Florida 32726*; and Franklin F. Snelson, Jr., *Department of Biological Science, University of Central Florida, Orlando, Florida 32816.*

Mangrove Rivulus

Rivulus marmoratus

FAMILY APLOCHEILIDAE

Order Cyprinodontiformes

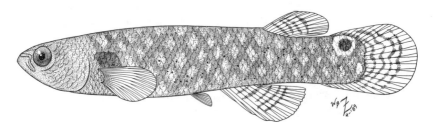

Mangrove rivulus, *Rivulus marmoratus* Poey, 1880. UF 59150. Adult, 37.6 mm SL. Ocean side of northern Key Largo, Monroe County, Florida. 25 March 1960.

OTHER NAMES: Rivulus.

DESCRIPTION: This is the only species of *Rivulus* found in North America. It is most similar superficially to killifishes of the genus *Fundulus*, from which it differs in possessing tubular anterior nares. It resembles the species of *Fundulus* in having a relatively long slender body, the dorsal and anal fin situated on the posterior third of the body, and a rounded caudal fin. As is true of some species of *Fundulus*, the dorsal-fin origin is situated distinctly posterior to the caudal fin. *Rivulus marmoratus* also differs from all other Florida killifishes in coloration. Overall body coloration is dark brown to almost maroon in wild specimens, with the sides of the body speckled with small black spots against a reticulated background. A prominent ocellus is situated on the upper part of the caudal-peduncle base in hermaphrodites. Males (which have only rarely been collected in Florida) lack the ocellus, and in addition they have a red-orange cast to the flanks and fins. Maximum total length given by Snelson (1978) is about 60 mm, but the largest specimen (of 51) recorded by Huehner et al. (1985) from Big Mangrove Key in the Florida Keys had a total length of only 49 mm (average size of specimens examined = 24 mm TL).

TAXONOMIC REMARKS: Seegers (1984) reduced *R. marmoratus* (type locality, Cuba) to a subspecies of *Rivulus ocellatus* Hensel 1868, the type locality of which is believed to be near Rio de Janeiro. He also retained *R. marmoratus bonairensis* Hoedeman 1958, which was described from Bonaire, as a subspecies. Only limited morphometric and meristic data

Distribution map of *Rivulus marmoratus*. Possible subspecies not distinguished on inset. If populations in South America (presently called *R. ocellatus*) are conspecific with *R. marmoratus*, range of species would extend southward to southern Brazil.

were presented, however. Seegers included black-and-white photographs of live specimens from Rio de Janeiro (*R. ocellatus ocellatus*) and Guadeloupe (*R. ocellatus bonairensis*). The individuals illustrated appear to be the same species, and they possess a pigmentation pattern similar to that found in a series of 11 specimens from Yucatan (UF 77253). It is entirely possible that the assessment of relationships by Seegers is correct and that *R. ocellatus* should be the correct name for the Florida population of *Rivulus*. Nevertheless, we feel that the data presented are not sufficiently complete to prove this categorically, and for the time being we retain the name *R. marmoratus* for the Florida population.

The genus *Rivulus* has usually been placed in the family Cyprinodontidae. It was recently transferred to the family Aplocheilidae, a group that traditionally had included only old-world genera (Nelson 1984). This revised classification is followed here.

RANGE: If Seegers (1984) is correct, the overall range of this species (*R. ocellatus*) extends from southern Florida south throughout the West Indies to coastal areas of northern South America (Cervigon 1973; Taphorn 1980) and south at least to Rio de Janeiro, Brazil. The range of *R. ocellatus marmoratus* has been defined as southern Florida, Cuba, the Bahamas, Jamaica, and Yucatan (Seegers 1984); it has also been collected on both Grand Cayman and Little Cayman islands (Huehner et al. 1985; UF 47430 [Little Cayman Island]). Although the inset map depicting the overall range that accompanies the present account shows it not to be present in Mexico west of the tip of the Yucatan peninsula, this may not be exactly accurate. In Florida, the mangrove rivulus occurs in coastal localities on the Atlantic coast as far north as Indian River County and the Melbourne area in Brevard County. According to the spot-distribution map accompanying this account, there appears to be a wide distributional gap to the south, between Indian River and Dade counties; however, we assume this to be a collecting artifact and believe the species to have (or to have once had) a general distribution along the lower east Florida coast. The species occurs in Dade County south throughout the Florida Keys (Fowler 1928; Gilbert and Burgess 1980; Huehner et al. 1985), and on the west coast in Collier County almost to Ft. Myers (Hastings 1969; Brockmann 1975). Although Loftus and Kushlan (1987) did not find it during their survey of extreme southern Florida, it almost certainly is present in coastal areas bordering Florida Bay (W. F. Loftus, personal communication). We cannot substantiate the reported occurrence of this species in the St. Petersburg area (Snelson 1978). A distribution map of

R. marmoratus (with localities spotted for the Florida portion of its range) appears in Gilbert and Burgess (1980).

HABITAT: Florida collections of the mangrove rivulus have been taken in or adjacent to mangrove swamps and high saltmarsh areas (Huehner et al. 1985; Abel et al. 1987; Davis et al. 1990). Specimens are most often collected in shallow stagnant water with heavy leaf litter, in isolated dry-ing pools, or in crab burrows (see discussion below). Fish will actually leave the water by burrowing through leaf litter (Huehner et al. 1985), and Brockmann (1975) reported a living specimen far from water in damp peat on Marco Island, Florida. The fish has been taken from a wide range of salinities, including fresh water, but most collections are from water of 20–35 ppt. Taylor (1989, 1990) has provided new insights into the presumed rarity of this species by demonstrating that it is widely dis-tributed and locally common (more than 350 collected) in the burrows of the great land crab, *Cardisoma guanhumi*, along the Indian River la-goon. Up to 26 individuals have been collected from a single crab bur-row. Beds of saltwort (*Batis maritima*) and glasswort (*Salicornia* spp.) seem to be especially attractive sites for land crab burrows along the east coast; burrows of other crab species may also be utilized, particularly along the west Florida coast, where *C. guanhumi* is not common. Addi-tional specimens have been found in this habitat in south Florida and the Florida Keys (Davis et al. 1990).

LIFE HISTORY AND ECOLOGY: The most striking aspect of the man-grove rivulus is its unique mode of reproduction. In Florida, at least, it functions as a synchronous self-fertilizing hermaphrodite, the only such example known among vertebrate animals. Harrington (1961, 1971) first investigated this phenomenon and described an ovotestis that simultane-ously produces eggs and sperm. An individual fertilizes its own eggs in-ternally, as has been conclusively proved by the laying of fertilized eggs by individual fish kept in total isolation from the egg stage onward. Since both eggs and sperm are produced by one parent, the young are geneti-cally identical to the parent; this unusually high degree of homozygosity places captive-reared specimens of the fish in high demand for use in ge-netic, immunochemical, and bioassay research. Male fish (gonochrists) are very rare in Florida but have been reported to be more common in the West Indies (Kristensen 1970) and Central America (Davis et al. 1990). Males are of two types, termed primary and secondary. Primary males develop directly from fertilized eggs, without going through the hermaphroditic phase. Primary males may also be produced from eggs incubated at low temperatures (Harrington 1967, 1971). Secondary males develop from hermaphroditic fish under certain ecological and experimental conditions. Normal biparental reproduction has not been demonstrated for the Florida population but has been reported from the West Indies (Kristensen 1970 [referring to *bonairensis*]); however, these observations have since been questioned, so that the function of males in this species remains an intriguing and still unanswered question. Little is known of the reproductive life history of *R. marmoratus* in the wild. Ritchie and Davis (1986) reported circumstantial evidence for aestivation or diapause of eggs in a mangrove forest substrate, and Taylor (1990) indicated that fish dwelling in crab burrows may deposit their eggs outside the burrow on the damp marsh surface, where they develop and hatch.

Huehner et al. (1985) examined stomach contents of 21 individuals from Big Mangrove Key. Four stomachs were empty, and they found combinations of mosquito larvae, springtails, polychaetes, copepods, small insects, fish scales, and vegetable matter in the remaining 17 individuals. Snelson (1978) also recorded small crabs and snails among the food items eaten. Taylor (1989) documented an instance of cannibalism in individuals dwelling in crab burrows. In captivity, *R. marmoratus* does poorly unless provided with live food (Harrington and Rivas 1958).

BASIS OF STATUS CLASSIFICATION: The mangrove rivulus is normally collected only accidentally, and at the time of the first FCREPA report (Snelson 1978) was known from only a few localities and from relatively few specimens. Most collections were from the Florida east coast, but even these were probably represented by a total of no more than 50 wild-caught specimens (R. W. Harrington also raised a number of individuals in captivity as offspring of specimens captured earlier). In addition, the coastal habitat inhabited by this species is especially vulnerable to human encroachment and development, and on this basis the species was accorded "threatened" status. Subsequently, William Dunson (Pennsylvania State University) on several occasions collected specimens in the Florida Keys incidental to other research projects, and Huehner et al. (1985) reported the collection of 51 specimens at one locality in the Florida Keys. W. P. Davis (personal communication) reported having collected over 100 individuals from Collier County, and Taylor's collections from the Indian River area total more than 350 specimens. It now appears that the species probably is generally distributed in favorable habitats along both coasts of lower peninsular Florida, although it has undoubtedly been eliminated from many areas, particularly along the lower east coast. The species probably also occurs along the southern rim of peninsular Florida, in the area bordering Florida Bay, although Loftus and Kushlan (1987) failed to collect any specimens during their extensive survey of southern Florida south of the Tamiami Trail (U.S. Highway 41). They did cite literature references, however, relating to the occurrence of this species in or near their area of study (Tabb and Manning 1961; Odum 1971). Ogden et al. (1976) identified mangrove rivulus among the food remains of wood storks from southern Florida. William F. Loftus (personal communication) feels that his and Kushlan's failure to collect this species during their survey was due both to the fact that their collections were confined to freshwater situations and also that they did not collect in the precise habitat (crab burrows) where this fish most likely would be found. Based on the above, the species almost certainly occurs within the boundaries of Everglades National Park. Considering the relatively wide distribution of *R. marmoratus* in coastal areas of southern Florida, as well as the protection afforded the species by the National Park, we feel that the species should properly be changed from "threatened" status to the category "of special concern." We acknowledge, however, that the species occurs in an unusually vulnerable habitat as far as human encroachment is concerned.

RECOMMENDATIONS: Continue to search for additional localities, particularly in areas bordering Florida Bay and within Everglades National Park. Studies on the life history and population dynamics of this species are underway.

ACKNOWLEDGMENTS: We would like to thank William P. Davis, Environmental Protection Agency, Pensacola, Florida, who reviewed this account and offered many valuable recommendations and suggestions.

Literature Cited

Abel, D. C., C. C. Koenig, and W. P. Davis. 1987. Emersion in the mangrove forest fish *Rivulus marmoratus*: a unique response to hydrogen sulfide. Environ. Biol. Fishes 18(1):67–72.

Brockmann, F. W. 1975. An unusual habitat for the fish *Rivulus marmoratus*. Fla. Sci. 38:35–36.

Cervigon, F. 1973. Los peces marinos de Venezuela. Complemento III. Contrib. Cient. Univ. Oriente 4:3–70.

Davis, W. P., D. S. Taylor, and B. J. Turner. 1990. Field observations of the ecology and habits of mangrove rivulus (*Rivulus marmoratus*) in Belize and Florida. Ichthyol. Explor. Freshwaters 1(2):123–134.

Fowler, H. W. 1928. Fishes from Florida and the West Indies. Proc. Acad. Nat. Sci. Phila. 80:451–473.

Gilbert, C. R., and G. H. Burgess. 1980. *Rivulus marmoratus* Poey, Rivulus. Page 536 *in* D. S. Lee et al., eds., Atlas of North American freshwater fishes. North Carolina State Museum of Natural History, Raleigh. i–x+854 pp.

Harrington, R. W., Jr. 1961. Oviparous hermaphroditic fish with internal self-fertilization. Science 134(3492):1749–1750.

———. 1967. Environmentally controlled induction of primary male gonochrists from eggs of the self-fertilizing hermaphroditic fish, *Rivulus marmoratus* Poey. Biol. Bull. Woods Hole, Mass. 132:174–199.

———. 1971. How ecological and genetic factors interact to determine when self-fertilizing hermaphrodites of *Rivulus marmoratus* change into functional secondary males, with a reappraisal of the modes of intersexuality among fishes. Copeia 1971(3):389–432.

Harrington, R. W., Jr., and L. R. Rivas. 1958. The discovery in Florida of the cyprinodont fish, *Rivulus marmoratus*, with a redescription and ecological notes. Copeia 1958(2):125–130.

Hastings, R. W. 1969. *Rivulus marmoratus* Poey from the west coast of Florida. Q. J. Fla. Acad. Sci. 32(1):37–38.

Huehner, M. K., M. E. Schramm, and M. D. Hens. 1985. Notes on the behavior and ecology of the killifish *Rivulus marmoratus* Poey 1880 (Cyprinodontidae). Fla. Sci. 48(1):1–7.

Kristensen, I. 1970. Competition in three cyprinodont fish species in the Netherland Antilles. Stud. Fauna Curacao Carib. Isl. Utig. Natuurw. Studkring. Suriname 32:82–101.

Loftus, W. F., and J. A. Kushlan. 1987. Freshwater fishes of southern Florida. Bull. Fla. St. Mus. Biol. Sci. 31(4):147–344.

Nelson, J. S. 1984. Fishes of the world. Wiley, New York. xv+523 pp.

Odum, W. E. 1971. Pathways of energy flow in a south Florida estuary. Univ. Miami Sea Grant Tech. Bull. 7.

Ogden, J. D., J. A. Kushlan, and J. T. Tilmant. 1976. Prey selectivity by the wood stork. Condor 78:324–330.

Ritchie, S. A., and W. P. Davis. 1986. Evidence for embryonic diapause in *Rivulus marmoratus*: laboratory and field observations. J. Amer. Killifish Assoc. 19(1):103–108.

Seegers, L. 1984. Zur revision der *Rivulus*-arten Sudost-Brasiliens, mit einer Neubeschreibung von *Rivulus luelingi* n. sp. und. *Rivulus caudomarginatus* n. sp. (Pisces: Cyprinodontidae: Rivulinae). Zool. Beitr. N.F. 28:271–320.

Snelson, F. F., Jr. 1978. Rivulus, *Rivulus marmoratus* Poey. Pages 18–19 *in* Carter R. Gilbert, ed., Rare and endangered biota of Florida. Vol. 4. Fishes. University Presses of Florida, Gainesville. 58 pp.

Tabb, D. C., and R. B. Manning. 1961. A checklist of the flora and fauna of northern Florida Bay and adjacent brackish waters of the Florida mainland collected during the period July, 1957 through September, 1960. Bull. Mar. Sci. Gulf Carib. 11:552–649.

Taphorn, D. C. 1980. First record of *Rivulus marmoratus* Poey, 1880 from the South American continent. Zool. Meded. 55:127–129.

Taylor, D. S. 1989. Observations on the ecology of the killifish *Rivulus marmoratus* Poey (Cyprinodontidae) in an infrequently flooded mangrove swamp. Northeast Gulf Sci. 10(1):63–68.

———. 1990. Adaptive specializations of the cyprinodont fish *Rivulus marmoratus*. Fla. Sci. 53(3):239–248.

Prepared by: D. Scott Taylor, *Brevard Mosquito Control District, Titusville, Florida 32780*; and Franklin F. Snelson, Jr., *Department of Biological Sciences, University of Central Florida, Orlando, Florida 32816*.

Mangrove Gambusia

Gambusia rhizophorae

FAMILY POECILIIDAE

Order Cyprinodontiformes

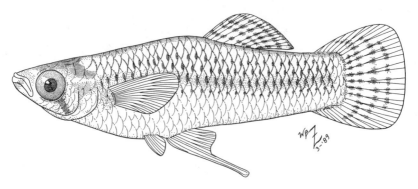

Mangrove gambusia, *Gambusia rhizophorae* Rivas, 1969. UF 34915. Adult male, 29.5 mm SL. Artificial stream, tributary to Snapper Creek Canal, in Parrot Jungle, South Miami, Dade County, Florida. 23 January 1981.

OTHER NAMES: Mangrove mosquitofish.

DESCRIPTION: *Gambusia rhizophorae* belongs to the *Gambusia punctata* species group of the subgenus *Gambusia* Poey, as defined by Rivas (1963). The four subgenera comprising the genus *Gambusia*, as well as the individual species groups, are distinguished entirely by gonopodial characters, which have been discussed and illustrated by Rivas (1963, 1969). The mangrove gambusia is characterized by having the spots overshadowing (vs. not overshadowing) the reticulate pattern formed by dark margins of the scale pockets; sides of body with four to six (usually five) longitudinal rows of conspicuous dark spots, the lowermost along the row of scales below the midlateral row, sometimes another row below the latter; dorsal fin crossed by two or three rows of spots; caudal fin crossed by two to four rows of spots; gill rakers on outer (first) arch usually 15 or 16 (range 14–18); and branched caudal rays usually 16 (range 15–17).

208

It is distinguished from its closest congener, *G. punctata*, in having the
dorsal rays usually 9 (vs. usually 10 or 11, range 8–10); lateral scales usually 29 or 30 (vs. usually 31 or 32, range 28–31); origin of anal fin
midway between tip of mandible and middle of caudal base or nearer to
caudal base in males (vs. nearer to tip of mandible than middle of caudal
base); depressed dorsal fin shorter than distance between tip of snout and
insertion of pectoral fin in males (vs. equal to or [usually] longer than
this distance); dorsal base equal to or shorter (vs. longer) than snout in
females; and ray three spines in gonopodium of males usually 13–16 (vs.
usually 10–12; range 13 to 17).

Distribution map of *Gambusia rhizophorae*.

RANGE *Gambusia rhizophorae* has a limited distribution, being restricted to extreme southeastern Florida and northwestern Cuba in and around Havana. In Florida, it occurs as far north as Ft. Lauderdale, south to extreme eastern Florida Bay, and throughout much of the Florida Keys west to Key West (Getter 1980, 1982).

HABITAT: The mangrove gambusia occurs mostly in brackish and salt water, where it is found around red mangrove roots. Although salinities at collection sites in Florida ranged from 13.0 to 53.0 ppt, it can tolerate fresh water in aquaria and has been recorded from natural fresh waters in Cuba (Getter 1982). *Gambusia holbrooki*, the only other member of the genus known from Florida, may occur syntopically with *G. rhizophorae* in red mangrove habitats, but replaces the mangrove gambusia in freshwater habitats around the state.

LIFE HISTORY AND ECOLOGY: Getter (1976) studied the systematics, distribution, and biology of *G. rhizophorae* and subsequently summarized part of this work in two publications (Getter 1980, 1982). He indicated that the species feeds on floating terrestrial insects, is sexually inactive in winter and reaches its reproductive peak in spring, has broods ranging in size from 2 to 65 individuals (mean 13.4), and apparently only lives one year or less (Getter 1980). It also hybridizes naturally with *G. holbrooki*. Getter (1982) also found the acute lower temperature tolerance to be 17° C and determined that the northern limit of distribution in Florida corresponds very closely with the 16.7° C isotherm. He theorized that "failure of the mangrove mosquitofish to be found in fresh waters of southern Florida or in Florida Bay . . . may be due to the inability of the species to move across this isotherm which would require the species to tolerate lower temperature." He also determined that the fertility index of the species corresponds very closely with temperature and that females are not reproductively viable when temperatures drop too low. He reasoned that this might also be a factor contributing to the failure of this species to invade the cooler freshwater habitats in Florida.

As indicated, *G. rhizophorae* occurs syntopically with *G. holbrooki* in Florida. In Cuba, it may occur syntopically with *Gambusia puncticulata* and sympatrically (but not syntopically) with *G. punctata*. Rivas (1969) indicated that wherever *G. rhizophorae* has been found with either *G. holbrooki* or *G. punctata*, it is greatly outnumbered by the last two species. Nothing was said by him regarding the relative abundance of *G. puncticulata* and *G. rhizophorae*. Franklin F. Snelson (*in* Gilbert 1978) indicated that *G. rhizophorae* appears to be more nocturnal than *G. holbrooki*, and this probably is an important factor in segregating the two species eco-logically where they occur together.

SPECIALIZED OR UNIQUE CHARACTERISTICS: The mangrove gambu-sia, although not strictly endemic to southern Florida, nevertheless is found only in a very limited area elsewhere. Thus, it is one of the more unusual biotic elements in the state.

BASIS OF STATUS CLASSIFICATION: The statement regarding status classification that appeared in the earlier FCREPA account (1978) is also applicable here. The mangrove gambusia remains in the category of "spe-cial concern" because of its restriction to southern Florida, where much of its range is confined to the Miami area and the adjacent Florida Keys. Both of these areas are under heavy pressure because of development and increasing human population. Its ecological restriction to mangrove areas, however, could be a positive factor contributing to continued survival in the area. Franklin F. Snelson (personal communication) has indicated that he was recently unable to locate the species in several areas where he had found it earlier; however, since this was apparently based on limited collecting effort, it is much too early to tell whether this might be indica-tive of a general decline in the species.

RECOMMENDATIONS: Preserve suitable mangrove areas where *Gambu-sia rhizophorae* is known to or might possibly occur.

Literature Cited

Published Information

Getter, C. D. 1980. *Gambusia rhizophorae* Rivas, Mangrove gambusia. Page 545 *in* D. S. Lee et al., eds., Atlas of North American freshwater fishes. North Caro-lina State Museum of Natural History, Raleigh. i–x+854 pp.

———. 1982. Temperature limitations to the distribution of mangrove mosquito-fish in Florida. Fla. Sci. 45(3):196–200.

Gilbert, C. R. 1978. Mangrove gambusia, *Gambusia rhizophorae* Rivas. Pages 55–56 *in* Carter R. Gilbert, ed., Rare and endangered biota of Florida. Vol. 4. Fishes. University Presses of Florida, Gainesville. 58 pp.

Rivas, L. R. 1963. Subgenera and species groups in the poeciliid fish genus *Gam-busia* Poey. Copeia 1963(2):331–347.

———. 1969. A revision of the poeciliid fishes of the *Gambusia punctata* species group, with descriptions of two new species. Copeia 1969(4): 778–795.

Unpublished Information

Getter, C. D. 1976. The systematics and biology of *Gambusia rhizophorae*, with an account of its hybridization with *Gambusia affinis* and *Gambusia punctata*. M.Sc. thesis, University of Miami, Coral Gables.

Prepared by: Carter R. Gilbert, *Florida Museum of Natural History, University of Florida, Gainesville, Florida 32611.*

Key Silverside

Menidia conchorum

FAMILY ATHERINIDAE

Order Atheriniformes

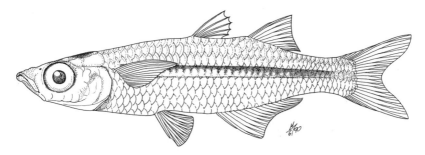

Key silverside, *Menidia conchorum* Hildebrand and Ginsburg, 1927. UF 77204. Adult, 38.0 mm SL. Grassy Key, Monroe County, Florida. 27 August 1978.

OTHER NAMES: None.

DESCRIPTION: *Menidia conchorum* is the smallest known species of *Menidia*, the largest specimen recorded measuring only 53 mm (about 2 in) SL. It is distinguished from the other six members of the genus by a lower anal-ray count (usually 12–15 vs. usually 16–18); fewer branchial lateral-line scales (usually 33–36 vs. usually 37–39); and fewer total vertebrae (usually 36–38 vs. usually 39–41).

TAXONOMIC REMARKS: Although the characters listed above appear to provide a clearcut separation of *M. conchorum* from the closely related and morphologically similar *Menidia peninsulae* and *Menidia beryllina*, none will permit absolute separation throughout their entire geographic ranges. In addition, the level of distinctiveness also differs according to geographic area. The most extreme example involves separation of *M. conchorum* from *M. beryllina* specimens from Key Largo; there one obtains only about a 25% separation in anal-ray counts and no separation at

213

all in lateral-line scale or vertebral counts, as opposed to an 80%–90% separation for specimens from elsewhere. Specimens of *M. beryllina* from Key Largo are thus extremely difficult to distinguish from *M. conchorum* (which does not occur there), even though these two species (based on electrophoretic data) are less intimately related than is *M. conchorum* to *M. peninsulae* (see subsequent discussion). *Menidia peninsulae* does not occur in the Florida Keys.

It may be assumed that the characters given by Chernoff et al. (1981) to separate *M. peninsulae* from *M. beryllina* will (for reasons to be discussed below) also permit separation of *M. conchorum* and *M. beryllina*, although substantiating data have not yet been formally presented. They

Distribution map of *Menidia conchorum*.

found that the distance between the origin of the spinous dorsal and anal fins is greater for *M. peninsulae* than for *M. beryllina* (9%–11% vs. 4%–6% of SL) and that this difference is also reflected in the number of vertebrae between these two points (four in *M. peninsulae* vs. two in *M. beryllina*).

The systematics of the genus *Menidia* are extremely complex. Clinal variation in meristic characters within species is common, and some species are very similar morphologically. In addition, the genus displays some interesting and complex sex mechanisms, as shown by the all-female species *Menidia clarkhubbsi*, which was recently described from coastal Texas (Echelle and Mosier 1982). Electrophoretic studies have proved invaluable in resolving a number of taxonomic problems and in establishing phylogenetic relationships within the genus (Johnson 1975). One such study (Duggins et al. 1986) has shown that *M. conchorum* not only is much more closely related to *M. peninsulae* than to the morphologically similar *M. beryllina* but in fact is electrophoretically indistinguishable from *M. peninsulae*. The geographically closest populations of *M. peninsulae*, however, apparently occur in the Sebastian Inlet area on the lower east coast of Florida and around Marco Island on the west coast. *Menidia beryllina* ranges south into the upper Florida Keys (Key Largo), however, where it comes in very close geographic proximity to the most northern populations of *M. conchorum*. Meristic counts for the Key Largo population of *M. beryllina* are unusually low, represent the end of a north-south cline, and are virtually identical to those of *M. conchorum*. *Menidia peninsulae* and *M. beryllina* exhibit similar meristic clines elsewhere. It could be predicted that were the geographic range of the former species to extend southward into the northern Florida Keys, individuals would display the same meristic characteristics as *M. beryllina*, and that it would also grade imperceptibly into *M. conchorum*. It was on this basis that Duggins et al. (1986) chose to regard *M. conchorum* as conspecific with *M. peninsulae*.

RANGE: This species is known from the Florida Keys (Key West to Long Key) in Monroe County, Florida.

HABITAT: Duggins et al. (1986) listed the habitat of *M. conchorum* as shallow, protected, coraline pools surrounded by mangroves and often mats of organic debris. Although essentially a marine fish, it is nevertheless tolerant of a wide range of salinities. Aquatic vegetation (*Thalassia, Diplanthera, Acetabularia*) is often but not always present.

LIFE HISTORY AND ECOLOGY: The biology of this species was studied

by Charles Getter of the University of Miami. He found that the key silverside subsists on a diet of animal microorganisms, with copepods,
mysids, isopods, amphipods, and insects the most important. Females of
M. conchorum with well-developed eggs in the ovary were collected on 10
January (Robins and Getter 1975). Based on this observation, the spawning period probably occurs during middle to late winter. The numerous
eggs have long, thread-like garnitures attached to a single stalk. Duggins
et al. (1986) listed seven fish species (five cyprinodontids, one poeciliid,
and one belonid) regularly collected together with *M. conchorum*. They
indicated that the hardhead silverside (*Atherinomorus stipes*), which Robbins (1969) and Gilbert (1978) had indicated as being a common asso-
ciate of *M. conchorum*, is usually found in more exposed open waters, and
they collected the two together only once, on Rockland Key. *Menidia conchorum* is a diurnal species and occurs in fast-moving schools. Duggins et
al. (1986) hypothesized that the rapid-swimming capability and inaccess-
ible habitat are primarily responsible for the difficulties others have experienced collecting the fish during the day. They found that the fish is
more easily collected at night, when it is found in more shallow water
(<10 cm deep) among black mangrove rhizomes, where it presumably is
less vulnerable to predation.

SPECIALIZED OR UNIQUE CHARACTERISTICS: *Menidia conchorum* is
entirely confined to the Florida Keys. It is of scientific interest because of
the historical and biological implications of its limited range and its present geographical separation from the closely related (and perhaps conspecific) *M. peninsulae*. The debate as to whether the key silverside should
be considered a distinct species does not detract from the fact that it represents a distinct and geographically isolated taxonomic unit.

BASIS OF STATUS CLASSIFICATION: The key silverside is currently classified as "threatened" by the state of Florida based largely on the original
recommendations of the first FCREPA committee. When the first report
was prepared, *M. conchorum* was known only from a few localities on Key
West, Big Pine, and Cudjo keys. At that time, the species was reported as
having disappeared from Key West and that situation apparently still
holds true. Subsequently, however, the species was collected in conjunction with studies by Duggins, at other localities on Big Pine Key, as well
as on Rockland, Grassy, and Long keys; and there are present in the Florida Museum of Natural History a total of 17 cataloged lots totaling 418
specimens that were collected during this time. Although the fish cannot
really be considered common, at the same time its supposed rarity un-

doubtedly results in large degree from its elusiveness and the inaccessibility of its habitat to routine collecting. Based on this, we recommend downgrading *M. conchorum* to the category "of special concern."

RECOMMENDATIONS: Populations of the key silverside should be periodically monitored to ensure that additional habitat degradation has not occurred, and additional effort should be made to find additional populations.

Literature Cited

Published Information

Chernoff, B., J. V. Conner, and C. F. Bryan. 1981. Systematics of the *Menidia beryllina* complex (Pisces: Atherinidae) from the Gulf of Mexico and its tributaries. Copeia 1981(2):319–336.

Duggins, C. F., Jr., A. A. Karlin, K. Relyea, and R. W. Yerger. 1986. Systematics of the key silverside, *Menidia conchorum* with comments on other *Menidia* species (Pisces: Atherinidae). Tulane Stud. Zool. Bot. 25(2):133–150.

Echelle, A. A., and D. T. Mosher. 1982. *Menidia clarkhubbsi*, n.sp. (Pisces: Atherinidae), an all-female species. Copeia 1982(4):533–540.

Gilbert, C. R. 1978. Key silverside, *Menidia conchorum* Hildebrand and Ginsburg. Pages 1–2 *in* C. R. Gilbert, ed., Rare and endangered biota of Florida. Vol. 4. Fishes. University Presses of Florida, Gainesville. 58 pp.

Johnson, M. S. 1975. Biochemical systematics of the atherinid genus *Menidia*. Copeia 1975(4):662–691.

Unpublished information

Robbins, T. W. 1969. A systematic study of the silversides *Membras* Bonaparte and *Menidia* Linnaeus (Atherinidae, Teleostei). Ph.D. diss., Cornell University, Ithaca.

Robins, C. R., and C. D. Getter. 1975. The biology and management of the Key silverside, *Menidia conchorum*, an endangered, endemic Florida species. Research proposal submitted to U.S.F.W. Service. 9 pp.

Prepared by: Carter R. Gilbert, *Florida Museum of Natural History, University of Florida, Gainesville, Florida 32611.*

Striped Croaker

Bairdiella sanctaeluciae

FAMILY SCIAENIDAE

Order Perciformes

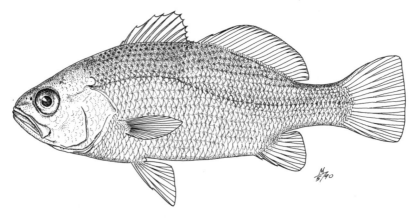

Striped croaker, *Bairdiella sanctaeluciae* (Jordan, 1890). UF 12031. Adult, 134 mm SL. Atlantic Ocean S of Sebastian Inlet, Indian River County, Florida. 12–13 June 1964.

OTHER NAMES: Caimuire

DESCRIPTION: *Bairdiella sanctaeluciae* is distinguished from its closest relatives in Florida waters by the following characteristics: from *Bairdiella chrysoura* (silver perch) by lack of serrations on preopercular margin, second anal spine less than two-thirds the length of first anal-soft ray, and gold to rusty stripes on body in life; from *Bairdiella batabana* (blue croaker) by greater body depth (31.5% SL vs. 28.6% SL), higher total gill-raker count (23–26 vs. 18–22), and lower dorsal-fin ray count (XI–I, 23 [range 22–24] vs. XI–I,26 [range 25–29]); from *Odontoscion dentex* (reef croaker) by absence of canine teeth (particularly in lower jaw) and in lacking a black spot at base of pectoral fin; and from *Larimus fasciatus* (banded drum) in having neither an oblique mouth nor projecting lower

218

jaw and in having a higher anal-fin ray count (II,8 vs. II,5–6). The maximum body size is 260 mm SL (10.2 in).

RANGE: *Bairdiella sanctaeluciae* is a tropical species whose range is centered primarily in the Caribbean Sea, including the Central American coast and the Greater and Lesser Antilles south to Guyana; to the north it occurs disjunctly in the Gulf of Campeche and east-central Florida (Jordan and Evermann 1898; Evermann and Marsh 1900; Meek and Hildebrand 1925; Cervigon 1966; Gilbert and Kelso 1971; Gilmore 1977; Chao 1978). It was first recorded from Florida waters by C. R. Gilbert from collections made in the Atlantic Ocean south of Sebastian

Distribution map of *Bairdiella sanctaeluciae.*

Inlet, adjacent to the Indian River lagoon (Bailey et al. 1970; Gilbert 1973).

During fish surveys conducted from 1972 to 1988, striped croakers were consistently observed on near-shore rock-algal reef formations (depth 10 m or less) from Sebastian Inlet south to Jupiter Inlet but not north of 28°00′N or south of 26°58′N (R. G. Gilmore, personal observation). Adults have been captured on reef formations at depths to 30 m within the same latitudinal range (R. G. Gilmore, personal observation). The species has never been found during intensive studies of reef-fish populations elsewhere around the Florida peninsula. The very limited distribution on the east coast of Florida parallels that of several other fish species and may be attributed to the occurrence of the proper habitat under optimal hydrological conditions, undoubtedly promoted by the near-shore occurrence of the warm Florida current (Gilmore 1977).

HABITAT: Very little has been published on the habitat of *B. sanctaeluciae* in the Caribbean region, other than general statements that it occurs over mud and sand bottoms or around rocks (Cervigon 1966; Chao 1978). However, there is considerably more information on the habitat preference of Florida populations, based on surveys conducted between 1972 and 1988 using submersible vehicles for 70 dives and scuba gear for 82 dives (R. G. Gilmore, personal observation). Striped croakers prefer rock-reef habitats, which typically support luxuriant growths of attached algae. Juveniles (15–50 mm SL) have consistently been observed hovering over mats of accumulated algae, into which they retreat when disturbed. Juveniles are most abundant on near-shore reef formations at depths less than 10 m. Adults may occur on these same shallow reefs but prefer deeper formations to depths of 30 m.

Despite intensive quantitative sampling over the years, only one small juvenile striped croaker has ever been recorded from the adjacent Indian River lagoon, where it was captured adjacent to an ocean inlet (Gilmore 1977). Absence from the estuary precludes syntopy (cooccurrence at the same specific location or microhabitat) with its congener, *B. chrysoura*, which is an estuarine species. Striped croakers and reef croakers (*O. dentex*) are syntopic and are commonly observed under the same rock formation; however, the former species is usually represented by gregarious juveniles, whereas the reef croaker is restricted to solitary adults.

It is doubtful that Florida populations of *B. sanctaeluciae* occur over open mud or sand bottoms very often or for any length of time since this species has never been captured during a wide variety of trawling surveys made on the east Florida shelf over the past 40 years.

LIFE HISTORY AND ECOLOGY: Nothing is known regarding the life history and ecology of this species other than the information appearing above. Most observations have been of juveniles occurring in groups of 10 to 50 individuals. However, no quantitative studies have been conducted to determine population sizes. The algal community with which this species is closely associated likely harbors a unique group of invertebrates (e.g., shrimp; Chao 1978) on which this species presumably feeds.

SPECIALIZED OR UNIQUE CHARACTERISTICS: *Bairdiella sanctaeluciae* is one of a group of species of basically Caribbean affinities that maintains an isolated population along the east-central coast of Florida and that is presumed to have reached this area via transportation by the Gulf Stream. The striped croaker also is unusual with regard to the very specific habitat to which it is restricted.

BASIS OF STATUS CLASSIFICATION: The highly specific habitat occupied by the striped croaker is vulnerable to beachfront activities, especially beach-renourishment projects and dredge-and-fill operations, which serve to increase sedimentation and water turbidity and often cover rock formations directly. The algal community, which supports not only juvenile striped croakers but also a specific group of invertebrates, has received little study. The impact on this floral community and the unique species that it supports should be considered when evaluating all beach-renourishment projects, particularly those contemplated within the range of Florida populations of the striped croaker.

Although the habitat in which this species occurs is vulnerable to certain human activities and the length of Florida coast occupied by the species is not extensive, it nevertheless seems that assignment of "threatened" status is inappropriate at this time. Likewise, the species is common within the area to which it is confined. Considering these factors, we feel that the species is most properly placed in the category "of special concern."

RECOMMENDATIONS: Discourage dredge-and-fill operations in areas adjacent to near-shore rock and reef formations. Designate known reef croaker habitat as a wildlife preserve.

Literature Cited

Bailey, R. M., J. E. Fitch, E. S. Herald, E. A. Lachner, C. C. Lindsey, C. R. Robins, and W. B. Scott. 1970. A list of common and scientific names of fishes from the United States and Canada. Am. Fish. Soc. Spec. Publ. 6. 77 pp.

Chao, L. N. 1978. Sciaenidae. *In* W. Fischer, ed., FAO species identification sheets for fishery purposes: Western Central Atlantic (fishing area 31). Vol. 4.

Cervigon, F. M. 1966. Los peces marinos de Venezuela. Vol. 2. Fundacion La Salle de Ciencias Naturales, Caracas, pp. 449–951.

Evermann, B. W., and M. C. Marsh. 1900. The fishes of Porto Rico. *In* Investigations of the aquatic resources and fisheries of Porto Rico. Bull. U.S. Fish Comm. (1900) 20(1):51–350, pls. 1–46.

Gilbert, C. R. 1973. Characteristics of the western Atlantic reef-fish fauna. Q. J. Fla. Acad. Sci. (1972) 35(2–3):130–144.

Gilbert, C. R., and D. P. Kelso. 1971. Fishes of the Tortuguero area, Caribbean Costa Rica. Bull. Fla. St. Mus. Biol. Sci. 16(1):1–54.

Gilmore, R. G. 1977. Fishes of the Indian River lagoon and adjacent waters, Florida. Bull. Fla. St. Mus. Biol. Sci. 22(3):101–147.

Jordan, D. S., and B. W. Evermann. 1898. Fishes of North and Middle America. Bull. U.S. Nat. Mus. 47(2):v–xxx, 1241–2183.

Meek, S. E., and S. F. Hildebrand. 1925. The marine fishes of Panama. Field Mus. Nat. Hist. Publ. 226 (Zool. Ser.) 15:xv–xix, 331–707.

Prepared by: R. Grant Gilmore, *Harbor Branch Oceanographic Institution, Ft. Pierce, Florida 33450*; and Franklin F. Snelson, Jr., *Department of Biological Sciences, University of Central Florida, Orlando, Florida 32816.*

Spottail Goby

Gobionellus stigmaturus

FAMILY GOBIIDAE

Order Perciformes

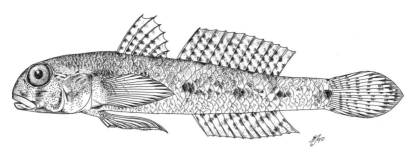

Spottail goby, *Gobionellus stigmaturus* (Goode and Bean, 1882). UF 37133. Adult male, 29.0 mm SL. Intercoastal waterway, N of Jupiter Inlet, Palm Beach County, Florida. 13 June 1983.

OTHER NAMES: None

DESCRIPTION: The spottail goby is a "coarse-scaled" species of *Gobionellus*, having 29–33 scales in the longitudinal series along the midside of the body, dorsal rays VI–12 (I,11), anal rays 13 (I,12), and pectoral-fin rays usually 16 (range 15–17). Other distinguishing characters include a completely scaled predorsal area, 10–12 scales anterior to dorsal-fin origin, except specimens from southern Florida, which have 4–7 predorsal scales in this area (this area largely or completely naked in all other coarse-scaled members of the genus except *Gobionellus smaragdus*); a narrow band of pigment paralleling posterior margin of cheek; a diffuse blotch of pigment on cheek under eye, extending from eye to upper lip; third dorsal spine in adult males not excessively long, not reaching origin of second dorsal fin; body and head marbled with pearly white and brown in life; five more-or-less diffuse spots along midside of body, the most posterior one situated at base of tail; diffuse narrow bars extending

223

downward and slightly forward from anterior three or four spots described above; dorsal and caudal fins with streaks of pigment comprised
of rows of spots.

RANGE: *Gobionellus stigmaturus* is known from Bermuda, Florida, Cuba,
Belize, and Panama (Pezold 1984), with Florida populations being limited to the southeast coast from Brevard to Monroe counties.

HABITAT: The spottail goby has been consistently collected in sea-grass
meadows during the cool-dry season (December to May) in Ft. Pierce
Inlet (Springer and McErlean 1962; Christensen 1965; Gilmore 1988).

Distribution map of *Gobionellus stigmaturus*.

The only detailed habitat-microhabitat observations for the species were made in Ft. Pierce Inlet during recent sea-grass fish-community studies (Gilmore 1988; R. G. Gilmore, personal observation). Spottail gobies have been observed primarily in vegetated areas with sand bottom in sea-grass meadows of *Syringodium filiforme* and *Halodule wrightii*. Some individuals have been observed in burrows on sandbars in very shallow water (<0.5 m depth), in areas situated between a steep inlet channel dropoff and a sea-grass meadow.

LIFE HISTORY AND ECOLOGY: *Gobionellus stigmaturus* appears to undergo seasonal migrations between sea-grass meadows and burrow areas. The species is more common in the former areas during winter and spring, in places where the water is typically deeper (ca. 1.0 m). Spottail gobies have not been seen at locations away from the Ft. Pierce Inlet and are gradually replaced by *Gobionellus boleosoma* and *G. smaragdus* as one approaches the mangrove-lined shore 100 m away. The principal microhabitat for this species thus appears to be a strictly marine environment at the outer edges of ocean inlet sea-grass meadows.

Sea-grass beds are subject to ecological changes from both natural and anthropogenic processes. Sediment movement through ocean inlets can be dramatic, particularly when associated with storm events, and sea-grass meadows may be periodically covered and uncovered at such times.

BASIS OF STATUS CLASSIFICATION: As indicated above, sea-grass beds are sensitive to direct and indirect disturbances. Dredge-and-fill operations, boat traffic, and "clamming" activities all have occurred throughout Florida historically. The indirect impact of poor water quality is more difficult to assess and is typically more insidious, but may be dramatic over a short period of time. Industrial, agricultural, and urban wastes enter estuarine waters at Ft. Pierce, the principal habitat study site for the spottail goby. The same likely holds true for certain other areas where the species occurs. Since gobies are highly dependent on appropriate microhabitat, any disturbance of the sediments and sea-grass meadows where this species is found could result in its extirpation. On the other hand, since its range encompasses a fairly long stretch of the southeastern Florida coastline (including part of the Florida Keys), localized extirpation should not seriously threaten the species throughout its entire range in the state. Under these circumstances, neither a "threatened" nor a "rare" classification would appear appropriate, and it consequently is placed in the category "of special concern."

RECOMMENDATIONS: Preserve inlet sea-grass ecosystems. Protect water quality in shallow estuaries, particularly near ocean inlets.

Literature Cited

Published Information

Springer, V. G., and A. J. McErlean. 1962. Seasonality of fishes on a south Florida shore. Bull. Mar. Sci. Gulf Carib. 12:39–60.

Unpublished Information

Christensen, R. F. 1965. An ichthyological survey of Jupiter Inlet and Loxahat-chee River, Florida. M.Sc. thesis, Florida State University, Tallahassee.

Gilmore, R. G. 1988. Subtropical seagrass fish communities: population dynamics, species guilds and microhabitat associations in the Indian River lagoon, Florida. Ph.D. diss., Florida Institute of Technology, Melbourne.

Pezold, F. L., III. 1984. A revision of the gobioid fish genus *Gobionellus*. Ph.D. diss., University of Texas, Austin.

Prepared by: R. Grant Gilmore, *Harbor Branch Oceanographic Institution, Ft. Pierce, Florida 33450*; and Carter R. Gilbert, *Florida Museum of Natural History, University of Florida, Gainesville, Florida 32611*.

Contributors

Writers

Carter R. Gilbert, Florida Museum of Natural History, University of Florida, Gainesville, Florida 32611

Stephen A. Bortone, Department of Biology, University of West Florida, Pensacola, Florida 32504

Noel M. Burkhead, U.S. Fish and Wildlife Service, National Fisheries Research Laboratory, 7920 NW 71st Street, Gainesville, Florida 32606

R. Grant Gilmore, Harbor Branch Oceanographic Foundation, Route 1, Box 196, Ft. Pierce, Florida 33450

William E. Johnson, Florida Game and Freshwater Fish Commission, P.O. Box 1093, Eustis, Florida 32726

William F. Loftus, South Florida Research Center, Everglades National Park, P.O. Box 279, Homestead, Florida 33030

Kenneth Relyea, Department of Biology, Armstrong State College, Savannah, Georgia 31419

Franklin F. Snelson, Department of Biological Sciences, University of Central Florida, P.O. Box 25000, Orlando, Florida 32816

D. Scott Taylor, Brevard Mosquito Control District, Titusville, Florida 32780

James D. Williams, U.S. Fish and Wildlife Service, National Fisheries Research Laboratory, 7920 NW 71st Street, Gainesville, Florida 32606

Ralph W. Yerger, 2917 Woodside Drive, Tallahassee, Florida 32312

Illustrators

Merald Clark, Florida Museum of Natural History, University of Florida, Gainesville, Florida 32611

Wendy Zomlefer, Florida Museum of Natural History, University of Florida, Gainesville, Florida 32611

Index

Note: Numbers in *italic type* denote illustration.